Praise for *Flat, Fluid, and Fast*

Workers today are more mobile than ever—whether they're tele-commuting from a kitchen table or relocating to another continent. How can you support these folks while ensuring you have the talent you need, where you need it, when you need it? *Flat, Fluid and Fast* has the answers. This incisive book explores the meaning of talent mobility, outlines the challenges you will face as a team leader with mobile employees, and provides an essential map for navigating the modern workplace.

—DANIEL H. PINK, author of *When, Drive* and *To Sell is Human*

There are major forces changing the nature of work today that business leaders confront every day. In *Flat, Fluid and Fast*, Kennedy tells leaders how to take advantage of the talent mobility revolution to successfully navigate the future of work, support workers through transitions and build talent strategies that attract, retain and engage workers. Every business and talent leader must read it!

—DAMON BERKHAUG, Global Head of
Talent Acquisition, LAM Research

Kennedy provides a powerful book on how businesses, careers and teams are changing amid disruptions and new generations in the workplace. *Flat, Fluid and Fast* tells us how these forces can help create opportunities for businesses, workers and the economy as a whole. It is a must-read for anyone interested in how to grow jobs and create policies to support the new world of work.

—STEPHANE KASRIEL, CEO of Upwork, the world's
largest freelancing website, and World Economic Forum Co-Chair,
Global Futures Council on the New Social Contract

The future of work will increasingly involve humans collaborating with other humans to design work for machines. In *Flat, Fluid and Fast*, Brynne Kennedy provides a practical, insightful and well-informed guide for leveraging the mobility revolution to create a more connected, motivated and effective workforce. It's a must read for every inspiring leader!

—GREG SATELL, author of *Cascades* and *Mapping Innovation*

The talent mobility revolution is changing almost everything about the way we attract, retain and engage workers. *Flat, Fluid and Fast* takes the reader on an innovative, eye-opening journey to learn how savvy business leaders are successfully navigating the Future of Work.

—PEGGY SMITH, President and CEO, Worldwide ERC, a trade body that educates and connects more than 250,000 corporations, thought leaders, learners and mobile people

Flat, Fluid and Fast is an important and insightful read that explores both the history of people development inside of companies, and also how this is changing in revolutionary ways. Kennedy provides a set of tools and way of thinking that are indispensable in a world of rapid technical and sociological change.

—ROB SIEGEL, Lecturer in Management, Stanford Graduate School of Business

Global talent mobility is now a hallmark of high-performing organizations. Brynne's book is a wonderful overview of this critical area, filled with important best-practices for every organization.

—JOSH BERSIN, Global Industry Analyst

FLAT,

Fluid,

AND

FAST

Harness the Talent Mobility Revolution
to Drive Employee Engagement,
Accelerate Innovation,
and Unleash Growth

BRYNNE KENNEDY

New York Chicago San Francisco Athens London Madrid
Mexico City Milan New Delhi Singapore Sydney Toronto

1 2 3 4 5 6 7 8 9   LCR   24 23 22 21 20 19

ISBN: 978-1-260-45727-8
MHID: 1-260-45727-3

e-ISBN: 978-1-260-45728-5
e-MHID: 1-260-45728-1

Library of Congress Cataloging-in-Publication Data

Names: Kennedy, Brynne, author.
Title: Flat, fluid, and fast : harness the talent mobility revolution to drive employee
    engagement, accelerate innovation, and unleash growth / Brynne Kennedy.
Description: New York : McGrawHill, [2019] | Includes bibliographical references
    and index.
Identifiers: LCCN 2019026999 (print) | LCCN 2019027000 (ebook) | ISBN
    9781260457278 (hardcover) | ISBN 9781260457285 (ebook)
Subjects: LCSH: Manpower planning. | Labor mobility. | Personnel management.
Classification: LCC HF5549.5.M3 K45 2019 (print) | LCC HF5549.5.M3 (ebook) |
    DDC 658.3/14—dc23
LC record available at https://lccn.loc.gov/2019026999
LC ebook record available at https://lccn.loc.gov/2019027000

McGraw-Hill Education books are available at special quantity discounts to use as premiums and sales promotions or for use in corporate training programs. To contact a representative, please e-mail us at bulksales@mheducation.com.

For my mother, Katherine. Thank you for showing me tenacity, empathy, and altruism— in business and life. You are my inspiration.

For Team Topia. To colleagues, customers, investors, and partners, thank you for opening my eyes to the future of work and for the privilege of building a company with you.

Contents

Acknowledgments   vii

Introduction: Welcome to the Talent Mobility Revolution   xi

SECTION 1
SETTING UP A FLAT, FLUID, AND FAST COMPANY

1 Rethinking Your Definition of Talent Mobility   3

2 Restructuring Your Organization for Talent Mobility   27

3 Redesigning Your Offices for New Ways of Work   49

SECTION 2
REDESIGNING WORK TO BE FLAT, FLUID, AND FAST

4 Rearchitecting Roles to Be Dynamic Jobs   71

5 Evolving Teams and Managers for Dynamic Jobs   93

6 Redefining Career Paths for the Talent Mobility Era   115

SECTION 3

OPERATING A FLAT, FLUID, AND FAST COMPANY

7 Creating Policies to Manage Talent Mobility   141

8 Transforming Compensation and Benefits
for Talent Mobility   167

9 Transforming Systems and Operations for
Talent Mobility   191

CONCLUSION

UNLEASHING THE FLAT, FLUID, AND FAST ECONOMY

10 Transforming, Launching, and Incentivizing
Flat, Fluid, and Fast Work   219

Index   241

Acknowledgments

I'd like to start by thanking my Co-Founder, Steve Black, for being my partner on the journey of talent mobility. Without your belief, dedication, and partnership, Topia never would have been possible. Thank you for being our biggest cheerleader, hardest worker, and most stabilizing force. I cannot thank you enough.

I'm grateful to everyone who worked at Topia through the years and came together across various stages of the company to support relocations for countless families, understand the Talent Mobility Revolution, and create a playbook for it. There are so many people without whom Topia and the solutions discussed here would not have been possible. I want to specifically acknowledge and thank Steve Giles, Rachael King, Peter Almasi, and Sten Tamkivi as invaluable members of the founding team.

Thank you to all of Topia's customers over the years. Thank you for sharing your expertise and your transformations. Thank you to our partners who contributed to understanding the Talent Mobility Revolution and serving customers.

Thank you to Topia's investors, specifically NEA, NewView Capital, and Notion Capital, and Jos White and Ravi Viswanathan. Thank you Kevin Eyres and John Mullins for being the first to believe. Thank you Shashank Samant and Mike Ettling for being invaluable Board members.

Thank you to my executive coaches through the years. Thank you Kevin Eyres and Whit Mitchell for your tireless work in those early years. Thank you John Hamm for guiding me through the toughest and most impactful parts of the journey, and always pushing me to be my best.

Thank you to Stanford Business School, Columbia Business School, and Berkshire Community College for the opportunity to teach about talent mobility and learn from you and your students. Thank you Rob Siegel, Jeff Immelt, Brendan Burns, and Ellen Shanahan.

Thank you to TechNet for discussions on the future of work and talent mobility with government leaders in California and Washington, DC. Thank you John Chambers and Andrea Deveau for inspiring me to think further about policies for our future.

I am grateful to everyone who shared expertise for this book, both formally and informally. Thank you, Steve Black, Sten Tamkivi, Rachael King, Jacky Cohen, Silver Keskkula, Peggy Smith, Robert Horsley, Eric Halverson, Nick Pond, Ed Hannibal, Sean Collins, Catherine Stewart, Susanna Warner, Kerwin Guillermo, Sjoerd Gehring, Stephane Kasriel, Jessica Herrin, Krish Ramakrishnan, Stacy Brown-Philpot, Manon DeFelice, Joanna Riley, Anne McPherson, Tana Graves, Nadine North, Daniel Zahler, Brendan Burns, and many more. Thank you Blake Kavanaugh for your research work.

Thank you, Vanessa Chu, Becky Yang, Carla Holtze, and Asti Khachatryan for being my regenerative community of businesswomen since Lehman Brothers. Thank you to my London Business School classmates, specifically Emily Perry, Marilyn Muffs, Sonal Gradischnig, Ayesha Fuller, David Tran, Peter Lewin, Jodi Ingham, and Greg Uckele for encouraging me through the early days of Topia and beyond. Thank you Francis DeSouza for always telling me that my wildest ideas and more are possible.

Writing a book for the first time is an experience of exponential learning. It would not have been possible without the incredible support of my wonderful agent, Joelle Delbourgo, and my editor Noah Schwartzberg at McGraw Hill. You instantly understood the Talent Mobility Revolution and its impact on our businesses, workers, and economy. You both have been incredible partners in this journey. Thank you.

Finally, I want to give the biggest thank you to my family without whom none of this would be possible. Thank you for encouraging me and supporting me through building Topia, writing this book, and pursuing every project in life. Most of all, thank you for always reminding me that our work is the result of many people—and that our greatest accomplishment is how we give back to others. Thank you, Mom, Porter, Erin, Molly, Tom, Carol, Mark, Robin, Doug, David, Ellen, Bob, Barbara, Katy, Bet, Anne, Tana, Nate, and Mike. Thank you, Dad, Mama, Papa, Julia, and Grandma Edna, who are here in spirit.

Welcome to the Talent Mobility Revolution

It's five years in the future.

Automation, globalization, and new demographics wreak havoc on the workforce. Artificial intelligence creates new jobs and makes old ones obsolete at a pace that was previously unimaginable. Millennials and Generation Z now make up 60 percent of the workforce. They interact via smartphones and apps, and switch jobs regularly. Their careers span full-time employment, freelance work, and learning or everything at the same time. They see work disrupted and new work created. They have more jobs than their parents had job titles. Work is conducted anywhere: a home office in Tahoe, a beach in Cape Cod, a coworking space in Sacramento, a long-distance commute between New York and London. Workers depend on frictionless movement—across geographies, locations, jobs, and employment for projects, training, tours of duty, opportunities, fulfillment, career progression, salary, family needs, and more.

This ceaseless pressure pushes companies and policy makers to support a different world of work, to make it easier and more seamless for individuals to work everywhere, to better and more fully support workers whose jobs are threatened, and for companies to fill jobs with workers based anywhere. Jobs are created in suburban and rural areas. Workers no longer go to an office every day. Managers rethink how they hire workers and operate companies. Economic mobility is again unleashed across America.

Internationally, competition is fiercer than ever, further complicated by skill shortages in some countries and surpluses in others.

Countries are competing, too, each rewriting its own policies to keep jobs from slipping across borders and to attract the best and brightest to start companies on their shores. The global flow—of goods, capital, ideas, and talent—is more powerful than ever. Companies that can tap into this flow succeed. Workers that adapt to this new economy thrive. Governments that update programs to support everyone do right by their citizens.

This is the *Talent Mobility Revolution*. Business leaders, workers, and policy makers all know it. Today, they're asking the same questions: *How do we navigate the future of jobs? How do we make our companies and communities disruption-proof? How do we help our workers transition and ensure they are supported?* It's what they're talking about at cafés, at conferences, in boardrooms, and in government offices. The answer is in this book.

My name is Brynne Kennedy, and I'm the founder of Topia, a company that I ran as CEO for nine years that helps organizations and workers adapt to this perfect storm of business trends with a relocation and talent mobility software solution. I got the idea for Topia while working around the world for a traditional bank and experiencing the frustration of relocation—one of the most stressful experiences a family can endure. Through this, I realized that the world was changing—that we were on the cusp of a great Talent Mobility Revolution. I watched as globalization, automation, and demographic change took hold and increasingly disrupted jobs, companies, and communities. And I watched as employees like me started to work in different ways.

I have spent most of the last decade studying these disruptions, building solutions to address them, and helping people navigate them. In 2010, I founded Topia, one of the first companies to tackle relocation and talent mobility through technology, now a $32 billion industry segment. While building Topia, I raised more than $100 million from the world's leading investors, created hundreds of jobs, and grew the company to operate globally. We worked with hundreds of companies and helped tens of thousands of families move more easily—from finding new homes, to enrolling kids in new schools, to getting acclimated in new towns. I have had the pleasure of both helping families in their most intimate moments and learning from companies as they transform for a new world of work.

At the same time, I have seen many new companies designed from the beginning for a new world of work—with talent mobility at their core. Many of these companies have become both blueprints and solutions for the future of jobs. Some of them are now the most coveted employers for top talent.

I have spoken regularly to business leaders, workers, and policy makers on the Talent Mobility Revolution. When companies sought to reinvent their organizations, I brainstormed with them. When policy makers wanted to learn about the future of jobs, I presented to them. When workers wanted to know what's ahead, I talked to them. When students wanted to prepare for their future careers, I taught them. And today, I am running for US Congress in California District 4 to help lead our community and economy into a future that benefits all workers.

In other words, I know what's coming better than most do. And I wrote this book because the vast majority of organizations and workers are not ready. In fact, our whole country is not ready. Not even close. It's time to completely rethink our concept of jobs—to transform traditional companies, start companies in new ways, and rethink government policy to create a new work contract that provides economic opportunity for workers throughout America. To thrive in the future, our companies, workers, and economy must be agile. They must become *Flat, Fluid, and Fast.*

This book is a playbook for business leaders, workers, and policy makers to take action amid the forces of globalization, automation, and demographic change—the forces driving the Talent Mobility Revolution. This book is structured in nine chapters, each covering a component of work and how it will change amid these forces. You can think of this as a nine-step playbook for talent mobility transformation—to become a *Flat, Fluid, and*

Fast Company (*F3 Company*). We start by looking at the definition of talent mobility, and then move to the organizational design, offices, jobs, teams, career paths, policies, benefits, and systems of the future. The final chapter, Chapter 10, looks at how to apply these principles at a traditional company or start a new company with them at the core. I finish the book with a discussion on the new work contract we need in America—a set of policies to unleash a *Flat, Fluid, and Fast* economy that benefits all of our companies and workers and ensures that the United States remains the most economically competitive and innovative nation in the world.

Although not every concept in this book applies to every situation, the vast majority of these principles can be applied across companies, teams, and careers in the new economy. The book can be read end to end as a complete playbook or by diving in and out of specific chapters to look at particular topics. Each chapter is structured in three sections, looking at the traditional way of work, the new way of work, and how to transform for the future.

Finally, I must note that our workforce includes many different kinds of workers—from the knowledge workers discussed in this book, to the teachers that educate our children, retail clerks who we buy goods from, and firefighters, nurses, and janitors who serve our communities among so many others. Certain of the forces discussed in this book have negatively impacted our working and middle classes, doing away with stable employment, benefits and wage growth, and collective bargaining, together curtailing the American Dream for so many families. Much of what we cover is targeted at leaders, teams, and knowledge workers at our largest and fastest-growing companies. The policy proposals I outline in the final chapter will help ensure all workers can organize and benefit in this new economy.

We're right on the cusp of the Talent Mobility Revolution. Globalization, automation, and demographic change will continue to change our economy in significant ways. This can be an incredible opportunity—to create jobs, accelerate innovation, and unlock flexibility—across our economy. Or it can be catastrophic, disrupting our workers, companies, and economy.

Flat, Fluid, and Fast is the definitive playbook for successful transformation amid the Talent Mobility Revolution. It is the culmination of more than a decade of work, where I experienced these forces, studied what was happening, and built a business around it. It is based on my experiences with countless companies, business leaders, and families, as well as discussions at colleges, business schools, and government halls around the world.

Today, we have an opportunity to do right by all of our workers—to create policies and opportunities for our future jobs. Leaders who adopt the principles in this book will be doing a service to their companies and communities.

SETTING UP A FLAT, FLUID, AND FAST COMPANY

Rethinking Your Definition
of Talent Mobility

In 2010, I was sitting at a relocation industry conference listening to people talk about the term "talent mobility." I had just started my MBA at London Business School, fresh off working in finance, which had brought me from the United States to Asia to Europe. I couldn't believe how cumbersome and frustrating it had been to move for work. So, as I started business school, I decided to take a closer look at the outdated relocation industry and how I could make it easier for families everywhere to move. This catapulted me into becoming an entrepreneur (like my mother, a small business owner of 47 years) and founding Topia, a relocation and HR software company that enables talent mobility for the Fortune 1000 and the employees who work there. Since then, Topia has helped tens of thousands of families move, created hundreds of jobs, and grown to global operations.

At that point, however, I knew virtually nothing about the nuts and bolts of corporate relocation or talent management or human resources. I had talked my way into a "consulting" role with the Forum for Expatriate Management, a horribly named but incredibly large corporate relocation conference group, where I figured I'd learn why things were so outdated and what kind of business was needed for the future. And that is how I found myself sitting in an ugly-carpeted hotel ballroom drinking stale coffee and listening to HR professionals talk about talent mobility.

The problem was that no one at the conference, and I later learned anywhere else, actually knew what talent mobility meant. For most people at the conference, it was a sexier label for corporate relocation, a way to jazz up a staid industry in the back-office of big companies. For others, it referred to people who moved between companies or jobs within companies—a sexier label for internal and external recruiting. For some, it referred to people whose jobs were displaced by automation and had to find another form of work. For still others, it meant employees who had mobile phones.

Nearly 10 years later, we still don't have a good definition for talent mobility—even though talent mobility is defining us. Growing disruptions to the way we work and the jobs we do means that today more people move, for many more reasons, for many more durations, and in many more configurations. They move between countries. They move between cities. They move between jobs. They move between teams. They move between careers. They move between their home and office. They move between traditional employment and freelance work. My generation will work across more careers than our parents did *companies*.

I have spent most of the last decade in meetings discussing talent mobility and the future of jobs—with business leaders, government officials, industry analysts, investors, journalists, consultants, employees, and customers of Topia. In these discussions, we consistently talked about how unleashing talent mobility is the key to traditional companies transforming to win the war on global talent, creating new jobs that can be done anywhere and evolving jobs in the face of a changing economy. The problem, however, is that most of the world is still just as confused as the corporate relocation professionals were in 2010. We still don't have a clear definition of talent mobility. And we don't understand how it can be used to support businesses, workers, and families in the face of change.

It's well known today that globalization, automation, and demographic change are upending the way we work. We have seen storied companies overtaken by upstart new competitors, the gig (or freelance) economy emerge to account for a growing share of jobs, escalating demand for job flexibility and autonomy from millennial workers, and communities decimated by globalization, automation, and unpredictable work. It's less clear, however, what our companies and country should do in the face of these trends, which together have created the Talent Mobility Revolution. This book gives you the answer.

To succeed amid the Talent Mobility Revolution—in the future of jobs—companies must first know what talent mobility exactly means. In this first chapter, we provide an applicable definition of talent mobility that you can use as your guiding framework for transformation. From there, we can look at how business leaders can reinvent their companies, how workers can best be supported through change, and how government leaders must rethink policies to foster a new economy that benefits everyone.

Companies and managers that are stuck in the past with traditional definitions of business operations, human resources, and corporate relocation will fail in the twenty-first century. Success today comes from being a *Flat, Fluid, and Fast Company* (an *F3 Company*). Once you understand what talent mobility means today, you'll understand how it impacts all parts of your business and talent strategy, and how to transform in the face of the seismic macro trends of globalization, automation, and demographic change.

The Traditional Company Lexicon

Human resources (HR) can be traced to the ideas of two men in the nineteenth century—Robert Owen, a Scottish social reformer, and Charles Babbage, a mechanical engineer. Although the term *human resources* did not emerge until later, these two men are generally regarded as the first to see that the well-being of workers made them more effective and productive for companies. The first formal human resources department is generally believed to have been the result of a large worker strike at the National Cash Register Company in 1901. After this strike, the company established a "personnel" department responsible for record keeping, workplace safety, wage management, and employee grievances—the world's first HR department.*

Through the early twentieth century, with trade unions and personnel management departments growing, the traditional human resources discipline started to take hold. As employment legislation passed, including the National Labor Relations Act (NLRA) of 1935 that protected certain rights of employees and employers, and companies grew larger and more complex, HR departments became responsible for ensuring companies were compliant with state and federal employment laws and that workers were protected. As HR evolved through the twentieth century, the discipline evolved to include traditional HR operations to manage employees, recruiting to hire employees, and corporate relocation to move employees. For decades, this is how HR was set up and defined.

How Traditional HR Departments Managed Employees

Traditional HR operations were responsible for exactly what the name said—managing the operations of the company's *human resources*. Employees were considered resources that the company needed to manage to get work done. Traditional activities included paying their compensation, administering their benefits, conducting their annual performance reviews, and ensuring compliance with labor laws. Business leaders sometimes perceived traditional HR departments as a type of operational policeman—keeping companies out of trouble and ensuring people got pay, benefits, and performance reviews on time.

Topia's first VP People, Rachael King, had an impressive career across companies like Cisco, Vodafone, and AXA before joining

---

* Fast Company, "Welcome to the New Era of Human Resources," May 20, 2015, https://www.fastcompany.com/3045829/welcome-to-the-new-era-of-human-resources.

Topia in 2014. She remembers her early career as "operational HR," with work largely done on files and paper. "When I started in HR, the jobs were transactional," says King. "As my career has evolved, so has the HR discipline. I saw a more strategic side of HR gradually develop, and I became a greater partner to the business. But even as HR grew in strategic importance, we still had to knock down the door to business leaders to get them to take us seriously. Today, however, my role is increasingly seen as a true partner to the CEO, like at Topia."

Peggy Smith is CEO of Worldwide ERC, a trade body that educates and connects more than 250,000 corporations, thought leaders, learners, and mobile people. She has had a front-row seat to the evolution of HR operations across her member companies.

"Over the last 10 years, I've seen a retooling of the broader HR function from tactical (compliance, annual reviews, offer letters, etc.) to strategic (workforce and succession planning, critical skill deployment, and the like). Companies now recognize that talent is not a resource to be managed, but a critical asset to business success," says Smith. "HR functions are now expected to have the business acumen to both manage talent and drive the results needed."

How Traditional HR Departments Hired Employees

As companies grew and needed to hire workers more regularly, the recruiting function became an important part of the traditional HR department. The purpose of the recruiting department was to source candidates for open full-time roles, convince them that they should join the company, and complete the hiring process. In nearly all cases, recruiting was done with external candidates in the relevant local market, often in partnership with external recruiters who maintained a database of candidates. Company recruiters would schedule and conduct interviews, negotiate compensation and benefits, and execute offer letters with the selected candidate. Over time, graduate recruiting programs sprung up where recruiters would go to college campuses to source and interview candidates for entry-level roles, often as a part of a broader graduate program. Other than campus recruiting programs, it was rare to source candidates from afar. Recruiting focused on local hiring for full-time roles for jobs done in an office.

How Traditional HR Teams Moved Employees

Corporate relocation departments came about when an employee needed to move to a new office location, generally the result of international expansion of the company or some type of knowledge transfer or training that was required in a different market. Generally, about 3 to 5 percent of staff moved like this each year. In these circumstances, a manager asked an employee to relocate, and after the employee said yes, he or she interacted with the corporate relocation department, a part of the broader HR organization, to manage the details of the move. These moves were generally either full relocations, a permanent move to a new location, or expatriate assignments, a three-to-five-year engagement where the employee and family would relocate and then return back home. Packages were full of benefits—housing, cars, school support, tax, and immigration support, etc.—to entice families to relocate or accept assignments and carry out work that the company needed done. The corporate relocation department was the back-office function that made all of this happen—with no hiccups for the employee or with local laws. No one really thought much about corporate relocation beyond this.

In 2006, I joined Lehman Brothers as an investment banker after college and interacted with these very departments—HR, recruiting, and corporate relocation. After learning Mandarin and studying China in depth in college, I talked my way into an investment banking job in Hong Kong instead of the traditional analyst program starting in New York. After accepting the offer, I was handed over to the corporate relocation team to process my relocation from the United States to Hong Kong—sending them into a tailspin since I didn't fit the model of an existing employee relocating at the request of the company. A year later, bored with writing pitch decks in a cubicle in Hong Kong, I again talked my way into an opportunity to long-distance commute to India to work on the country's largest initial public offering at the time. Again, falling outside of the definition of traditional corporate relocation, the bank didn't know how to handle me. Instead I got a travel visa and hotel room for nearly a year, and I crossed my fingers every time I entered the country that I wouldn't be stopped at the border for spending so much time working in India. With these experiences—and similar ones I saw my colleagues and friends starting to have—I knew that the traditional definition of corporate relocation was changing. I knew that I was witnessing a systemic shift in the way we work, and that companies would have to adapt.

"Corporate relocation has historically been a caretaker-oriented, operational role for a small portion of relocations and expatriate assignments, largely for mid- and senior-level employees. There was a heavy focus on ensuring all went smoothly regarding compliance, and that the employee could get from point A to B and start work as quickly as possible," says Peggy Smith. "But now corporate relocation has evolved to be just one part of a much broader definition of talent mobility that is at the heart of today's successful economy, job creation, and company operations."

The Building Blocks of Talent Mobility Today

With the forces of globalization, demographic change, and automation, we are seeing a fundamental shift in the nature of the HR department. *F3 Companies* now recognize that talent mobility—and the ability to leverage employee *movement* to drive employee engagement, accelerate innovation, and unleash growth—gives them a competitive advantage. The way they think about their workforce, strategy, and operations must be redefined with talent mobility at their core. To tap into the Talent Mobility Revolution,

F3 Companies transform from running traditional HR departments to putting talent mobility at the core of their whole business to unlock work from everywhere. This transformation starts with defining what talent mobility means. *Talent mobility is the movement of employees across geographies, jobs, locations, and employment classifications.* We discuss each of these four building blocks of talent mobility in this chapter—and then how they influence different parts of your business in subsequent chapters.

Geographic Movement

Employees today move geographically more than ever. But these moves are not only the traditional relocations and assignments of yesteryear that you're probably thinking of. (In fact, traditional relocations are waning in the United States.) Rather, when we say moves, we mean many different configurations of geographic movement from commuting to short-term projects to frequent travel. Workers today move for an ever-greater set of reasons and depend on frictionless geographic mobility for training programs, career progression, continued engagement, lifestyle, fulfillment, salary, family needs, and much more. Increasingly, this geographic movement doesn't only come from companies asking employees to move to fulfill a business need, but from employees raising their hands for personal reasons, and *growth* and *learning* to fulfill their own career ambitions.

In our definition of talent mobility, geographic movement includes six configurations:

- *Relocations.* The traditional one-way permanent move
- *Expatriate assignment.* The traditional three-to-five-year move with a return home
- *Long-distance commute.* Regular work across two locations with travel between them (e.g., working every other week between Sacramento and San Diego)
- *Frequent travel (aka, the road warrior).* Regular work across many locations with travel in between them

- *Short-term projects.* Structured fixed-term work in a given location
- *Rotation and training programs.* Structured fixed-term work in multiple locations

Since founding Topia in 2010, I have seen this evolution happen firsthand. When I founded the company, most of the businesses I spoke to had a traditional corporate relocation department responsible only for relocations and expatriate assignments. Today, Topia's most innovative customers now define geographic mobility to include all of the major configurations of geographic mobility—and many of them have rebranded their corporate relocation departments as talent mobility departments. These companies use long-distance recruiting to fill talent needs, host training programs for workers around the world, regularly deploy people to open new markets or conduct short-term projects in different places, embrace commuting and frequent travel as a way to balance employees' work and personal needs, and hire people who live outside of traditional urban hubs.

Each year at Topia, we host Customer Advisory Board meetings where we bring together our customers to discuss upcoming product developments and hear their feedback. Almost always these conversations include discussions about the many more ways employees are moving today, and the complexity this brings to the talent mobility teams who have to manage it. I recall discussions about frequent travel across states and countries, which kicked off tax challenges, and high performers who wanted to move to other locations and commute to their jobs—*should* the company allow this? And *how* could the company do this if it had no entity in the location where the employee wanted to live? The general consensus in all these conversations was that employees today move for many reasons and in many ways—all of which should be included and managed under one talent mobility umbrella.

Eric Halverson joined eBay 15 years ago to build its talent mobility program. Over that time, he has led the transformation of eBay's geographic movement from a small number of domestic relocations and expatriate assignments to frequent geographic mobility—including sharp growth in short-term project moves, rotational and training programs, commuting, and frequent business travel in recent years. Today, a large portion of the company falls into the frequent business traveler classification.

Halverson started this transformation by reviewing with HR leadership and specific business unit leaders throughout the company the changing demographics of employees and their preferences for greater geographic mobility—and the different and more frequent configurations it would entail. He educated the company on how opportunities for geographic movement could be leveraged as a part of recruiting, developing, and retaining top talent, particularly in the fierce talent wars between top technology companies. Halverson created frameworks to enable employees to work across different locations and scenarios, including business-directed geographic movement and self-initiated geographic movement—like we discussed at the Customer Advisory Board meetings.

The result is that, as Halverson says, "eBay now recognizes that this is how employees today work and it helps us to attract and retain the talent we need—in a very competitive recruiting environment. Geographic movement, coupled with flexible remote work scenarios, is a key pillar of both our business and talent strategy."

"Today, there is an expectation that work is frictionless," says Nick Pond, who leads EY's People Advisory and Consulting services, advising the world's largest companies on their talent mobility strategies. "People see movement as part of their career learning, experiences, and life. We are seeing a huge increase in geographic movement across our global clients, particularly in frequent short-term moves and extended business travel, which allow employees to get work experience in different places while balancing personal and family needs."*

---

* Interview with Nick Pond, Partner, EY People Advisory, December 17, 2018.

F3 FOCUS

F3 Companies identify and include all six types of geographic movement—relocations, expatriate assignments, long-distance commuting, frequent business travel, short-term projects, and rotational and training programs—as part of their definition of talent mobility. They harness geographic movement to attract, retain, and deploy their talent in the face of rapidly changing global business needs, technology disruptions, and employee demands.

Job Movement

Underlying all of this geographic movement is a stark increase in employees moving between jobs within companies. Today, an employee may start her career as a customer service rep, then move to a sales role, before working for some time in marketing, before becoming a project manager. Much of today's workforce watched the promise of a job for life erode for their parents amid the 2008 recession. This recession threw away the long-held social contract where workers traded autonomy and flexibility for the stability and benefits that came from a traditional job. Today's generation of workers are realistic about disruptions that may occur to their jobs, and may instead seek autonomy, flexibility, and continuous learning in their careers. They want to build a tool kit of skills that they can leverage across different opportunities throughout their career. Workers often now look at their careers as a series of different job segments, or *tours of duty*, a phrase coined by LinkedIn Co-Founder Reid Hoffman, with Chris Yeh and Ben Casnocha, in their 2014 book, *The Alliance*. Employees today expect to have many career segments rather than a "job for life."

With disruptions to jobs more frequent and employees demanding tours of duty, job movement is on the rise within companies. Facilitating it is an increasingly important part of attracting and engaging top talent, and having the agility to respond to opportunities and disruptions that arise for your company. To do so, companies must rethink how they structure and staff work, something we'll discuss in detail in Section 2.

Job movement includes three types of tours of duty:

- *Engagement tour of duty.* An employee who is disengaged with a current job and requests a new job. Companies that don't make this happen often lose employees to another company or to work in the freelance economy.
- *Disruption tour of duty.* An employee whose job has been disrupted or made obsolete, often as the result of automation. These employees now can be moved to a new job, and must be supported well through the transition. Companies that don't make this happen lose institutional and cultural knowledge.
- *Geographic tour of duty.* An employee who is moved to a new job to gain experience in a new market or fill a business need there. Companies that don't make this happen often lose out to their more agile competitors.

Kerwin Guillermo leads HP's Global Talent Mobility function and has transformed the traditional corporate relocation function to include dynamic job movement. Guillermo first joined HP as a part of the Talent Acquisition team Asia, which also included traditional corporate relocation in the region. He progressed through the organization to eventually lead Global Talent Mobility, where he set off to transform the way HP thought about talent mobility, and bring more dynamic job movement into the company's traditional definition.

Fresh off reading Simon Sinek's book, *Start with Why*, Guillermo says he approached his new role by thinking hard about "the why of mobility—both in terms of how it achieves company objectives and each employee's objectives, particularly for millennial employees." He knew that it would be difficult to align a large, complex, global company like HP around a new definition of talent mobility, so he set out to rapidly show value to business leaders through increasing job movement.

Guillermo knew that HP's business and staffing leaders traditionally looked to local hiring to fill new jobs. He thought that if he could show that talent mobility can offer diverse talent and business solutions to rapidly fill jobs and skills needs with internal talent, the company would start to think about job movement—and tours of duty—as a key part of its talent mobility definition and business strategy. Similarly, he knew that HP employees were increasingly looking for tours of duty as a part of their careers. Including job movement in the traditional talent mobility definition would help attract, retain, and engage the talent the company needed to succeed.

Guillermo cites examples of matching employees with emerging skills, like artificial intelligence, data science, or cybersecurity with jobs across the company, and where employees from "mature skill markets," like the United States and United Kingdom, were matched to tours of duty in "growing skill markets" like China or the Czech Republic.

"My first success in clarifying the definition and perceived value of talent mobility was quickly filling 'difficult-to-fill' jobs that were revenue-generating and would previously go unfilled for over 120 days with traditional local recruiting processes. Filling that vacancy could be directly attributed to revenue generation, showing the clear benefit of talent mobility," says Guillermo.

"These real experiences, that benefited the business, really expanded people's understanding that talent mobility is not just corporate relocation anymore. It is about dynamically matching people with skills to jobs that need those skills. By doing this, we were also responding to our employees' increasing demands for more career phases and skills development."*

---

* Interview with Kerwin Guillermo, VP Talent Mobility, December 27, 2018.

Robert Horsley is both the Executive Director of Fragomen, the world's largest private immigration firm, and the Chairman Emeritus of Worldwide ERC, the trade body where Peggy Smith is CEO. Through these roles, he sees growing job movement at companies like HP.

"I am seeing work happening in smaller segments that build on themselves," says Horsley. "We can think of this as a modularization of the workforce, similar to what we've known as the traditional internship. These 'modules' happen in one place with one team, and then they end, and a new one starts, often in a different place, with a different team, not unlike the nonlinear way a film is made. This is a new iteration of job movement, and should be part of our definition of talent mobility."*

F3 FOCUS

F3 Companies identify and include the three types of job movement—engagement tours of duty, disruption tours of duty, and geographic tours of duty—as part of their definition of talent mobility. They harness these to attract, retain, and deploy their talent in the face of rapidly changing business needs and disruptions. They include job movement as a key part of their employee value proposition for their workers.

Location Movement

In addition to growing geographic and job movement, work today has a growing amount of flexible and remote (or distributed) work. Companies eager to reduce costs and carbon footprint and to support employees with flexibility and work-life balance embrace

---

* Interview with Robert Horsley, Executive Director, Fragomen, December 6, 2018.

flexible work arrangements as an important part of their business and talent strategy. Location movement, or remote and flexible work, is the third building block of talent mobility.

Many companies, however, don't yet define or manage location movement in a cohesive manner. Rather location movement often emerges as a series of one-off allowances managed haphazardly across the different business areas. With growth in distributed work comes the need to manage employee collaboration and compliance, plus new opportunities to hire from a larger talent pool. Location movement must be a deliberate part of talent mobility definition and strategy.

Location movement includes two types of distributed work:

- **Work-from-home.** Full- or part-time work done from a home office
- **Work-from-anywhere.** Full- or part-time work done from outside the company office, including in coworking spaces, cafés, and while traveling

Companies like Automattic, which owns popular content management platform WordPress.com, have made remote work a key part of their business strategy and employee value proposition. Automattic has 877 employees across 68 countries, all of whom work remotely. At Automattic, employees can truly work from anywhere: a home office, a beach, or a local café or coworking space. (The company even provides an "office stipend" for those who prefer to work around others and leverage a local coworking space.)* Similarly, companies like HP, where Kerwin Guillermo leads talent mobility, have moved away from "office face time" to partial work-from-home models, where staff comes into the office to collaborate or work on specific projects using "hot desks" in the office. Like employees moving between geographies, these employees are

---

* Interview with Catherine Stewart, CBO at Automattic.

moving—from external work locations to an internal office location—and this should be included as part of the talent mobility definition and managed as part of one cohesive strategy.

From 2016 to 2018, Jing Liao was the Chief Human Resources Officer for rapidly growing Silicon Valley lending company SoFi, where she saw a surge in employees asking to work-from-anywhere—a frequent request from today's millennial staff.

"Every week, I have employees coming into my office and asking to move to some location and work from there," said Liao at the Bay Area Mobility Management Conference. She then went on to cite a recent example where a high potential engineer wanted to spend some time exploring Mexico while still working at SoFi, and she had to figure out how to make this work.

"As a company, we need to make this happen, or we will lose our talent to our competitors. It's very difficult to manage, but it's critical for our success—and the success of so many other companies—with today's millennial workforce," said Liao.[*]

Stephane Kasriel, CEO of NASDAQ-listed company Upwork, the world's largest freelancer platform, says that nearly two-thirds of companies (63 percent) now have full-time employees who work outside the office.[†] Upwork, like Automattic, lives this—it has about 400 people who work from a company office and about 1,000 who work remotely.[‡] "Companies that refuse to properly support a remote workforce risk losing their best people and turning away tomorrow's top talent," says Kasriel.

* Discussion on a panel at 2017 Bay Area Mobility Management Conference.
† Upwork, Future Workforce Report, 2018.
‡ Interview with Stephane Kasriel, CEO, Upwork, December 4, 2018.

F3 COMPANY FOCUS

F3 Companies identify and include the two types of location movement—work-from-home and work-from-anywhere—as a part of their talent mobility definition. They harness location movement to control costs, reduce their carbon footprint, and empower today's workers to work how and where they want to, helping them win the global war on talent and bringing jobs to people all over the country.

Employment Movement

The rise of the freelance or gig workforce has created a fourth type of movement for our talent mobility definition: employment movement. Companies today increasingly have a workforce that includes both traditional full-time employees (FTEs) and freelancers—workers who contribute their skills on demand for a particular job, project, or team as microentrepreneurs. Companies have historically used contractors for specific fixed-term work, but today staffing models are evolving to include dynamic skills matching with teams regularly made up of FTEs and freelancers. Similarly, workers increasingly look at their careers as having both full-time work and freelance gigs—a given worker may work as an FTE at one company and freelance across gigs at the same time, or may have different career segments moving between full-time work and freelance gig work. The definition of talent mobility should include managing an expanded definition of the workforce and workers' movement between classifications.

Employment movement includes four classifications of workers and their movement:

- *Employees (FTEs).* Workers hired full-time with traditional employment benefits, protections, and contract provisions.

- *Contractors.* Workers hired for specific, fixed-term work with particular requirements for the amount of work that can be done so as to not classify workers as FTEs. Often called a 1099 worker in the United States to signify the tax treatment (workers' income is reported to the IRS on Form 1099) and independent nature of the work.
- *Freelancers.* Workers hired to complete high-value, specific work (e.g., engineering or design). Often freelance workers are hired on demand when their skills are needed, and frequently they work remotely.
- *Gig workers.* Workers hired to complete work that is short and simple in nature (e.g., a delivery or translation of a specific document). Often gig workers are hired on demand when needed, and frequently they work remotely, augmenting their principal income.

These four classifications of workers are reinventing the way companies define their workforce and manage movement between types of work. This has also spurred a vigorous debate among policy makers in the United States about employment benefits, protections, and tax treatment for this growing cohort of freelance workers, and whether a new worker classification is needed under federal labor law (see Chapter 10 for a full discussion of this).

Today's workforce can now be defined as including both a traditional workforce and a new workforce:

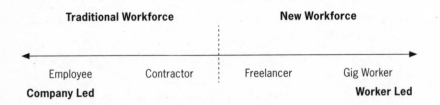

Stella and Dot is a company that was founded with employment movement and an expanded definition of the workforce at its core.

The company has both full-time employees and contract workers as a part of its business model. Stella and Dot sells jewelry, bags, and other accessories both directly on its website and through a large group of social sellers, freelance microentrepreneurs that manage their own independent businesses selling Stella and Dot's products. It's common for FTEs to also work as sellers—both working full-time at the company and independently as members of the freelance economy. Stella and Dot thinks of the company's workforce as including both its FTEs and freelance workers and regularly brings together its top sellers to interact with FTEs, something we'll discuss in more detail in subsequent chapters.

Like at Stella and Dot, one of the principles of employment movement is flexibility—workers have the choice to use their skills when they want to, whether as independent microentrepreneurs in the freelance economy or as a part of a team at a Fortune 500 company.

"For large, traditional companies to survive digital transformation [and disruptions], we must rethink their talent models." says Stephane Kasriel. "Innovative companies adopt more agile approaches to sourcing talent—often finding skills they need online among a growing workforce of independent professionals." According to Upwork, 9 out of 10 hiring managers said they were open to working with freelancers in 2018.*

"We must use an expanded definition of the workforce, and tie flexibility and learning into today's employment model," says Peggy Smith. "Employees increasingly are choosing what type of work they want to have—whether full-time, working as a part of the freelance economy or taking a career break for an adventure, or to volunteer somewhere. Throughout all of this what you're seeing is people placing a greater value on skills development and their time. My generation was about money and stability. This one is about time and experiences. This is why I see the full employment

---

* https://www.upwork.com/press/2018/02/06/fortune-500-enterprises/.

model as under attack, and why employment movement and different staffing models are such an important part of talent mobility."

F3 FOCUS

F3 Companies know that their workforce is evolving beyond just full-time employees. They include employment movement and all four classifications of workers—FTEs, contractors, freelancers, and gig workers—as part of their workforce definition and their talent mobility strategy. They harness employment movement to unlock agility to respond to disruptions and opportunities as they occur.

The New Lexicon of Talent Mobility

The Talent Mobility Revolution is driven by the forces of globalization, automation, and demographic change. Talent mobility should be defined as all types of employee movement across geographies, jobs, locations, and employment classifications. Unlocking this helps companies win the war on talent and create business agility, ensuring they can respond to disruptions and opportunities as they hit.

However, just like in 2010 at the relocation conference, there remains significant confusion about how to bring these four building blocks together into a single definition of talent mobility that can underpin a new business and talent strategy. While building Topia, I met with countless investors, analysts, and customers who looked at me with blank stares when I talked about talent mobility. They asked me if I actually meant recruiting, movement between companies. Or if I meant relocation. Or meant the growing amount of remote and virtual work. Actually, I'd say, these are all part of talent mobility—and this is the future of your company.

Today, I still ask company leaders and managers I meet how they define talent mobility. The most forward-looking companies have evolved to include geographic, job, and employment mobility under their talent mobility definition, but few have brought all four building blocks together to harness the new workforce in an intentional and efficient way.

The definition of talent mobility today must include geographic, job, location, and employment mobility. Put together, it should look like this:

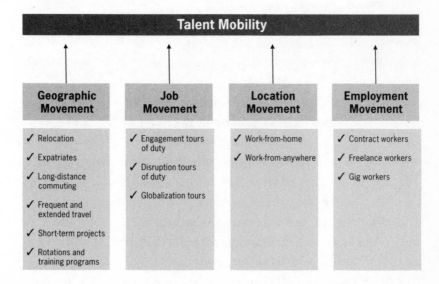

Talent Mobility			
Geographic Movement	**Job Movement**	**Location Movement**	**Employment Movement**
✓ Relocation	✓ Engagement tours of duty	✓ Work-from-home	✓ Contract workers
✓ Expatriates	✓ Disruption tours of duty	✓ Work-from-anywhere	✓ Freelance workers
✓ Long-distance commuting	✓ Globalization tours		✓ Gig workers
✓ Frequent and extended travel			
✓ Short-term projects			
✓ Rotations and training programs			

Companies—from pharmaceutical manufacturers to investment banks to technology companies like HP, are taking steps to define talent mobility like the blueprint in the figure. In 2018, I was speaking about the Talent Mobility Revolution, and the new definition of talent mobility, at a conference when the Head of Talent Mobility at a Fortune 500 financial services company approached me. She told me that her company was taking steps to do exactly what I was talking about—bring together the various forms of employee movement into a single talent mobility area, and she had recently been appointed to lead this initiative. Another Topia customer—a global bank—started to redefine talent mobility and reorganize around it in 2017. The firm had appointed a new head of human resources, who was not from a traditional HR background. Upon taking his new role, he had reorganized around talent mobility, uniting geographic, job, and employment movement under a single umbrella, now defined as talent mobility. With this updated definition and reorganization, I had been called to discuss the operations and systems to manage this new talent mobility area, something we'll cover in Section 3.

Peggy Smith regularly advises companies on talent mobility transformation, as part of her role as CEO of Worldwide ERC. She believes we are just at the beginning of this transformation, however.

"The definition of talent mobility is being rewritten," says Smith. "Movement doesn't need to mean crossing a state or regional border, as 'corporate relocation' historically did. I worry that most companies and leaders still only understand talent mobility with a physical manifestation. But today, talent mobility includes all types of mobile talent—virtual and remote work, contingent workers, frequent travelers and commuters, short-term moves for tours of duty or projects, or new jobs internally at the company, *and* relocations and expatriate assignments.

Smith continues, "Talent mobility means you're able to move people resources in and out as you need them, whether physical or virtual, full-time or contingent."

Some might say it's the human equivalent of scalability. This talent mobility revolution isn't exclusive to crossing a border. Companies must transform along these lines to be positioned for the future. Not many have figured out how to do this yet—especially larger companies—but it's coming, and that's what many of my conversations with employers are about these days."

F3 FOCUS

F3 Companies define talent mobility to include all forms of employee movement: geographic, job, location, and employment movement. They know that talent mobility is the core of their business and talent strategy—and to attracting, retaining, and enabling today's top talent. Company managers are the orchestrators of talent mobility, seamlessly coordinating movement between different places, jobs, and employment types as opportunities and disruptions hit.

This Talent Mobility Revolution is what I saw starting more than a decade ago at Lehman Brothers, and what made me found and build Topia. What I also saw was that the vast majority of companies were not ready for this revolution, and instead risked being left behind by more nimble and agile competitors. Most companies hadn't even recognized this revolution was happening, let alone defined talent mobility and its components. Many still haven't.

Defining talent mobility is the first step to succeeding amid the Talent Mobility Revolution. But the vast majority of companies haven't even done this first step. Any business leader who wants to survive in the next 10 years must become an expert at talent mobility and leverage it for strategic advantage.

CHAPTER SUMMARY

- The Talent Mobility Revolution started a decade ago amid the macro forces of globalization, automation, and demographic change. It is now rapidly accelerating.
- Disruption is the norm in the Talent Mobility Revolution. Companies need to build adaptability into their business and talent strategies to respond to changes and opportunities as they happen and access skills when and where they need them.
- To succeed in today's rapidly changing business world, companies must transform their traditional HR department to be a talent mobility department that unleashes agility and movement throughout the company.
- The building blocks of talent mobility are geographic, job, location, and employment movement. Companies must rewrite their definition of talent mobility to include all of these.
- Companies and workers increasingly demand work in tours of duty across geographies and jobs. To attract, retain, and engage top talent, companies must make geographic and job movement a core part of their talent mobility definition and strategy.
- Companies and workers are adopting more distributed and remote work models. To successfully manage and enable this, companies must include location movement as a part of their talent mobility definition and strategy.
- Companies now define their workforce to include FTEs, contractors, freelancers, and gig workers. To harness this expanded workforce, companies must make employment movement and managing an expanded workforce part of their talent mobility definition and strategy.

Restructuring Your Organization for Talent Mobility

One of my favorite parts about building Topia was working through the organizational design we needed to make our business work. We were one of the first companies to tackle the complex talent mobility space—starting with supporting families with relocations—and that meant there were few precedents for how to organize ourselves.

As we founded the company, we built innovative software and had all the standard functions of a rapidly growing technology company, but we also managed a concierge business to support relocating employees and their families with moving their stuff, securing housing, and finding schools, managed complex finances on behalf of our corporate customers, and coordinated with a global supply chain that included many different services across more than 100 countries. We wanted to be like traditional relocation service companies, but not too much like them. We wanted to be like the Big 4 consulting firms who populated the space, but not too much like them. We wanted to be a world-class software company, but we knew that relocation required much more human support than a traditional software company.

Every few months, as we grew or entered new business areas, Rachael King, Topia's VP People from 2014 to 2018, would come to my desk and start the org design conversation. Rachael, an HR expert with experience at Cisco and Vodafone, was one of my first executive hires at Topia. I knew that, as we built a complex company in an emerging business area, how we organized ourselves and the culture we built could make or break our success. Every few months—with a whiteboard nearby—we looked at what we were trying to achieve and how to do it. We looked at where the people and functions we needed currently sat in our company—often across different teams or geographies—and how we might restructure to bring them together into a new design. We'd then move people and functions from certain parts of the company and unify them in another, or create a new team to tackle new problems. We documented all of this on a whiteboard before putting it into action.

In 2017, we decided to shift a part of our business area to be delivered by a partner. For a variety of operational and financial reasons, this made the most sense for our business and customers. Executing it was not as simple, however. To make this shift, we kicked off a cross-functional project that required creating a new business area. Like we had done so many times before, we pulled team members with specific skills—operations experts from our finance team, customer experts from our concierge team (called Move Advocates), supply chain experts, engineering, and product experts—to create a new business area to complete this project and then manage it. This required restructuring some teams and creating new ones with a different assortment of skills and functions.

This is much the same scenario that today's business leaders face amid the Talent Mobility Revolution. There are no playbooks or precedents for what this revolution means, or how companies should change their organizational design to succeed. Traditional companies are not set up to respond to and capitalize on this revolution; rather they continue to operate with an outdated organizational design and team structures. The majority of companies have the components of talent mobility—geographic, job, location, and employment movement—fragmented across different parts of their companies with different teams managing them. This makes it complicated to have a unified business and talent strategy—and to truly unlock business agility.

To succeed amid the Talent Mobility Revolution—in the future of jobs—companies must dynamically reorganize and unite all parts of talent mobility in a single department managed by a newly created Chief Talent Mobility Officer (CTMO). With a clear talent mobility definition and updated organizational design, we can then look at how companies and business leaders should reinvent their physical office spaces and operations for business success, which we'll cover in subsequent chapters.

Companies and business leaders that are stuck in the past with a traditional view of organizational design and leadership roles will fail in the Talent Mobility Revolution. *F3 Companies* make agility the core of their business strategy. They reinvent their organizational design around talent mobility, uniting all of the building blocks in a single department that seamlessly interacts across all areas of the business to respond to disruptions and opportunities from the seismic forces of globalization, automation, and demographic changes. This chapter looks at how to successfully reorganize for talent mobility.

Traditional Company Design

For decades, companies have organized with a standard set of organizational functions—or departments—each responsible for specific business activities. These functions emerged to bring order to the many activities happening across companies and the many employees working at a company. Together these functions, how they interact with each other, and the reporting lines within them colloquially became known as the organizational design, or org design, a type of company blueprint for who did what and reported to whom. If business leaders wanted to, they could literally print a page with their entire company's functions, reporting hierarchy, and what each employee did.

Employees for their part typically worked in one of these functional areas and grew their career by progressing through different levels. Junior engineers became senior engineers and then engineering managers and senior engineering managers. There was a defined set of activities handled by each department, and as employees progressed in a given specialization, they acquired expertise in that area. Outside of some specific companies that actively facilitated rotations across departments, there was little movement of employees between business areas.

How Companies Historically Organized

Company organizational design developed with a standard set of departments: sales, marketing, finance, operations, engineering, manufacturing, legal, and human resources. As businesses evolved, departments like procurement (to handle purchasing), travel (to manage employee travel), product (to innovate and design new offerings), and customer service (to manage customer relationships) emerged, among others. Each of these departments has a standard set of activities that it carries out with a leader who plans and directs work. As we discussed in the last chapter, for human resources these activities included recruiting, employee compensation and benefits, corporate relocation, performance management and reviews, and the operations and compliance related to hiring and managing staff.

With defined functional areas, it was not uncommon for silos to emerge between the different parts of the business. In certain instances, this caused challenges, but for the most part, in a stable business environment, these silos were manageable—teams came to work each day, completed their tasks, and then went home. Limited interaction was required across different departments, as innovation cycles were slow and new disruptions and opportunities infrequent.

In 2006, Lehman Brothers was still set up like this. The bank had a clearly defined organizational structure and hierarchy where everyone clearly understood their role and expectations. There was limited interaction across departments, unless required for the normal course of business operations. As an investment banker in the corporate finance area, I rarely interacted with the sales and trading, technology, or administrative teams, for example. The team that I worked with and the managers that I worked for were consistent—and we developed into a kind of specialized work tribe where everyone knew their place and value.

"Traditional company structures were vertical with many levels and grades. Employees did set work that was centrally planned for long periods of time and measured by annual performance reviews," says Rachael King, who has seen the evolution of company organizational design throughout her career.

The Chief Human Resources Officer

The Chief Human Resource Officer (CHRO), or VP HR, was the traditional leader of the human resources department. Typically, she had a set of direct reports who were responsible for managing the different HR departmental functions. CHROs were experts in HR operations, and generally had deep technical knowledge of compliance with labor laws, compensation, benefits, and recruiting. They generally developed this expertise through a career in the HR area and, in many cases, by earning HR qualifications at universities. Historically, HR leaders came from an HR background, and there was little movement from other business areas into HR and vice versa.

The traditional CHRO was an administrative or operational role, often referred to as personnel coordinators or bureaucracy by others across the business. In the last decade, as business leaders started recognizing the critical role of talent attraction and retention to their financial success, the CHRO role started evolving from being viewed as an administrator to being included as a partner in business and staffing decisions. In today's Talent Mobility Rev-olution, the CHRO role is further transforming—moving from a business partner to a new cross-functional role that drives business strategy and agility.

"Historically, if you were in HR, you studied HR in school and earned some kind of certification or professional qualification. You progressed into HR leadership roles by putting in time in the HR business area and developing your HR expertise," says Rachael King. "Now, you don't need to come from an HR background to lead an HR organization. In fact, business leaders are increasingly becoming HR leaders. The CHRO job is now much more about driving the talent agenda, culture, and business strategy."

In the 2015 *Harvard Business Review* article "People Before Strategy: A New Role for the CHRO," Ram Charan, Dominic Barton, and Dennis Carey discussed the changing nature of the CHRO role and the relationship with the CEO, comparing the CHRO's shift from an administrative to strategic focus as similar to that of the CFO in prior decades. This shift has accelerated over the last five years and continues amid the Talent Mobility Revolution.

"It's time for HR to make the same leap that the finance func-tion has made in recent decades and become a true partner to the CEO," they wrote in 2015. "Just as the CFO helps the CEO lead the business by raising and allocating financial resources, the CHRO should help the CEO by building and assigning talent, especially key people, and working to unleash the organization's energy.

"CEOs might complain that their CHROs are too bogged down in administrative tasks, or that they don't understand the business. But let's be clear: it's up to the CEO to elevate HR and bridge any gaps that prevent the CHRO from becoming a strategic partner."*

---

* Ram Charan, Dominic Barton, and Dennis Carey, "People Before Strategy: A New Role for the CHRO," *Harvard Business Review*, July–August 2015.

Talent Mobility Fragmented Across the Company

In traditional company org design, the components of talent mobility—geographic, job, location, and employment movement—are spread across multiple different business areas. In fact, in this model, the CHRO doesn't even manage or influence some of them. Rather they are spread across different company functions and leaders, with significant variances across companies. This makes it near impossible to execute a cohesive talent mobility strategy—and unleash the agility needed to respond to the frequent disruptions and opportunities created by the seismic macro trends of globalization, automation, and demographic change.

Although it varies across companies, here is where the key building blocks of talent mobility sit generally in a traditional company:

- *Relocations.* Traditionally handled by Corporate Relocation, a part of HR
- *Expatriate assignments.* Traditionally handled by Corporate Relocation, a part of HR
- *Long distance commutes.* Traditionally handled by Travel, a part of Procurement, or an executive assistant
- *Frequent travel.* Traditionally handled by Travel, a part of Procurement, or by an executive assistant
- *Short-term projects.* Traditionally handled by Corporate Relocation, a part of HR, or by the business unit manager directly
- *Rotation and training programs.* Traditionally handled by HR, but not by Corporate Relocation
- *Engagement, disruption, or globalization tours of duty.* Traditionally handled by the business unit manager, sometimes, but not always, in partnership with Recruiting
- *Work-from-home and work-from-anywhere.* Traditionally handled by Real Estate, in partnership with the business unit manager

- *Contractors, freelancers, and gig workers.* Traditionally handled by the business unit directly or by Procurement
- *Immigration requirements for employee movement.* Traditionally handled by Legal
- *Tax requirements for employee movement.* Traditionally handled by Tax, as a part of Finance
- *Budgets for employee movement.* Traditionally handled by Finance

Does that sound confusing? It is. In traditional company organizational design, the components of talent mobility are spread across many business areas—corporate relocation, recruiting, real estate, legal, travel, procurement, HR, tax, finance, plus the business units themselves. With all this confusion and the pace of business today, it's not uncommon for managers to initiate and handle employee movement themselves, creating operational and compliance complexity. I have seen this time and time again in my own career and in the companies that I worked with as Founder and CEO of Topia.

In 2007, while working at Lehman Brothers, I accepted an opportunity to leave Hong Kong and work for a number of months in Delhi, India. At the time, Lehman Brothers was advising India's largest real estate developer, DLF, on a $23 billion initial public offering (IPO), the largest in Indian history. The deal was at a critical stage and needed an extra pair of hands. I jumped at the opportunity to join in. This kicked off my own talent mobility experience—a short-term project, long-distance commute, frequent travel, and work-from-anywhere sojourn. It also opened my eyes to the fragmented, inefficient, and complex talent mobility activities at a traditional company.

After I accepted the opportunity, someone from the legal team immediately called me to get my Indian travel visa started. Then the travel team called to book my flights and hotel. Then my boss—the business unit manager—told me that I needed to get a car and driver, which was de rigueur in Delhi, especially for a solo 23-year-old female. "Book it and expense it via your EA," he said. Realizing that, as a part of this work, I'd be working-from-anywhere, I knew I needed better connectivity than the standard corporate laptop with a blocked USB port and slow virtual private network (VPN) provided. So I called the IT department to help get me set up for this more remote working scenario. Despite living and working in India for close to nine months, I never interacted with anyone from the HR or finance team.

My experience in India was a lens into the Talent Mobility Revolution—and the importance of employee movement for the future of jobs. It also gave me a lens into the different activities required to make dynamic talent mobility happen—and just how fragmented they were across departments and people at traditional companies like Lehman Brothers. What was supposed to be a frictionless process to get me on the ground in India as soon as possible was anything but. I knew companies would need a dramatically different org design to succeed in the Talent Mobility Revolution and to deploy workers when and where they needed them.

"We are starting to see companies recognize that talent mobility should be one organization within companies and start to structure it like that," says Nick Pond, who is the Mobility Leader for EY's People Advisory Services. "Companies are starting to see companies take a unified approach to talent mobility and redesign strategic workforce planning around the concept of 'build, buy, move.' Talent mobility is inherent in the employee journey. Cutting-edge companies now know that a cohesive talent mobility strategy and function is key to making this happen."

Talent Mobility Company Design

With the forces of globalization, demographic change, and automation, *F3 Companies* now recognize that talent mobility—the ability to leverage employee movement to drive employee engagement, accelerate innovation, and unleash growth—gives them a competitive advantage. With a clear definition for talent mobility in place, companies then reorganize to unify the fragmented components of talent mobility under one department with one leader. Only with alignment and accountability can companies succeed amid the Talent Mobility Revolution.

A Single Talent Mobility Function

I have attended HR conferences every year for the last nine years. At these conferences, there was always a discussion about whether global mobility (e.g., corporate relocation) should report into the talent function or into the compensation and benefits function. After a lot of spirited debate, attendees nearly always conclude that it should report to talent. Then they go back to work and not much changes.

I always sat through these conversations a bit perplexed, feeling that so many companies were entirely missing the point. Corporate relocation should not report into the talent function. It is a building block of an entirely new talent mobility business strategy. To succeed amid the Talent Mobility Revolution, companies must combine all types of employee movement—geographic (e.g., legacy corporate relocation), job, location, and employment—into a single talent mobility business area. Talent mobility should be a new organization—on par with operations or finance or sales—that replaces and expands the traditional HR organization and unites the areas of talent mobility fragmented across companies today. In the dynamic twenty-first-century business environment, characterized by seismic shifts from globalization, automation and demographic change, talent mobility is the basis of business and people strategy. It should report directly to the CEO with a single leader accountable for business agility as disruptions and opportunities strike.

Here is what the new talent mobility function should include for each of our four types of employee movement:

- *Geographic movement.* Management of all planning, tracking, benefits, pay, budgets, taxes, immigration, compliance, operations, and policies related to geographic movement; management of all workforce planning for business expansion into new geographies; management of all personal needs for relocating employees and their families; management of the supply chain partners who support mobile employees (such as relocation and real estate companies)

- *Job movement.* Management of internal and external recruiting, employer brand, job marketplace and matching, skills categorization, and onboarding and offboarding for hiring and firing workers; management of learning programs that support job tours of duty and career development; management of all operations and policies across the company related to employee job movement

- *Location movement.* Management of all policies and operations for work-from-home and work-from-anywhere arrangements, including flexible work structures, benefits, and compliance; management of all systems that enable work everywhere including virtual collaboration and messaging software; management of all real estate and space planning aligned to the employee footprint

- *Employment movement.* Management of all policies, operations, systems, and compliance for hiring, firing, and staffing contractors, freelancers, and gig workers across teams; management of benefits and worker protections for freelancers; management of the processes for managers to select workers for projects from a broader workforce pool including all four worker classifications

In addition to these four vertical areas, the new talent mobility function should be responsible for a set of horizontal human resources functions that include the traditional HR department responsibilities. The talent mobility area should manage these across the whole workforce, including all four worker classifications.

The horizontal talent mobility activities include:

- Payroll and systems (see Chapter 9)
- Performance, compensation, and leveling (see Chapter 6)
- Benefits, health, and wellness (see Chapter 8)

This new talent mobility function centralizes all aspects of managing the company's workforce and interfaces regularly with other company departments—like an octopus stretching and retracting its tentacles far and wide. It reports to the CEO and collaborates closely on business strategy and rapidly responds as disruptions and opportunities hit.

The talent mobility function should look like this:

One of the world's largest pharmaceutical companies recently went through a transformation to create a unified talent mobility department and hired a new Global VP to lead this. His remit included reorganizing and modernizing the talent mobility area to unify geographic, job, and employment movement, and the systems, operations, policies, partners, and onboarding and offboarding processes needed to make talent mobility a success. He set to work in both digitizing and modernizing each of these individual areas—for example evolving traditional corporate relocation to be broader, digitally enabled geographic movement, and including contingent (or freelance) workers in the definition of the workforce. To do this, he broke traditional org design conventions and silos to unite the components of talent mobility in a single functional area.

"I did consulting work like this for a long time," he told me. "I love helping traditional companies get ready for the future. Designing a single talent mobility function to unlock company agility is an important first step on the journey of transformation for companies."

"We've got companies today operating in a global business environment that's filled with disruptions from technology and competitors. And there's a wave of new types of employees—like remote and contingent workers, and individuals that crave purpose and adventure—that they want to attract to their firms," says Robert Horsley, Chairman Emeritus of Worldwide ERC® and Executive Director of Fragomen, the world's largest immigration firm. He sees a multitude of traditional companies starting to transform amid the talent mobility revolution.

"At the same time, we've got a generation of people saying, 'I want to work where I want and when I want,' whether it's at the office in Hartford, at the client site in Hungary, or in their own home," continues Horsley. "To achieve this, companies are adopting what I call a 'mobile workforce mindset,' asking 'How do I acquire, develop and deploy my people through the lens of talent mobility?' Companies are starting to reorganize around these principles with a single talent mobility area at the core. But it's still really early days. And most companies are not yet there yet."

F3 FOCUS

F3 Companies know that the Talent Mobility Revolution is creating disruptions and opportunities to their business at an unimaginably fast pace. To harness this revolution and respond as changes hit, they unite all parts of talent mobility and people operations under a single new talent mobility business area reporting directly to the CEO and accountable for business agility.

Bringing the Talent Mobility Pieces Together

To create a single new talent mobility function, business leaders must bring together the components of talent mobility—geographic, job, location, and employment movement—into a new business area. They include the operations within each component, as well as the horizontal people operations areas, within this new talent mobility area. This might seem simple here. But it's not. As discussed above, the talent mobility activities have historically been spread across a variety of departments and business owners in a traditional company. This means that, to transform for talent mobility, leaders must break down silos across their traditional org design to move and combine activities into a new area. This is easier said than done.

In traditional organizations, talent mobility activities are spread across a complex patchwork of company departments, such as HR, travel, finance, tax, legal, real estate, IT, and individual business units—creating immense friction for talent mobility like I encountered at Lehman Brothers when moving to India.

Once you've defined talent mobility and built the blueprint for your new talent mobility business area, it's time to identify where the components of talent mobility currently sit in your company and then create a plan to bring them together into a single new business area.

Here are the steps you should follow to bring the talent mobility pieces together and reorganize for agility:

- Update your definition of talent mobility to include geographic, job, location, and employment movement (see Chapter 1 for details).
- Appoint a Chief Talent Mobility Officer to lead your new function, partnering with the CEO and accountable for leading your reorganization and your new function (see next section for details).
- Create a schema for the talent mobility business function, including geographic, job, location, and employment movement, plus key horizontal people operations (follow the diagram in this chapter).
- Using your schema, create the org design for your new talent mobility business function, deciding how you will staff the various areas and remit of each manager. Create your org design without using specific employee names; rather focus on the structure and remit of each job first.
- Once you have your schema and org design, create a single working document that everyone working on the transformation team can refer back to and know what the end goal is.
- Identify where the components of talent mobility are in your current org design. Which departments do they sit in? Who manages them? What do the team structures look like? Who else do they interact with and impact in the company? (A whiteboard helps a lot here!)
- Looking at your schema and the activities spread across your current org, next identify if there are any parts of your new talent mobility function that the company is not yet

doing. You will need to create a new team and operational processes for these (for example, leveraging the freelance economy for staffing).

- Once you've designed your schema and org, and identified where the current components are in your company and those that you'll need to develop, it's time to create your new talent mobility function. To do this, move the current teams from across your company under a single new talent mobility organization, and create the new teams you will then staff.

After watching this transformation proceed, Robert Horsley believes that ". . . all parts of companies will be tied to talent mobility in the future. There should be no specific discussion of when someone is mobile or not—because all employees are," says Horsley. "I see companies across the world moving in this direction, starting to combine geographic and job movement, and increasingly thinking about how to pull other areas under the talent mobility umbrella. To do this, companies should be thinking bigger and more broadly about how talent mobility can be the basis of agility and success. A transformation of their thinking, organizational designs and leadership around talent mobility is needed to do this. Everything in the company that's workforce-related should be aligned with a workforce that is seeking to be more mobile, however you define mobility."

F3 FOCUS

F3 Companies reorganize and create a single new business area that combines all of the pieces of talent mobility. They identify where these pieces currently sit in their company and unite them in a new business area, and they create new teams to tackle parts of talent mobility that they haven't done previously, such as employment movement. With this organizational design, they harness the benefits of talent mobility for their business and workers.

The Chief Talent Mobility Officer

Once the new talent mobility department is created, it's time to appoint the leader for it. The leader of the new talent mobility business area is the Chief Talent Mobility Officer, or CTMO, who is accountable for business agility.

Role and Remit: From CHRO to CTMO

The CTMO, a new take on the traditional CHRO, is the executive role that brings together talent and business strategy for companies staring down the Talent Mobility Revolution. The CTMO should report directly to the CEO and function as a close partner in creating business and workforce strategies amid today's constantly changing business environment. If the company sees a business opportunity in China, it's the CEO and CTMO who should look at how to tackle it. If the company is losing talent to more agile competitors that allow employees to work from anywhere in the country, it's the CEO and CTMO that should lead the design of new policies, systems, and cultural norms to unleash more location movement. If the company faces a shortage of specific skills, the CTMO should look at how to fill them between geographic, job, and employment movement. If jobs are overtaken by artificial intelligence, it's the CTMO who should identify new job opportunities and learning paths for the affected employees, and ensure they are supported through transitions to new jobs.

While the traditional CHRO has historically been as focused on compliance, operations, and, in recent years, business partnership, the CTMO takes this a step further. The CTMO is fully accountable for business agility—ensuring the company has the skills and people it needs for its strategies and operations. The CTMO looks at the workforce as including all classifications of employees and seamlessly orchestrates movement within it. The CTMO is a combined talent and business role. She must understand the inner workings of the company's business, respond to the macro trends creating regular disruptions and opportunities, and manage a complex and diverse workforce inside and outside the company. Appointing a strong CTMO, often with a strong business background, and creating a close partnership between the CEO and CTMO is a critical part of business success amid the Talent Mobility Revolution.

Although the concept of a CTMO is new, companies have started on this journey by hiring people with business and consulting backgrounds to lead their talent mobility teams and transformations. Although these leaders often report to a traditional CHRO who is responsible for traditional HR operations, their remit and influence is vast across the company, and roles often involve more business orientation than traditional HR roles. In my role as Founder and CEO of Topia, I have seen this start to play out at many of our customers across the Fortune 1000. At one customer, a large financial services firm, a new CHRO was recently appointed from a prior role in finance. At another, the CHRO is leading a project, in conjunction with the business, to transform the entire company into having what they call a liquid workforce, rooted in talent mobility.

Catalant Technologies is a software platform that companies use to access and manage workers—including FTEs, alumni, retirees, and independent consultants. In its survey and report "Reimagining Work 2020: How Winning Executives are Building an Agile Workforce," 52 percent of companies said that both the CEO and CHRO or Chief Talent Officer are the key stakeholders in driving the future of work.*

As the Talent Mobility Revolution increasingly takes hold, the most forward-thinking companies will transform the CHROs into CTMOs responsible for their future of work strategy working as close partners to the CEO, Board, and business leaders.

---

* Catalant, "Reimagining Work 2020: How Winning Executives are Building an Agile Workforce," https://gocatalant.com/wp-content/uploads/2018/04/reimagining-work-2020-full-report-2018-04-09.pdf.

F3 FOCUS

F3 Companies evolve the traditional CHRO role into a new Chief Talent Mobility Officer (CTMO) job that leads the newly created talent mobility business area. The CTMO reports to the CEO and is a close working peer. She is accountable for business agility, rapidly responding to disruptions and opportunities from the Talent Mobility Revolution as they strike.

The CTMO Profile and Skill Set

With a clear talent mobility definition, new talent mobility organization, and CTMO job designed, it's time to look at what the CTMO skill set should be. A great Chief Talent Mobility Officer requires a different skill set than a traditional HR professional. The CTMO must be business-oriented, strategic, and innovative, able to juggle a complex set of emerging trends inside and outside of the company.

The CTMO may come from an HR or business background, but must be experienced and skilled in creation, transformation, and leadership across a dynamically changing business. He must be able to quickly identify opportunities, rapidly iterate as disruptions hit, and continuously align a complex set of stakeholders inside and outside of the company. While the traditional CHRO has deep expertise in the technical aspects of HR, the CTMO is more of a general business leader who has the emotional quotient (EQ) to understand and engage a diverse workforce. The CTMO does not need specific technical expertise in the talent mobility and people operations functions; rather the CTMO must be able to orchestrate the interlocking talent and business strategies across the company and manage experts in given HR areas.

Summarized, the CTMO profile and skill set looks like this:

- A strategic thinker, who understands the interplay between business and talent strategy
- Creative, innovative, and agile, with the ability to see the future, make it happen, and respond to disruptions and opportunities as they arise
- Deeply collaborative and able to work closely with the CEO and diverse business leaders in a matrix structure to respond to opportunities and disruptions
- A great communicator with the ability to persuade, influence, and align teams behind new jobs, projects, and strategies
- A strong orchestrator and manager who can set work priorities, rapidly get people where they're needed to complete work, and enable people for success
- A leader with good financial and operational acumen who can assess talent and business strategy across financial, operational, and compliance requirements to get the right people in the right place without any problems for the company

Although evolving a CHRO into a CTMO is new and companies are just making a start toward it, there has been a consistent evolution in the traditional CHRO role over the last few years with increasing numbers of business leaders moving laterally into the role. In the 2017 *Harvard Business Review* article "Why More Business Executives Should Consider Becoming a CHRO," authors John Boudreau, Peter Navin, and David Creelman discuss four reasons why those with nontraditional HR backgrounds may succeed as twenty-first-century HR leaders: a focus on business results, not only people outcomes; their role in pushing fellow leaders, not just supporting them; their desire to embrace opportunity, not only reduce risk; and their application of diverse business skills to the role.* These are the

---

* John Boudreau, Peter Navin, and David Creelman, "Why More Executives Should Consider Becoming a CHRO," *Harvard Business Review*, May 3, 2017.

same perspectives and skills that are needed for a CTMO who can drive business success amid the Talent Mobility Revolution.

"Companies and individuals need to make an investment to transform for talent mobility," says Peggy Smith. "Work is being completely rewritten through agile projects—and a new talent mobility leader at the highest levels of the organization must enable that."

F3 FOCUS

F3 Companies transform with talent mobility at their core, creating a talent mobility function led by a CTMO, who is a strategic talent and business leader. The CTMO is a senior executive responsible for business agility and orchestrating movement across a diverse internal and external workforce so that they are ready to respond as disruptions and opportunities hit.

This Talent Mobility Revolution is what I saw starting at Lehman Brothers as a young banker navigating fragmentation and friction as I moved to India. I saw the Talent Mobility Revolution accelerate through my nine years as Founder and CEO of Topia. As it did, the most forward-thinking companies started to redefine talent mobility, create a new business area that unified its parts, and appoint talent mobility leaders with strong business orientations to lead this transformation. But these critical reorganizations and the evolution of the CHRO into the CTMO are in a very early stage. While some companies have made steps down this path, virtually no companies or teams have made the full transformation into an agile organization with talent mobility at its core and all of its parts unified in a single business area and strategy.

Reorganizing for talent mobility is the second step to succeeding in the Talent Mobility Revolution. To win in the twenty-first century, amid the seismic trends of globalization, automation, and demographic change, companies must restructure their teams and departments for agility. Those that make this shift will succeed. Those that do not will be left behind and leave their workers exposed.

CHAPTER SUMMARY

- Traditional company org design is not set up for success amid the Talent Mobility Revolution. To succeed, companies must create a single new talent mobility business area.
- The new talent mobility department should include all activities related to geographic, job, location, and employment mobility, as well as the traditional operational activities for managing staff.
- The new talent mobility function should think of the workforce, and its remit, as including all internal (FTEs) and external (freelance) workers, and seamlessly manage them as one workforce.
- To create the new talent mobility function, companies should identify where activities are currently done in the company as well as those new areas that need to be developed and then unite them all in a new function with a single leader.
- Companies should evolve the traditional CHRO role into a CTMO that leads the talent mobility function and is responsible for business and talent agility.
- Companies should look for CTMOs that have a strong business background and can effectively partner with the CEO to dynamically respond to disruptions and opportunities as they occur.

Redesigning Your Offices
for New Ways of Work

On a cold evening in December, I was sitting at a restaurant in Berlin after speaking at the annual TechCrunch Disrupt Conference. I was deep in the details of the financial plan for Topia's next year when Daniel, a fellow American with a laptop, sat down next to me and struck up a conversation. I learned that Daniel was a consultant who lived in LA, traveled frequently, and worked from pretty much anywhere he was—hotels, planes, coworking spaces, client offices, or his own company offices. Today, he was working at a restaurant in Berlin, just like me.

In the Talent Mobility Revolution with increasing location movement, companies are reinventing the role of an office and resetting expectations about where and how employees work. Like Daniel, employees today work from *everywhere*, valuing the flexibility, autonomy, and work-life integration that comes from blending work at offices, public spaces, and in the home. This, coupled with the growth of long-distance commuting and frequent travel, has changed the way companies design their offices and given birth to coworking spaces like WeWork (now valued at more than $20 billion). In this new era of jobs, people can now work from bustling urban hubs, small rural districts, or planned suburbs—in all parts of the world.

49

In 2017, Topia acquired Teleport, a start-up based in Tallinn, Estonia, with a distributed team working remotely throughout the world. Teleport was founded by Sten Tamkivi (who became Topia's Chief Product Officer) and Silver Keskkula (who became Topia's VP Data Science and Research). Tamkivi and Keskkula were veterans of Skype, and they founded Teleport to help individuals "find their best place to live and work" by leveraging a complex set of data and algorithms about cost and quality of life. At Topia, we always had a lot of geographic movement—frequent travel and some relocations—from our global operations. But acquiring Teleport was our first foray into the location movement of the Talent Mobility Revolution. Teleport had team members working all over the world—from a user experience designer in Germany to a data scientist in Canada to global nomads that literally worked everywhere (I even saw a picture of Keskkula working from a laptop on a beach in the Galapagos Islands). Their remote work culture was an important part of their DNA, talent strategy, and operating norms. They had even produced a manifesto detailing the principals of running a distributed organization with lots of remote work.

As we brought our two companies together, we combined Topia's principally office-based culture and Teleport's distributed culture. We had urban office hubs and embraced geographic and location movement for our employees. If our team members needed to work from home sometimes, they did. If they needed to work from coffee shops or restaurants while traveling (like I was in Berlin), they did. And, when they needed to collaborate, they came together in one of our offices that we redesigned over time to inspire creation and connection. Topia, like many *F3 Companies*, operated like a rubber band—team members could disperse to work remotely and then come together in our office spaces to collaborate and connect.

Over my nine years at Topia, I have seen companies built like Teleport with a distributed work culture, and companies built like

Lehman Brothers with an office work culture. In recent years, I have seen increasing numbers of traditional companies embrace location movement and transform their policies and physical spaces for greater remote work—benefiting from lower real estate costs, reduced carbon footprints, expanded talent pools, and higher staff engagement and retention, particularly for women balancing family and career needs, and millennials valuing autonomy and flexibility. These companies know that today's talent works differently. They work from home, work from holidays, work from planes, work from cafés, and work from coworking spaces. And they do this from everywhere in the world.

To succeed amid the Talent Mobility Revolution—and find, attract, and engage today's workers—companies must dispense with the notion that work is done only in an office with employees punching in at 9 a.m., five days per week. Instead, they must embrace distributed and remote work as a key part of their business and talent strategy.

Companies and business leaders that are stuck in the past with a traditional view of office work will fail to attract and engage the talent they need for success in the twenty-first century. *F3 Companies* rethink the purpose, design, and location of their offices, welcoming location movement as a core part of their operations. Today's talent works differently. Companies that don't transform their operations and offices for it will be left behind by those that do. This chapter looks at how to redesign your physical office spaces for talent mobility and remote work.

The Traditional Office

In the medieval era, itinerant tradesmen carried their wares into a town, set up shop in the village square, and sold what they could before moving on. "Chapmen," for example, sold books, paper, pens, and ink. In a typical town, the market for writing supplies would quickly be exhausted—few could read or write—at which point it would be time to pack up and move on.

As university towns sprang up during the early Renaissance, some clever chapmen realized that steady business from professors and students made it feasible to stay in one place. No more trudging through the countryside with a cart full of valuable goods. A fixed place of business would be easier, safer, and more profitable. These stationary sellers—"stationers," hence "stationery"—adapted to the new environment and thrived. This model of fixed physical offices endured for centuries, even as technology made it possible to work from all over the world and stay connected.

The Purpose of the Traditional Office

The purpose of the traditional office was daily work. Like at school, it was expected that employees come to work at the office each day and stay for a fixed number of hours—usually 9 to 5 with an hour lunch break. Work included daily tasks, as well as meetings—often in conference rooms—and conference calls. Contribution at work was measured to an extent by output, but largely by the concept of "face time": how long and often an employee was seen at the office. The reward for coming to work each day and clocking regular hours was a steady promotion ladder within a given department or team.

If employees couldn't make it to work one day—say, due to illness or childcare challenges—they "called in" to their manager and stayed home, generally forgoing any work and meetings that day. If this happened too frequently, they could be overlooked for promotions or receive negative performance reviews. With this traditional expectation of office attendance and hours, the workforce naturally developed with one spouse working in the office and one spouse caring for the home and children, popularized by the many sitcoms about the company man and his family—without location movement and work flexibility, it was difficult to balance the needs of work and family. The workforce also developed with the notion that work was local. Communities developed around companies and manufacturing plants, sometimes relying on a single employer to provide jobs. If business tides changed, communities and families were exposed.

Lehman Brothers was set up as a traditional office environment. Work was from the office, and we all moved to the cities nearest to where the office was. We were expected to be in the office, not anywhere else, when working. And everyone was. I arrived each morning by 9 a.m., worked from my cubicle, and stayed in the office until my boss left. If I finished my work early, I stayed until the end of the day and pretended to still be working. If I had a doctor's appointment or home delivery or family issue, I asked my boss for time off and logged it in our internal system. If I didn't put in the "face time" expected, my annual performance review and bonus showed it. If anyone on our team left early, colleagues whispered about it.

To accomplish this, Lehman Brothers made it next to impossible to get work done from anywhere but the office. BlackBerrys were only given to staff at a particular level. E-mail was blocked on personal smartphones. If you needed to access files from outside the physical office building, you had to use a virtual private network (VPN) that took minutes to connect—if it ever did. Virtual collaboration tools were nonexistent. No video conferencing, messaging, or network connection outside the physical office building. There was literally no concept of location movement or remote working. Everyone worked the same hours in the same way in the same place.

Krish Ramakrishnan founded the videoconferencing platform BlueJeans to enable a different way of working than at Lehman Brothers. Through the course of growing BlueJeans, he has seen an evolution in the role of the office for work.

"In prior decades, people went to work to do work," says Ramakrishnan. "Companies wanted to get things done so they forced people to colocate in the office during the workday. The office was for working with colleagues. If you needed to get work done outside of office hours, however, there was a significant time lag. With growing virtual work now—and the changing purpose of an office—work now comes to you. And it can be done anytime and from anywhere."

The Design of the Traditional Office

Traditional offices were often sterile and large, designed with the assumption that 100 percent of the employees would be in the office 100 percent of the time. Generally junior-level staff worked from cubicles while managers had offices, a manifestation of the hierarchy at the core of a traditional company. Offices generally increased in size with manager seniority—and almost always they had imposing desks, physical walls, and doors that could be shut when needed. For the most part, employees worked with desktop computers and landline phones.

Offices had conference rooms for meetings and a small kitchenette area—much like you would find in a hotel suite—with a basic coffee machine and empty refrigerators where employees could store a lunch they may have brought to work that day. Save for conference rooms and a basic table that may be in the kitchenette area, offices rarely had any sort of spaces for collaboration (today, often called "breakout areas")—no couches, armchairs, or communal tables for connection and collaboration. I've seen countless traditional offices designed like this—and often felt energy ooze from my body as I entered them. Lehman Brothers was set up like this—as are many of the traditional relocation, tax, and immigration firms that Topia works with (although in recent years, many have started to also transform their physical spaces). As recently as 2015, I visited one of these companies and learned that not only was their office designed with traditional cubicles, but the height of their cubicles and length of their lunch breaks grew with seniority—a perk of tenure!

In 2018, Topia acquired a company that had built software and expertise for managing the complex tax, compliance, and financial requirements of expatriates, an important part of the talent mobility systems roadmap (see Chapter 9 for more details). Like Teleport, its culture was different than Topia—it had a more traditional office design with cubicles for most team members and offices located in a separate part of the building, often with closed doors. As we combined the two companies, we redesigned the office for collaboration and connection, removing cubicles and walled offices and introducing communal tables, breakout spaces, and glass meeting rooms and phone booths.

"The traditional office was where all work was done," says Sten Tamkivi. "But the irony is, you could actually go into the office, work alone in a cubicle all day, and never talk to anyone else. There wasn't a concept of the office being about collaboration, connection, or inspiration. Rather, it was just the place you went to do your work, access your files, and use your desktop computer. The irony is that with this setup, it is actually more efficient to work alone from home and not have to commute into an office."

The Location of the Traditional Office

As traditional companies developed with the expectation that all staff would be in the office all the time, their office footprints grew. Due to space and cost constraints, traditional offices started to move outside of cities and set up in suburban office parks. These office parks were often large and characterless, proximate to but outside of cities, and often requiring a commute from employees. This image of the "commuting office man" was popularized by the British sitcom *The Office*, where employees work in a corporate office park in Slough, England, outside of London. (After living in London, I can personally attest to the fact that Slough is very much a traditional office park!)

In 2004, I interned at Mellon Bank. Thrilled to have my first company job and envisioning a summer working in New York, I was surprised to later learn that my internship would actually be in suburban New Jersey. Each morning, I got on a company minibus that took me and others from downtown Manhattan to a generic office park next to the New Jersey Turnpike. I worked 9 to 5 in my cubicle, ate lunch at the corporate cafeteria, and had meetings in walled-off conference rooms with doors shut. While I liked the work, at the end of that summer, I vowed that my next job would be in a different location that didn't require a commute to an office park!

The New Talent Mobility Office

As location movement and remote work grows amid the Talent Mobility Revolution, companies are rethinking the purpose, design, and location of their offices. As workforce demographics shift, companies must take a different approach to their office footprint and workplace environments to attract and engage today's workers, especially millennials. Seventy-eight percent of millennials see workplace quality as important when choosing an employer, and 69 percent will trade other benefits for better workspace.*

The Purpose of Today's Offices

Today's workforce operates like a rubber band—people work from distributed locations and come together in office spaces to collaborate, connect, and create. Companies today do not expect employees to be in the office every day for a set number of hours, like they did in prior years. The purpose of offices today is not attendance, but community. Offices function as a hub for workers to come together, and where energy, ideas, and personal relationships are cultivated. These personal relationships are important for building the trust required for effective work in distributed teams. Some employees come into the office every day—welcoming the community and routine—but for many, office attendance is not a daily activity. Rather,

---

* CBRE, "Millennial Myths and Realities," 2016.

they see office attendance as a set of dynamic interactions that form a part of their work-life integration—a new way of working that allows them to balance families, location preferences (for example living in a rural community), and other interests (for example working on projects as a part of the gig economy).

Manon DeFelice is an expert on location movement. She founded Inkwell to match people to jobs with flexible work and locations. As she built Inkwell, she has seen escalating demand for remote work and the role of offices changing.

"I saw a huge brain drain of talent demanding different ways of working and leaving companies when they didn't get them. People just didn't want to be in the office every day 9 to 5," said DeFelice. "I also saw huge numbers of people flocking to cities and suburbs without any options to work flexibly from rural locations and commute to offices as and when they needed," she continues.

"My husband is from West Virginia, and then moved to New York to work in finance. If he could have worked in West Virginia without the expectation of being in the office every day, then he probably would have stayed there and also contributed to the microeconomy there."

"Many traditional companies still need to rethink their offices to be about collaboration and community, not attendance," emphasizes DeFelice. "Location movement and flexible work is in demand for all of today's workforce—and must be a key part of company strategy." DeFelice says that transformation of office purpose starts with designing a culture where people know that "if you're not around you can still be working."

"Traditional managers sometimes struggle without seeing their people every day," says Tamkivi. "They need to move to measuring objectives and output, instead of face time. Their philosophy must become—where you do work doesn't matter, as long as you get the results. Put simply, there must be a total cultural transformation starting at the very top of a team or company."

F3 FOCUS

F3 Companies rethink the purpose of their offices and swap expectations of attendance for inspiring collaboration. They know that embracing location movement and flexible work is critical to winning the global war on talent, building a diverse workforce, and managing their costs and carbon footprint. With this strategy, they can attract and retain the people they need to succeed amid the Talent Mobility Revolution.

How Offices Should Be Designed Today

Today's offices generally have smaller physical footprints than the large corporate spaces of yesteryear. They are designed to stimulate energy and inspiration. They get rid of cubicles and walled-offices—removing physical barriers to collaboration and connection—and instead create open plan space with desks side by side, managers seated near their employees, and conference rooms easily accessible and often visible through glass walls.

With a focus on collaboration and creativity, today's offices generally have many breakout areas: corners filled with couches, armchairs, and inspiring art pieces or plants where employees can come together to brainstorm and ideate without the formality of a conference room or the distraction of being in the middle of other colleagues. With an open plan and desks adjacent to one another, you'll also often find phone booths for taking confidential calls. Kitchens stocked with food and treats are *de rigueur*—as are large communal tables for sharing meals, happy hour drinks, or work discussions. The purpose of these spaces is to inspire cross-functional innovation, creativity, and relationship building among staff.

Offices may be designed with assigned desks, where each employee has a specific desk even if he may not be physically in the office each day, or with hot desks, where employees do not have an assigned desk but rather pick an open one when they are in the office. Hot desking fully embraces location movement and allows companies to significantly reduce their physical footprint and real estate costs on the assumption that all employees are not in the office at the same time. Some companies even adopt fixed schedules for hot desking where certain employees come into the office on certain days, while others work from anywhere, and then swap. According to CBRE's 2018 America's Occupier Survey, 75 percent of companies today have assigned desks, but just 48 percent of them expect to operate an assigned desk office environment within three years.*

Skype was founded in 2003 in Estonia. Sten Tamkivi was an early employee, working at the company for eight years and growing to lead various business areas as a General Manager. Skype always operated on *F3* principles, expecting workers to work flexibly, be autonomous, and live and travel around the world from their Estonian hub. Tamkivi recalls that when they moved to their first full office building, they designed it intentionally to inspire collaboration and connection—not face time. They put desks on all four floors, and all of the meeting rooms on the second and fourth floors and the cafeteria on the third floor. The idea was that no matter where your desks were, you might run into someone you didn't normally see when going to lunch or to a meeting. Their belief was that if people came into the office to sit in a cubicle or closed office alone all day, then they could be doing that anywhere. In fact, it probably made more sense for them to stay home to work alone, rather than taking time for a commute. Rather, they designed the office to expose people to one another and spur random moments of collaboration.

According to global real estate consultancy CBRE, 25 percent of companies anticipate migrating toward activity-based, unassigned workplace strategies (or hot desking) "to meet the evolving needs of talent and workstyles." Forty-five percent of landlords say

---

* The CBRE Institute, "Solving for the Future with the Agility, America's Occupier Survey Report 2018."

flexibility of use was the most important occupier trend for real estate in 2018.*

"Unlike generations of white-collar workers before them, modern employees want—and often demand—flexible spaces that are conducive to thinking and that help them perform the tasks required of them," says Adam Jezard in the *World Economic Forum* article "The Traditional Office is Dead. Here's Why." "Additionally, many companies are complaining of difficulty hiring and retaining millennials, and a barnlike office with little daylight and row upon row of desks is unlikely to help."[†]

F3 FOCUS

F3 Companies redesign their physical spaces to inspire collaboration, creativity, and connection. They swap cubicles and closed conference rooms for open-plan spaces and inspiring breakout areas where employees can work together informally. With this design, they drive employee engagement, accelerate innovation, and unleash growth.

Where to Locate Offices Today

With frequent location mobility and physical spaces designed for collaboration and inspiration, companies are increasingly setting up offices in urban, city center locations. These office locations incorporate the dynamism of the city—and often become a part of urban regeneration projects. With city center locations, employees can get a coffee at local cafés, lunch at a nearby restaurants, and have one-on-one meetings while walking through the urban

---

* The CBRE Institute, "Solving for the Future with the Agility, America's Occupier Survey Report 2018."
† Adam Jezard, "The Traditional Office is Dead. Here's Why," World Economic Forum, November 1, 2017.

downtown. This connection with the city inspires further creativity and easier connectivity with other professionals and creatives, contributing to both the work and society experience. Many millennial workers increasingly prefer to live in cities.

In Silicon Valley—a place filled with *F3 Companies*—this "flight to the city" is well underway. In a drive to attract top talent and inspire creativity, many of today's high-flying technology companies have opened offices in downtown San Francisco instead of suburban Silicon Valley (Menlo Park, Mountain View, and Palo Alto) where software companies were historically based. Companies such as Stripe, Uber, Pinterest, Square, Slack, and Lyft have all made this choice. Companies like LinkedIn, Workday, and Upwork, which were historically based outside of San Francisco, have opened offices in the city. Many venture capital funds have added smaller, high-energy city locations to their suburban Silicon Valley footprints as their employee demographics have shifted.

A 2018 paper published in the journal *Regional Studies* by Adam Okulicz-Kozaryn of Rutgers University and Rubia Valente of Baruch College investigates the happiness of different generations. The study shows that millennials are happiest in larger, more urban environments.* In order to attract, retain, and engage the largest cohort of the workforce, today's companies move their office locations back to urban centers and enable flexible work and commuting around them.

F3 FOCUS

F3 Companies know that today's talent looks to offices to inspire ideas and collaboration and increasingly prefers to work from urban locations when in the office. They set up city offices where physical spaces and employees can interact with the surrounding city to enhance creativity and innovation.

---

* Richard Florida, "Millennials are Happiest in Cities," CityLab, June 29, 2018.

Swapping Offices for Fully Remote Work

In the talent mobility era, certain companies are taking location movement a step further and championing fully remote teams— both as work-from-home and work-from-anywhere models. These innovative companies entirely reject the concept of an office, and instead hire staff to work in a virtual setting—over videoconferences, messaging applications, and other software that fosters virtual collaboration.

Working from the Home Office

All *F3 Companies* embrace remote work as part of their employment models, offering the flexibility and work-life integration that is important to today's top talent. Cutting-edge companies take this a step further, however, and hire employees to almost exclusively work virtually, from their own homes. They do not have physical offices (or may just have a couple of small ones) but rather operate virtual teams where employees collaborate digitally, using modern technology systems like videoconferencing, file sharing, and messaging applications to complete work (see Chapter 9 for further details on collaboration systems).

Typically, work-from-home companies bring their employees together in one or multiple annual all-company meetings, hosted in a given location (often a hotel), often over a week. They generally also hold team meetings in a similar fashion, bringing together specific teams for a period of time to plan, collaborate, and build relationships. What these companies save on the overhead of physical office spaces, they often invest in systems for virtual work and travel budgets for employees to come together for these meetings. A significant amount of investment typically goes into these all-company and team meetings to ensure the time together is maximized and strong personal relationships are built that can support virtual working thereafter. Often these meetings involve business activities, such as planning and goal setting, annual and quarterly reviews, and strategy working sessions, as well as team social and team-building activities, generally based on collaborative problem solving (at Topia, we once did the "spaghetti challenge"—take pieces of dry spaghetti and marshmallows and see which team can build the coolest contraption!).

Work-from-home companies also recognize that an office can be an important form of social engagement and community for some employees. They balance their work-from-home culture with unique benefits that offer office work to employees who want it (see Chapter 8 for a full discussion on benefits)—expanding their notion of flexibility for employees. These companies offer an office stipend that employees can spend on a membership at a local coworking space, like WeWork, or on frequent coffees while working from a local café, offering the opportunity for the community and energy that working from home can lack for some employees.

F3 FOCUS

F3 Companies know that flexibility is key to attracting, retaining, and engaging today's top talent. Cutting edge *F3 Companies* embrace work-from-home models that allow employees to work virtually from home offices. They save money on office overhead costs, and instead invest in software to enable virtual work and regular in-person meetings.

Making Everywhere Your Office

Some companies expand their work-from-home definition to be work-from-everywhere. In work-from-everywhere models, companies recognize that distributed employees may not only be working from a home office, but may literally be working from *anywhere*—a café in California, airport in Alabama, train in Europe, or even a beach in the Galapagos Islands. The policies and norms of these companies are similar to work-from-home companies, but they tend to attract a growing class of travelers and digital nomads, like my friend Daniel from Berlin. Work-from-anywhere companies tend to have few, if any, physical offices, instead investing in virtual tools to keep employees connected and collaborating while remote.

Silver Keskkula, Co-Founder of Teleport (the company Topia acquired) is a data scientist and global nomad—a large part of the reason why Teleport developed with a work-from-everywhere culture. Like many top millennial and Gen Z creative and engineering professionals, Silver values location movement and the inspiration that comes with it. Silver decided, while living in Palo Alto and working at Skype, that he wanted to see the world. When building Teleport, he lived in Airbnbs around the world—literally working from all places in all corners of the world and gathering inspiration into the global products he was building.

At Automattic, which owns popular content management software WordPress.com, the center of gravity is virtual. Chief Business Officer Catherine Stewart says that with this model, "work happens all the time."

"We've designed our organization to be distributed, and our employees live and work all over the world," says Stewart. "Having a distributed organization helps us recruit top talent, and to better design and create products for a global audience."

Automattic has designed its company operations and systems to enable this virtual culture. Employees rely heavily on videoconferencing via Zoom, a messaging platform, Slack, and a proprietary internal system that teams use to communicate, log notes, and post updates. This is supported by a culture of sharing and transparency, where people regularly document notes from meetings they have, and tag others who may need to read them and comment.

"We record all of our videoconferences and put things in writing that a lot of other companies may not," says Stewart. "We save and share everything that might need to be referenced by someone working from a remote location alone in some part of the world. It provides a really good record for people to read and digest, and helps with alignment across our distributed model."

Automattic also recognizes the importance of face-to-face time for teams to ensure that relationships are built across the company. The company hosts an annual gathering, called the Grand Meet-up, in which employees convene in a single location. Individual teams also meet in person one or two times a year, for five to seven days at a time. Teams use this time for different reasons, but common ones include goal setting, weeklong hacks, and cross-functional projects.

The executive team also gets together regularly for important decisions, such as companywide OKRs and product roadmaps. Leaders are also expected to attend partner team meet-ups, meet with coworkers as needed, and host their various team meetings. This can mean significant travel for company leaders—up to 50 percent, says Stewart.

Finally, like many work-from-home and work-from-anywhere companies, Automattic recognizes that an office can be an important daily social venue for many people, particularly those who are extroverted, or a place to escape when home has distractions (or slow Wi-Fi). Automattic provides what they call a "coworking stipend" to employees that can be used to pay for space at a coworking space where a given employee may be based.

"Some people want to sit in an office every day. Others want to work from home," says Stewart.

One of the most difficult things about making this work-from-everywhere model work is time zones, says Stewart—something that we have also found challenging at Topia with a nine-hour time difference between our product and engineering centers in Tallinn, Estonia, and Bellevue, Washington.

"Time zones can be a significant constraint," says Stewart. "On my teams, I require that individuals have at least two hours of overlap in working time, twice per week. This means that if you decide to work from Asia, and the team you're considering joining is mostly based out of the United States and Europe, you will be committing to having calls at odd hours."

"For teams with structured work—e.g., customer support—teams take shifts relevant to their assigned time zone, ensuring no gaps in the global day for customers," continues Stewart.

Automattic has found its work-from-anywhere model to be a critical differentiator in attracting, retaining, and engaging top talent. It also allows the company to recruit from a global talent pool, hire from urban and rural locations, and welcome a breadth of perspectives and ideas that accelerates innovation and company growth. With this model, Automattic has truly harnessed the Talent Mobility Revolution.

Upwork follows a similar model of work-from-anywhere. "Our philosophy is to hire the best people, no matter where they are," says Kasriel. "This gives us the opportunity to access better, more affordable talent, and retain this talent through greater flexibility."

F3 FOCUS

F3 Companies like Teleport, Automattic, and Upwork embrace work-from-everywhere models that help them attract and retain workers who value location movement and autonomy as part of their work. These companies know that doing away with the traditional notion of work in an office allows them to access a larger talent pool, and attract and retain workers by offering autonomy and flexibility.

This Talent Mobility Revolution is what I saw starting more than a decade ago as I worked from airports, cafés, and client offices. It's what led me to found and build Topia, unlocking greater employee movement for companies around the world. What I saw was employees demanding more flexibility in where they work and seeking more inspiration and community from their company offices. As the demographics of the workforce continue to shift, the successful companies of the future will make location mobility a key part of their business, talent, and real estate strategies, transforming traditional office spaces into creative, agile spaces where employees come together to collaborate. In doing so, they also tap into a larger talent pool and extend job opportunities to communities farther afield.

Redesigning offices for talent mobility is the third step to succeeding in the Talent Mobility Revolution. Companies that embrace location movement and make the shift to flexible work models will attract, retain, and engage the world's top talent. Those that do not make this shift will lose the global talent war to the their more innovative competitors and not be ready to respond to disruptions and opportunities from globalization, automation, and demographic change.

Redesigning your offices for talent mobility is necessary to succeed in the Talent Mobility Revolution. Today's workers work differently. Companies that enable remote and flexible work—location movement—will attract and enable the workers they need to achieve their business goals. Those that don't will lose out.

In this section, we looked at how to set up an *F3 Company* and covered the first three steps to talent mobility transformation: (1) rethinking your definition of talent mobility, (2) restructuring for talent mobility and (3) redesigning your offices for new ways of work. With this foundation in place, we now turn to look at how to redesign work for an *F3 Company*. In Section 2, we look at how to rearchitect roles, evolve teams and managers, and redefine career paths.

CHAPTER SUMMARY

- Embracing location movement allows companies to access a larger talent. Companies should reinvent their work strategies to champion more flexible and remote work. With this they can bring jobs to more workers.
- Today's workers increasingly demand location movement and remote work. Companies must embrace this to attract, retain, and engage key talent.
- Companies must rethink the purpose of their offices. Business leaders should not expect that employees will work 9-to-5 in the office. Instead, employees come into offices to collaborate and create.
- Companies must redesign their office spaces to inspire innovation and creativity by removing cubicles and creating breakout areas where workers can interact informally.
- Companies should set up offices in urban locations, where workers can easily commute and interact with the city, gathering inspiration from the urban diversity and dynamism.
- Companies and business leaders must adopt flexible work arrangements, work-from-home, and work-from-anywhere models to succeed amid the Talent Mobility Revolution.

REDESIGNING WORK TO BE FLAT, FLUID, AND FAST

Rearchitecting Roles to Be Dynamic Jobs

We know the villain of the movie well: a cigar-chomping titan of industry who casually lays off thousands of trained, hard-working employees the moment he can get the job done cheaper by technology or outsourcing. With avarice in his eye, he picks up the phone, barks out an order, and watches as streams of disgruntled workers go through the factory doors. The next day, all those diligent American workers have been replaced by automation or globalization.

People with families and mortgages register for unemployment. A town empties out. The shops on Main Street shutter. Unfortunately, this is the story for far too many American cities that have been reliant on a single employer hiring local workers to fixed roles. These workers have not historically had the opportunity to leverage their skills into new work opportunities. But with location movement, remote work, and a shift from fixed roles to dynamic jobs, American workers no longer need to face this scenario as the economy shifts.

We have seen the effects of globalization over recent years, but we are just starting to come to terms with upcoming risks from automation. A 2018 Pew Research Center study asked 1,896 experts about the impact of emerging technologies. A whopping 48 percent projected "a future where robots and artificial intelligence have replaced a significant number of both blue- and white-collar workers." Oxford University researchers found that "42 percent of U.S. workers have a high probability of seeing their jobs automated over the next 20 years."[*] In fact, McKinsey Global Institute estimates that 50 percent of current jobs could technically be automated *today*.[†] But, according to Accenture, far fewer jobs will be lost to automation if people are able to reallocate and match their skills to tasks—or jobs—that require "uniquely human skills," such as complex analysis, communications, and activities that require social and human intelligence. Underlying this is the need to rethink the nature of jobs, moving from employment based on fixed roles to work based on dynamic jobs.

Today, disruption is progressing at a faster pace than ever before. Companies have increasing market opportunities and competitive threats with shorter innovation cycles, frequent geopolitical shocks, and growing amounts of automation replacing traditional roles. Traditional roles are being overtaken, while, at the same time, skills gaps permeate the workforce for new jobs. Employers are slow to adopt a more skills-based work structure. At the same time, as demographics have shifted, people increasingly value the flexibility, autonomy, and lifelong learning of working across a company, for different companies, and on different "gigs." A growing share of people—either out of desire or necessity—now "loan" their skills to companies when needed versus have companies "acquire" their whole working life and skill set. According to well-known HR analyst Josh Bersin from Bersin by Deloitte, 40 percent of the US

[*] Darrell M. West, "Will Robots and AI Take Your Job? The Economic and Political Consequences of Automation," Brookings (blog), April 18, 2018, https://www.brookings.edu/blog/techtank/2018/04/18/will-robots-and-ai-take-your-job-the-economic-and-political-consequences-of-automation/.
[†] James Manyika et al., "What the Future of Work Will Mean for Jobs, Skills, and Wages: Jobs Lost, Jobs Gained | McKinsey & Company," November 2017, https://www.mckinsey.com/featured-insights/future-of-organizations-and-work/jobs-lost-jobs-gained-what-the-future-of-work-will-mean-for-jobs-skills-and-wages.

workforce will be contingent workers by 2020.* The millennial and Gen Z workforce will work across more careers than their parents had job titles.

All of this means that, amid the Talent Mobility Revolution, the nature of work and what it means is fundamentally shifting. Agility is the currency of today's business environment. When disruptions hit (whether from automation, globalization, or competition) and opportunity knocks (whether for new business, product, or profit), companies must be able to seamlessly find, select, and enable people for new jobs. To do this, they are moving their employment model from one based on traditional roles, career paths, and full-time employment to one of dynamic jobs leveraging the skills of both full-time and freelance workers. Once a job has been completed, a worker goes on to the next one, which may be in a completely different team or business area, or even at a different company. (We define a *role* as a traditional, full-time job with a clear job description and *job* as a unit of work completed as a project over a specific time period.)

F3 Companies know that globalization, automation, and demographic changes—the Talent Mobility Revolution—bring increasing disruption and opportunities to their businesses and workers. These innovative companies redesign their organizations and employment models to be agile and responsive, rearchitecting traditional roles to be dynamic jobs where skills, not titles, are the currency of work. They are at the forefront of the Talent Mobility Revolution, creating a new work model that seamlessly responds to changes, attracts and retains top talent, and delivers value to businesses and workers. Adopting this model at companies across our country will help many workers transition well amid our shifting economy.

Companies and business leaders that remain in the past operating with traditional roles and org designs will fail amid the Talent Mobility Revolution. Work today requires rapid adaptability. *F3*

---

* Bersin by Deloitte, "What Is Talent in the Future of Work," June 27, 2018.

Companies deconstruct roles to be dynamic, skills-based work with flat organizational design and teams of employees, freelancers, and technology working together. Companies that can make this transition will succeed, responding gracefully to disruptions and opportunities as they occur, and supporting their workers through a shifting work landscape. Those companies that can't do this will fail. We look at how to rearchitect roles, teams, and career paths in this section, starting with a look at the shift from fixed roles to dynamic jobs.

Traditional Fixed Roles

I am from a family of entrepreneurs and small business owners. Some of them were successful. Some were not. My great-grandfather started a company called Fine Foods of Virginia, which grew to sell cookies and biscuits throughout the country. Another great-grandfather started a silk glove company called Niagara Maid that grew successfully and was later acquired by a European competitor. In more recent years, my grandfather tried to make a living breeding thoroughbred horses and producing items for their stalls. Unfortunately, he couldn't make ends meet with this work, and instead joined Mead Paper Company with a traditional role on the factory floor.

Mead Paper Company was an archetypal traditional company. People like my grandfather joined to work in a specific role with a consistent paycheck and benefits. If they wanted other work opportunities, there was virtually no way to apply or move to a different job internally. If they had other skills—like my grandfather—there was no way to promote them inside or outside the company to find new jobs where they might be used and valued.

How Traditional Companies Organized and Defined Roles

For decades, companies were set up like Mead Paper Company. Work was in traditional, fixed roles based on a long-held premise that specialization and role clarity drove productivity and output. Workers were hired to perform a specific role, defined by a job description that detailed the requirements of the job. Work was planned and dictated top-down by a manager, and each business area had layers of hierarchy within it. If the worker performed the role well, he was promoted through a career ladder in that given business area: for example, from quality control analyst to quality control manager to quality control vice president.

At traditional companies, there was little opportunity to expand work beyond the role's job description or to move between roles. When workers switched companies, it was often for a higher salary or promotion in the same business area, not to try a new business area. Rather, the workforce was set up with the premise that workers worked full-time at companies in defined roles in a set business area, where they performed set tasks each day.

Mercer, one of the world's leading consultancies, is seeing the shift in new ways of work and role definition. "Organizational role definition has been a workforce characteristic since Adam Smith demonstrated the productivity and economic benefits of designing specific roles to different activities in a hypothetical pin factory.* [But], in the digital era, we anticipate a significant shift from the traditional model—in which employees apply their skills in fixed roles defined through organizational hierarchy—to a more dynamic model with talented individuals applying skills in multiple, project-based settings."[†]

How Roles Were Filled and Terminated

When traditional organizations like Mead Paper Company had open roles, they recruited new employees for them. Recruiters looked for comparable companies and job titles to dictate the

---

* Adam Smith, *The Wealth of Nations*, 1776.
† Mercer and Oliver Wyman, "Delivering the Workforce of the Future," 2017, https://www.oliverwyman.com/our-expertise/insights/2017/oct/delivering-the-workforce-for-the-future.html.

experience needed to fill a given role. Hiring looked at what you had done, not what you could do with the competencies you'd developed. Recruiting was almost always done from candidates outside the company—the concept of internal recruiting from an internal talent pool was virtually nonexistent.

When companies faced disruptions to their roles—for example from technology advances on the factory floor—managers often faced the painful decision to lay off employees. Employees would be called to a meeting and told about the elimination of their positions. Traditional companies rarely looked at these affected employees as a valuable internal talent pool that could be moved into new work. The concept of transferrable skills and learning initiatives was virtually nonexistent, an entrenched perspective that still negatively impacts job opportunities for our workers today.

Challenges with internal recruiting and mobility continue to permeate most companies—causing significant missed opportunities. According to IBM's Smarter Workforce Institute, today just 19 percent of new positions are filled by lateral moves. Seventy-nine percent of HR professionals today believe internal mobility and recruiting is important to their talent management strategy, but only 30 percent are satisfied with their ability to meet goals in this area. More than 80 percent said that internal mobility reduced costs and improved employee satisfaction.* These challenges stem from the fact that managers are often misaligned and unwilling to support internal candidates, employees often don't have visibility on open opportunities and what skills are required for them, and at most companies, work is not yet deconstructed into dynamic jobs and the skills required for them, making it difficult to assess and match workers. To make this happen, talent mobility must be clearly defined, organized, and enabled—starting with deconstructing work into smaller chunks and redesigning roles as dynamic jobs.

---

* Haiyan Zhang and Hannah Hemmingham, "Making Moves: Internal Career Mobility and the Role of AI," IBM Smarter Workforce Institute, May 2018.

Redesigning Roles as Dynamic Jobs

In fall of 2018, Workday announced their "Vision for a Frictionless Talent Marketplace" in a blog post. The company would offer both a new skills and a jobs marketplace where companies could list open jobs that workers could apply for or be matched to. Workday, long at the forefront of the HR technology revolution, would now help companies transform for today's Talent Mobility Revolution.*

From Traditional Roles to Dynamic Jobs

With disruptions growing and workforce demographics shifting, *F3 Companies* dispense with the long-held notion that fixed roles in fixed teams are the most effective way to organize. Instead, forward-thinking companies are deconstructing their work into smaller pieces and redefining traditional roles to be dynamic jobs that can be done by employees, freelancers, or technology. Each dynamic job is a unit of work that requires particular skills—for example, a project manager needed while the company shifts a particular function to partner, or a communications expert needed as the company launches a new product, or a data scientist needed to analyze sales data. Together, these jobs and those who do them form a project and a team. Collectively, they form the work that needs to get done in the company.

Deconstructed work should result in three types of work: (1) work that is critical and differentiated for the company, and should be done by employees, (2) work that is important and contextual, and can be done by freelancers, and (3) work that is repetitive, and may be automated by technology over time. Work done by employees and freelancers should be set up as dynamic jobs with a defined project team and with clear objectives and outcomes for the team. Jobs are dynamic because they change as business conditions evolve and as disruptions and opportunities occur. When one job

---

* https://blogs.workday.com/our-vision-for-a-frictionless-talent-marketplace/

is completed or automated, another emerges. When a new business opportunity rears its head, requiring new skills, a new job is created. Workers no longer work in a fixed role with defined tasks set top-down by a manager. Rather, they leverage their skills to complete a mosaic of jobs across a company, completing one with one team of people and then moving on to another with a different team.

We saw this phenomenon happen firsthand when building Topia. As we built software to power relocation and talent mobility, we realized that we needed the skills and knowledge not only of traditional software sales executives and engineers but also of tax, immigration, and relocation experts. We designed a role called Solutions Consultants, initially conceiving of a full-time position that formed a part of the sales team and interacted with customers. Over time, however, it became clear that the unique skills of this team were in demand across multiple areas of our business for many different dynamic jobs—from product and engineering to sales and marketing, to implementation and customer success, to finance and relocation services. Our Solutions Consultants became critical resources—with unique skills that contributed to multiple dynamic jobs across the company.

According to research by Accenture in its report *Reworking the Revolution*, 46 percent of executives say that traditional job descriptions are obsolete as machines take on routine tasks and people move to project-based work. Twenty-nine percent of these leaders reported that they've extensively redesigned jobs.*

"The traditional notion of a job is shifting," says Mercer.

"Consider an accountant and a data scientist. The accountant (representing a traditional job definition) has a specific set of accountabilities and outputs in any context. An accountant at a consumer goods company, broadly speaking, performs a very similar job to an accountant at a financial services company. Now think of the data scientist, a job that didn't exist 10 years ago. We refer

---

* Ellyn Shook and Mark Knickrehm, "Reworking the Revolution," Accenture Strategy, https://www.accenture.com/t20180613T062119Z__w__/us-en/_acnmedia/PDF -69/Accenture-Reworking-the-Revolution-Jan-2018-POV.pdf#zoom=50.

to the data scientist as a 'job,' but the term actually encompasses the set of skills and knowledge that a person has, rather than the accountabilities and output the role requires. A data scientist working for the marketing department of a consumer goods company is a very different job compared to a data scientist working for the treasury department of a financial services organization. Both are called data scientists, but that is where the similarity ends. In the new digital era, this new breed of jobs, requiring multiple and diverse skills, will increasingly replace what we perceive as role specification."*

F3 FOCUS

F3 Companies throw away the age-old belief from Adam Smith that organizations are most effective with defined roles and specialization. They redefine traditional roles to be dynamic jobs—each requiring a set of skills—and create a dynamic jobs graph and marketplace to match people to opportunities. With this, *F3 Companies* are agile and ready to respond when disruptions or opportunities strike.

Deconstructing Work and Creating a Jobs Graph

After shifting their mindset from traditional roles to dynamic jobs, *F3 Companies* reorganize their work along a dynamic jobs graph. They deconstruct the work across their company, breaking down traditional roles into a set of projects with jobs requiring specific skills—like building a new product at Topia that often required engineering skills, product management skills, business development skills, and relocation domain expertise. Each project should be led by a project lead, who is accountable for completing the objectives, staffing the team, and managing it to success (see Chapter 5

---

* Delivering the Workforce of the Future," Mercer and Oliver Wyman, 2017.

for more details on dynamic teams and project leads). Together, these projects and the jobs required to complete them form a jobs marketplace for the company. Once the jobs marketplace is defined, companies must invest to promote their jobs and the skills they require to their workers. Depending on the scope of the job, it may be promoted only to employees, only to freelancers, or to a combination (see Chapter 5 for further details on teams).

At the same time, innovative companies are investing in new talent marketplace and recruiting systems to match workers to jobs using artificial intelligence. If automation disrupts a particular area of work, the affected workers can be automatically recommended for new jobs internally. If new work in new locations emerges, workers can be automatically recommended for geographic and job movement. If Project Leads are missing skills on a team, they can source a worker with the skills they need at the click of a button.

Most traditional companies are just at the starting line of deconstructing their work into dynamic jobs, so there are few case studies to point to. In 2017, one of America's largest companies started this journey, reorganizing around talent mobility and championing a new initiative to fill open and newly created roles with internal talent. As we speak, they are deconstructing work into projects, designing training programs to prepare talent for new jobs, and investing in technology platforms to facilitate talent matching and movement. When I asked why they were investing in this, they put it simply: "We have many jobs being replaced by automation. At the same time, we have many jobs open and struggle to recruit people with the skills we need. As jobs are disrupted, we believe it's cheaper and more effective to recruit and train from an internal talent pool than an external one."

However, many technology companies—founded on the principles of agile software development—have been operating like this for decades and are now supporting traditional companies with their transformations.

Stephane Kasriel, CEO of Upwork, both supports companies' transformations to dynamic jobs and leads his own global agile organization with deconstructed work and dynamic jobs. Listed on NASDAQ in 2018, Upwork is the world's largest freelance market-place, used by 30 percent of the Fortune 500, including Samsung, Microsoft, and Procter & Gamble. Kasriel, who also cochairs the World Economic Forum's Global Future Council on the New Social Contract, became CEO in 2015 when oDesk and Elance merged to become Upwork.

oDesk and Elance were two of the first businesses in the freelance economy. Historically, these platforms were used by individuals and small businesses who lacked the resources and skills to, for example, design a brochure, create a basic website, or translate a document. They could hire a freelancer to complete the task generally at a lower rate than hiring an agency or other contractor locally. In the first year of Topia, we used oDesk to hire a front-end developer from Ukraine, an engineer from Poland, and workers for a variety of translation and data activities. Like Upwork itself, and other modern technology companies, we operated with project-based work and people from inside and outside our company staffed dynamically to these projects.

"At Upwork, we work in an agile way," says Kasriel. "We have dynamic projects with clear goals and we staff across this looking for the best talent and skills from across our global talent pool. But having been in Silicon Valley for a while, I don't think that agile work is unique. Most technology companies have done this for years."

F3 FOCUS

F3 Companies know that agility is critical for success amid the Talent Mobility Revolution. They deconstruct work into dynamic jobs, categorizing these on a jobs graph and creating a jobs marketplace. They promote these jobs to workers and match the skills that a job needs to the skills that a worker has.

Reclassifying Workers for Dynamic Jobs

In 2012, LinkedIn, the world's largest professional network, rolled out a new feature called Endorsements. User profiles now showed not only professional and educational history, but also the skills that a person had and others endorsed her for. Long before Workday announced its vision for a talent marketplace based on skills, LinkedIn was championing a new classification of the workforce: one based on skills rather than roles.

LinkedIn was early in embracing a broader trend to look at worker profiles as a combination of experience, education, *and* skills. Similarly, over recent years, various compensation benchmarking services have started to calibrate workers based on competencies, rather than titles, to benchmark salaries. This is exactly how *F3 Companies* look at the workforce today. Once they have deconstructed work into dynamic jobs, they consider an expanded definition of the workforce, including both employees and freelancers, and categorize them based on skills that can be matched to their open jobs.

Redefining Today's Workforce

Historically, companies have only considered their workforce to be their employees. They have hired these employees with an implied promise of job stability—a set number of working hours—and a standard set of employment benefits and protections—such as healthcare, pensions, and workforce safety protections. When they had open roles, they recruited employees to fill them. Occasionally, they have filled gaps in their companies with contractors provided by staffing firms. These firms maintained a database of contract workers who could be sourced and provided to companies to smooth peaks and troughs in their demand for workers. For decades, these workers have been classified by their tax status: "W2 workers" for employees with the benefits and taxes due for employment and "1099 workers" for contractors to denote their independent status and the different tax treatment. There was nothing in between. (In some instances, companies have abused the use of contractors leading to unpredictable work and unstable benefits and wages for much of the working class today.)

In recent years, however, the workforce has shifted to include two new classifications of workers: freelancers and gig workers. This has been driven both by employer and worker demands and by entrepreneurs who have capitalized on changing work models to develop new business models. Employers have increasingly realized that, with skills-based jobs and remote working models, they can find skills from a broader, more flexible, and more affordable talent pool than available only in their local market or through staffing agencies. Workers, for their part, have grown to value both autonomy and flexibility in their work, and realize that as disruptions occur to traditional employment, loaning their skills to multiple companies as "microentrepreneurs" may be an attractive avenue, and also allow them to work and live outside of urban locations. (Approximately 3,000 freelancers sign up to Upwork every day.)

After deconstructing work and creating a graph of dynamic jobs, companies start to match workers with jobs. Forward-looking companies define their workforce with all four classifications of workers and set up their talent marketplaces to include skills and job matching across all workers, depending on the work type. As discussed above, the best practice is to define which jobs should be kept with employees (those mission critical and differentiated for the company) and which jobs can be filled by freelancers and gig workers (those contextual or repetitive jobs that are required to run the company successfully, but not differentiated). If the company cannot find skills for the critical jobs in the employee pool, they may look outside the company at the freelance marketplace. At the same time, the company's own employees may be loaning their skills to other companies as a part of the freelance economy. The growth of employment movement—people working across employment classifications and companies—is a key part of the Talent Mobility Revolution and must form the foundation of the transformation to an *F3 Company*.

"Total talent management means that every human being who works at the company should be managed by HR. These companies think very proactively and holistically about getting work done," says Kasriel. "Traditionally full-time employees were managed by HR and contract or contingent workers were managed by procurement or the business unit. Hiring and staffing tended to be very reactive. If a manager needed to hire someone, they would go to HR and see if they could get headcount. If they did, recruiting for this role would swing into the traditional hiring cycle. If they couldn't get headcount, they would go to procurement and ask for some budget to hire a contractor temporarily. These companies were not making explicit, strategic decisions for workforce planning.

"The best companies today deconstruct work to be projects and then classify and staff the work that needs to be done across employees, freelancers, and automation initiatives. Our customers use Upwork to search for freelancers with the skills they need and match them to their dynamic jobs. This is not only replacing the traditional staffing-contractor model, but it's introducing a whole new strategic approach to getting work done at companies."

As Workday put it during the launch of its Talent Marketplace: "We must . . . add in external, non-employee talent—such as freelancers, independent consultants and contractors. Having the ability to quickly and painlessly source workers from a pool of skilled talent is vital for an organization that wants to stay competitive in a dynamic business environment."*

"Organizations have traditionally focused on one battleground for winning the war for talent: the internal workforce comprised of direct employees," says Mercer. "The workforce for the future will have a markedly different shape. Rather than managing only the internal workforce, the best companies will establish and manage an extended talent ecosystem, comprising multiple talent pools and spanning multiple generations. This ecosystem will provide

---

* Cristina Goldt, "Our Vision for a Frictionless Marketplace," October 2, 2018, https://blogs.workday.com/our-vision-for-a-frictionless-talent-marketplace/.

premium access to the latest skills, ideas, and experiences, allowing companies to adapt quickly to changes in their external environment while effectively managing their fixed costs."[*]

F3 FOCUS

F3 Companies know that to harness the Talent Mobility Revolution, they must expand their definition of the workforce to include all types of workers. These companies not only dynamically source skills from employees, but also tap into the freelance economy to match skills to jobs. *F3 Companies* know that strategically leveraging this broader workforce gives them a competitive advantage in the face of disruption and opportunity.

Classifying Workers with a Skills Graph

Once you've defined your workforce to include all four types of workers—employees, contractors, freelancers, and gig workers—you should then categorize the skills that they have creating a skills graph. Companies have historically classified employees in their HR system by their title, department, team, and manager. They have long thought about their employees' profiles as based on their experience across roles.

Agile companies instead classify their workers on a defined set of skills with a clear ontology for skills and competencies that is understood across the business. What skills does a worker excel at? What skills is he developing, and what learning must he do to acquire them? Innovative companies should also include employee preferences and personal details in their classifications—not only logging professional skills, but also storing immigration

---

* Mercer and Oliver Wyman, "Delivering the Workforce of the Future," 2017.

authorizations, language and cultural skills, and personal preferences in seeking a new job (for example, an employee may have a desire to work abroad for a given period of time or translate her analytics skills from a consulting role to a product role).

Like with deconstructing work to be dynamic jobs, it's early days for companies evolving their definition of their workforce and classifying their workers by skills. Workday's new "Skills Cloud" now identifies 55,000 verified skills that companies can use to classify workers, encouraging a standard ontology and framework. If it gets widespread adoption across companies, it could become the foundation of classifying employee skills—working with systems like Upwork to classify the entire workforce across employees and freelancers.

Censia, founded in 2018, is a company built to predictively match the best people to jobs for companies, using skills categorization and people modeling it has developed. Using complex technology and data science, Censia has mapped the global talent pool, aggregating data from thousands of publicly available sources for hundreds of millions of professionals and inferring skills patterns from this large data set. In essence, it has built a skills graph for the global workforce.

"Ninety percent of candidate data was created in the last two years. The idea that you can find information on people's skills is a relatively new concept," says Joanna Riley, founder of Censia. "But now people are putting that data out publicly, and it means that there is an opportunity to find talent in different ways, such as recruiting passive candidates for employment, leveraging internal mobility, or sourcing from the freelance economy.

"Most recruiting solutions out there are filtering technology. E.g., I want this type of profile with this background," continues Riley. "Censia draws on a massive skills graph to build intelligence to find and match candidates for enterprises—both from internal and external talent pools. More and more companies today are saying: 'I want great people who are skilled at X or Y, and I will teach them this industry or specific function.' Technologies need to respond by being able to clean and categorize skills data and seamlessly match talent to jobs."

F3 FOCUS

F3 *Companies* reclassify their workforce based on skills creating a skills graph with a standard ontology for skills and competencies. This skills graph then forms the foundation of matching workers to dynamic jobs and unleashing organizational agility. This agility helps companies accelerate employee engagement, innovation, and growth.

Matching Workers to Dynamic Jobs

Once traditional roles are redesigned as dynamic jobs and categorized on a jobs graph, and the workforce is defined to include all classifications of workers and categorized on a skills graph, you can build a talent marketplace that dynamically matches workers to jobs. *F3 Companies* set up systems, operations, and cultures where workers can easily apply for jobs that match their skills, or be automatically recommended to jobs by innovative matching technology. Companies should adopt a talent marketplace for employees (e.g., Workday) and a talent marketplace for freelancers (e.g., Upwork), and look at integrating them as a part of their systems roadmap (see Chapter 9) for comprehensive matching across the whole workforce.

Consulting firms have long operated in a project-driven world, staffing employees to projects as they come up. Certain of these firms have built their own internal talent marketplaces to facilitate this staffing model, but, for the most part, they haven't been user friendly or widely adopted. Companies today increasingly look to external partners to provide the systems that categorize worker skills and match them to dynamic jobs.

"We are living in a 'post-title world,'" says Joanna Riley, CEO and Founder of Censia. "Talent Marketplaces must be able to query for particular skills and recommend employees to fill jobs. Similarly, systems must make it easy for employees to understand what skills are required for a job and apply for it."

"A talent marketplace should flag open opportunities and provide bi-directional recommendations—between workers and work owners," said Workday in 2018. "For workers, this means recommendations on opportunities that will help them upskill or reskill to meet those requirements. This is important from an employee perspective because there tends to be little insight into what other jobs would be a good fit, and it would enable workers to be more active in steering their own career paths."*

F3 FOCUS

F3 Companies adopt a talent marketplace that matches workers to jobs. Workers can search for and apply to new jobs, and companies can source and select workers for jobs considering all classifications of workers to fill open jobs. *F3 Companies* then build a culture of movement and learning, embracing project-based work with clear goals and development initiatives for workers across teams and business areas.

Five Principels of a Jobs World

F3 Companies throw away the traditional notion of employment. They deconstruct work to be dynamic jobs, include employees and freelancers in their workforce, classify workers based on their skills

---

* Cristina Goldt, "Our Vision for a Frictionless Marketplace," October 2, 2018, https://blogs.workday.com/our-vision-for-a-frictionless-talent-marketplace/.

and competencies, and match workers to jobs with a talent marketplace. This is a fundamental redesign of the nature of work. It is widely discussed today among business and talent leaders. I have had countless conversations with Topia customers and partners about how to transform traditional companies to this agile world. But outside of modern technology companies that were founded with these principels at their core, few companies have made this transformation, and there are few case studies to look to. We therefore end this chapter by summarizing the five principles of a "Jobs World" to guide your transition from fixed roles to dynamic jobs.

The five principels of a Jobs World are:

1. Design work around jobs, not roles.
2. Define your workforce to include all workers.
3. Classify workers based on their skills and preferences.
4. Dynamically match and recommend workers for jobs.
5. Organize for frequent employee movement.

Design work around jobs, not roles. Traditional companies think in terms of set roles with fixed job descriptions and hierarchy. This static way of thinking about roles limits company agility and employee movement, making it hard to respond when disruptions and opportunities occur. *F3 Companies* deconstruct work, creating a blueprint of dynamic projects each with defined jobs and measurable objectives. This is called a jobs graph.

Define your workforce to include all workers. Traditional companies think of their workforce as including only employees. This narrow view of the workforce limits the talent that companies can tap into and the skills that they can leverage to complete work. For workers, it means a choice between stable employment and flexibility, a choice workers today increasingly don't want to make. *F3 Companies* recognize that today's workforce now includes four classifications of workers: employees, contractors, freelancers, and gig workers. They implement total talent management and strategically plan and manage their workers across all classifications.

Classify workers based on their skills and preferences. Traditional companies define employees by role and experience. Their systems classify workers by basic demographic detail, title, and manager, not by skills and competencies. This makes it impossible to source and match workers to jobs, based on the skills they have. *F3 Companies* categorize workers based on the skills, competencies, and preferences they have, developing a standard framework and ontology called a skills graph. With this information in hand, companies can respond to both disruption, quickly sorting the affected workers by their skills and matching them to new jobs, and opportunities, quickly identifying workers with the skills needed.

Dynamically match and recommend workers for jobs. Traditional companies hired employees to work in static roles. After designing a jobs graph and skills graph, *F3 Companies* adopt talent marketplaces to match and recommend employees for jobs as they arise. Think Tinder for jobs: workers identify what they can do, what they're interested in doing, what they're willing to learn, and where they're willing to go. Leadership identifies what they need done and where it needs to be done. The system does the work of connecting the two sides so that everyone ends up in the right seat at every point in time.

Organize for frequent employee movement. As workers are matched to jobs and undergo learning programs, *F3 Companies* easily support the geographic and location movement needed for workers to move to new jobs. If geographic mobility is required, *F3 Companies* leverage talent mobility technologies to seamlessly administer the process, managing interfaces and costs between business units; carrying out relocation, immigration, and tax activities for families; and helping workers match their personal preferences to the new location. If location movement or remote work is a part of new jobs, they champion virtual collaboration systems and remote working norms to enable it.

F3 FOCUS

F3 Companies structure their companies for talent mobility, following the five principles of a Jobs World. This new model of work gives them the agility and adaptability to capture opportunities as they arise and become *disruption-proof* in the face of today's seismic macro trends: globalization, automation, and demographic change.

This Talent Mobility Revolution is what I saw starting more than a decade ago at Lehman Brothers, a company very much built on traditional roles and employment. I saw companies increasingly looking for skills to support specific tasks—and people willing to do them in different employment constructs. I also saw peers leaving companies ever more frequently—the result of the 2008 recession and new demographics of workers who started to prioritize flexibility and autonomy over trust in large institutions. As I grew Topia, I saw this new world of work accelerating. Companies operating with dynamic jobs and agility were rapidly out-innovating competitors in products and profits. But most companies hadn't yet recognized what was ahead—that traditional roles would soon be replaced by dynamic jobs filled from an expanded workforce classified by skills.

Shifting from fixed roles to dynamic jobs is the fourth step to succeeding amid the Talent Mobility Revolution. Companies that can deconstruct their work into discrete projects and dynamically staff them based on skills will have the agility and adaptability for the twenty-first-century business environment.

CHAPTER SUMMARY

- Traditional companies defined work by fixed roles. Innovative companies today know that agility defines their success, so they throw this idea on its head and deconstruct work to be dynamic jobs with measurable objectives and goals tied to each project.

- Companies should categorize these dynamic jobs and detail jobs available, their project team, and the skills required. This is called a jobs graph.

- Companies should expand their definition of their workforce to include all four classifications of workers: employees, contractors, freelancers, and gig workers. They should manage these as one workforce, a concept called total talent management.

- Traditional companies classified workers by title, manager, and team. The workforce should be classified based on workers skills, the competency level they have for each, and their preferences. This is called the skills graph.

- Companies should adopt a talent marketplace that connects workers to jobs. Workers should both be encouraged to apply for jobs and matched to jobs.

- Companies should have one talent marketplace for employees and one for freelancers, uniting them through frictionless technology integration, something we discuss in detail in Chapter 9.

- Most companies are only at the very beginning of transforming their fixed roles to be dynamic jobs. To get started, they should follow the five principles for a Jobs World outlined in this chapter.

5

Evolving Teams and Managers for Dynamic Jobs

hen Topia was in its infancy in 2012, we never had enough people or money to do the work we needed. We had three employees: me, Co-Founder Steve Black, and our first engineer, Peter Almasi. Yet we were trying to build a relocation software product, sign up partners to deliver relocations worldwide, design a brand, set up basic operations, build relationships with potential customers, write a business plan, raise investment, and much more. Each of us did many different things each day—we "wore many hats" in start-up parlance—based on the skills we had and what needed to be done. I was an extroverted ex-banker with an MBA, so naturally the business plan, customers, and finance areas fell to me. Steve was an analytical ex-consultant with an operational brain, so managing the day-to-day logistics and product development fell to him. Peter was a brilliant engineer, so writing our first lines of code and designing our security infrastructure fell to him.

Quickly, however, it became clear that we would need to augment the three of us with more people. At that point, we didn't quite know what we needed in employees and we didn't have the revenue to hire and pay more full-time employees. So we had to get creative. We went to my MBA alma mater, London Business School, and recruited a group of part-time interns. We went to

freelancer platforms, ODesk and Elance, and hired remote workers to design basic web pages and marketing materials on demand.
And Peter hired a set of contractors who helped us build our product and branding. We also knew that we would almost always lack
the resources we needed (one of the cardinal rules of being an entrepreneur is that you always want more headcount than you have), so
we also made automation a key part of our strategy, immediately
building automated testing into our product to reduce the number of engineers we would need in the future, essentially pairing
humans with machines.

While I went on the road to raise money and build relationships, Steve kept this diverse team of employees, interns, freelancers,
contractors, and machines going—like a conductor managing a
symphony of different instruments and personalities. He led projects, set objectives and deadlines, coordinated deliverables, fostered
collaboration, and scaled hiring of freelancers up or down as
needed.

We didn't recognize it at the time, but in founding Topia like
this, we had created a blueprint for *F3 Companies* amid the Talent
Mobility Revolution. We were at the forefront of how *F3 Companies* would increasingly think about their workforce, teams, and
jobs. We had employees, contractors, freelancers, and gig economy
workers. We deconstructed work into projects and farmed work out
to our diverse array of workers to achieve the highest quality and
efficiency. At the same time, we thought often about automation—
how could we pair humans and machines as a team—to provide
more reliable software and services over time.

Today's forward-thinking companies think about teams and
management differently. Like Topia and certain of our customers,
they are redesigning their roles, teams, managers, and career paths
for the talent mobility era. They know that as fixed roles shift to
dynamic jobs, project teams will continually and fluidly shift in
composition as work gets started and completed. As automation and

artificial intelligence progresses, they increasingly think of teams as including both workers and machines—whether full robots like at Amazon distribution centers and certain medical clinics today, or the artificial intelligence that drives things like automated testing at Topia.

In this world, companies also redefine the purpose of a manager. Like Steve, company leaders today are increasingly conductors of work and workers, coordinating the projects that need to get done, by when and by whom. The concept of a single manager who plans, assigns, and assesses all of an employee's work is going away. Today's employees have managers who coach them on career progression, but they work day-to-day across many project leaders who orchestrate work and assess performance.

To succeed amid the Talent Mobility Revolution, agility is key. Creating dynamic teams for dynamic jobs allows companies to harness disruptions and opportunities as they occur by finding the skills that they need when they need them.

Companies and business leaders who operate out-of-date work models with static teams and roles will be left behind. Business leaders who want to succeed in the twenty-first century must rethink their definition of the workforce, the composition of their teams, and the role of their managers. Only with this new agile model in place will leaders harness the Talent Mobility Revolution to drive employee engagement, accelerate innovation, and unleash growth. In this chapter, we look at how to rethink teams and management for the Talent Mobility Revolution.

Traditional Teams and Managers

Since Adam Smith wrote *The Wealth of Nations* in 1776, companies have been designed on the premise that specialization—the division of labor—creates maximum efficiency and success. Today's companies have developed along this model, and many traditional companies today retain this structure. But the Talent Mobility Revolution is throwing the design of traditional teams and traditional management on its head.

How Traditional Companies Designed Teams

Traditional companies have a set of specific functions with defined teams that carry out their work. Teams are composed with a set of traditional roles defined by a static job description (see Chapter 4 for further details on the shift from roles to dynamic jobs), and a hierarchy in which junior employees are managed by more experienced employees who are in turn managed by managers and executives. If employees perform well in their roles and gain the necessary experience at the company, they may be eligible for a promotion or a salary increase. Experience is generally dictated by the time that an employee puts in at a given role. This structure, colloquially called "climbing the company ladder," has existed for much of the twentieth century—but in the twenty-first century, it must change.

Traditional teams were almost always made up solely of full-time employees. These workers were employed by the company—generally, dictated by an employment contract—and expected to work regularly in the office with regular hours, pay, and benefits. They had stable, predictable work and progressed through their career ladder over time. For the most part, these teams had the same people on them day in and day out—save for new employees who might be hired or those who may be let go. Occasionally teams would be augmented by part-time staff from a staffing agency, but for the most part, teams had few freelancers or gig workers. The team became an important sense of identity for employees, and much of an employee's career revolved around working with and socializing with members of the team.

When I worked at Lehman Brothers in 2006, teams were set up like this. As a first-year banking analyst, I was initially hired to a pool of analysts that was staffed across teams. However, after a year on the job, we were all "verticalized"—that is, assigned to a set team with a set manager that we would work with each day. Each team had a clear career ladder with a defined team hierarchy where managers managed those junior to them and so on. These managers were responsible for planning, assigning, and assessing work for those who reported to them. If we did well as an analyst, we had the opportunity to be promoted from analyst to associate to vice president to senior vice president, and so on—all within that given team. The team became an important sense of my identity. We worked long hours together, ate together, traveled together, and self-segregated to sit together in broader all-office meetings.

Teams were specialized in a multitude of ways. We had functional divisions: investment banking, equity capital markets, debt capital markets, sales, and trading. In banking, we further specialized into "industry teams"—such as industrials, consumer products, energy, financial services, and real estate—and "country teams"—such as India, China, and Japan. The idea was that with this structure, we could bring multiple teams to a client offering both industry and geographic expertise. For millennial employees like me, it got boring fast—many of us wanted to learn a multitude of skills, industries, and geographies, not specialize at age 23.

During my time at Lehman Brothers, I can't recall once meeting someone who wasn't a full-time employee. Teams only had full-time employees. If we needed to get something done and the team didn't have the skills to do it, someone had to learn (generally the analyst, e.g., me!) with a lot of late nights. There were no freelancers or gig workers to draw from.

Rachael King, Topia's first VP People, recalls how traditional companies organized like this in the earlier part of her career, before joining Cisco and then Topia.

"Company org design started as a vertical structure where you reported in an upward structure with many levels and grades. The manager of this vertical controlled work, annual performance reviews, promotions, and so on. Virtually everything was done in this vertical team," says King. "Companies then progressed into more of a matrix structure, where for example, I'd report into a global HR organization, but also into a location. This matrix has now evolved again into the project-based agile organizations we see as best practices today."

How Traditional Companies Managed Teams

Traditional companies like Lehman Brothers set up hierarchies that managed a team. A traditional manager was responsible for planning, assigning, and assessing work. He generally came from the team itself, progressing through its hierarchy, and was a specialist in the given business area after years working in it.

Adam Smith hit on the concept of management in his discussions of specialized business and production functions in the late 1700s. But the concept of management that most traditional companies use today emerged through the Industrial Revolution and twentieth century. As large-scale production grew during the Industrial Revolution, companies needed to develop a system to coordinate teams across far-reaching organization. Managers emerged to make this happen. Teams were led by a manager, or set of managers, who were principally responsible for execution and output. By 1881, the first management school—Wharton School—had been founded, and by the early 1900s the term *management* was widely used.

Through the twentieth century, as knowledge work emerged, management evolved. Managers' responsibilities evolved from being primarily focused on execution and output to a focus on coordinating and enabling knowledge workers. As noted by Rita Gunther McGrath in her *Harvard Business Review* article "Management's Three Eras: A Brief History," "The idea of what executives do changed from a concept of control and authority to a more participative coaching role."* With this shift, managers grew to be experts

---

* "Management's Three Eras: A Brief History," *Harvard Business Review*, July 30, 2014, https://hbr.org/2014/07/managements-three-eras-a-brief-history.

in their given business area—responsible for sharing their expertise and supporting employees to get their work got done.

At the same time, as companies grew global and more complex, company organizational designs were progressing from those of vertical, siloed teams to more of a matrix structure across functions and geographies, as Rachael King notes above. In these matrix structures, a manager may be responsible for the "terms and conditions" of employment and for coaching an employee on career progression, but might not be the same manager who is assigning work locally day-to-day. This evolution of org design and management was the prelude for the shift to the meritocratic, project-based org designs of the talent mobility era, where managers function principally as career coaches and work is assigned and assessed dynamically by different project leaders.

When I worked in real estate investment banking at Lehman Brothers, we had a traditional manager. He had worked at Lehman Brothers for more than a decade, climbing the ranks from entry-level analyst to senior vice president. By the time I worked for him in 2006, he was an absolute expert in real estate finance—managing his team through his knowledge, tenure, and relationships. He, and the ladder of managers below him, were responsible for planning our work, assigning it, and ensuring it got done on time. Today, he remains working in real estate finance with, presumably, an even greater amount of specialist knowledge and increasing management responsibilities. Many workers like me, however, would not follow this linear career path from entry level to manager in the same function.

"Company org designs are shifting, and with them, so are teams and managers," says Rachael King. "The traditional matrix org design has now evolved into a project-based org design. Employees still have managers but they are more coaches, with work and performance managed across projects by the project leaders that employees work for. Their feedback is then combined into a type of composite review that the manager can deliver with some coaching and advocacy for the employee. Put simply, the manager is your sponsor; she is not the person you are working for day to day. We will see an increasing decoupling of the manager and 'work leader' in the Talent Mobility Revolution."

Redesigning Teams for the Talent Mobility Era

Today's forward-thinking companies are moving away from traditional teams and managers. Rather, they design teams like Topia did in our early years—with dynamic projects that are staffed by an expanded workforce and augmented by technology. These teams form dynamically as projects start and then disband as projects are completed, with workers moving to a new project, generally with a new team. To enable this agile organization, companies deconstruct their work into smaller chunks and strategically plan which projects are core to the business and should be done by employees, which projects are contextual for the business and can be done by freelancers and what work is repetitive and should be automated through technology.

Extended Teams, Extended Potential

As we discussed in Chapter 4, in the talent mobility era, the definition of the workforce has expanded to include all four types of worker classifications: employees, contractors, freelancers, and gig workers. This extended view of the workforce offers greater potential for companies and team leaders to tap into the skills they need to complete work and to continually engage existing employees with diverse, high value work. (For clarity, we use the term *worker*, while certain *F3 Companies* still use the term *employee* to refer to all classifications.)

When projects start, leaders tap into their full workforce to source the skills they need to get for their project teams. Project teams may be all employees, all freelancers and contractors, or a combination of both. Freelancers and contractors may work and collaborate regularly in the office with little outward difference from employees, or they may work independently and remotely, never meeting members of the team and collaborating through virtual work tools. Or, in certain instances, they may be gig workers who complete specific tasks—for example running errands for a company event—with both in-person interaction and remote work.

This diverse team composition means that team members work everywhere—for example, you may find a single team with some people working in the office, some working from home in a rural location, and some working from a remote part of the world. In this new world of work, companies tap into an extended talent pool from around the world, efficiently pairing the skills they need with the people who have them, no matter where they are located.

As noted by *Accenture* in its 2017 report, "Shaping the Agile Workforce," "As talent and skills gaps grow, as many as 40 percent of companies experience shortages that drastically impact their ability to adapt and innovate."* And yet, many traditional companies continue to think about their workforce only as full-time employees who work from an office every day, and they continue to recruit for employees only from their local geographic area. At the same time, there are many qualified workers throughout the country looking for work, but not ready to move to high-cost, coastal urban locations where companies are generally located. With an extended definition of a team, companies can source talent from everywhere and provide vibrant job opportunities to skilled workers in other parts of the country. This is good for companies and good for the American economy.

Although this expanded view of work is new, the most innovative companies are starting to reframe their perspectives and gradually adopt freelancers as a part of their workforce. At Topia, we increasingly hired freelancers to augment our full-time employees as our

---

* Mary Lyons, Michael Blitz, and Nicholas Whittall, "Shaping the Agile Workforce," Accenture, 2017.

company grew. As discussed in Chapter 2, as companies reorganize for talent mobility, they include contingent (freelance) workers as a part of their new talent mobility department remit, recognizing that leveraging this expanded workforce would be an important part of their future agile organization. Procter and Gamble (P&G), a customer of Upwork, has adopted an expanded version of the workforce for staffing certain of its product research and development teams. It leverages Upwork to augment its teams with freelancers, and 60 percent of products developed with this approach were done at a lower cost than traditional methods.*

Still other companies in Silicon Valley have been designed with an expanded definition of the workforce in mind. Stella and Dot was founded in 2004 with a mission to create flexible economic opportunities for women. A part of this model was rethinking the definition of a workforce and how to enable it, something that many companies today are just starting to do.

Stella and Dot sells jewelry and accessories both directly to consumers online and through a large group of distributed sellers who are independent contractors. These microentrepreneurs manage their own sales and marketing, but the company provides merchandising, systems, and support for them.

Founder and CEO Jessica Herrin thinks about her full-time employees and independent sellers all as a part of the Stella and Dot workforce. "We completely view our sellers as part of our company—and we encourage our employees to do the selling experience also," says Herrin. "Our workforce is a community. We enable our sellers with online training, regional field meetings and executive development opportunities. We also bring our top sellers together each year for an annual conference where our employees and sellers come together to hear about new product launches and participate in training sessions. I also travel regularly to our major field locations and meet with our sellers—they are very much a part of the company."

---

* Mary Lyons, Michael Blitz, Nicholas Whittall, "Shaping the Agile Workforce," Accenture, 2017.

Stella and Dot was far ahead of its time in 2004 when developing this model and provides learnings for how companies today should think about working with an extended workforce. An extended workforce allows companies to access a broader talent pool and augment skills on project teams, including matching open jobs in low unemployment markets with skilled workers in higher unemployment markets. Companies today—from Procter and Gamble to Stella and Dot—are leveraging extended teams for their business success.

Bob Moritz, Global Chairman at PwC, highlights why and how this shift is happening in the World Economic Forum's article "4 Concerns That Keep CEOs Awake at Night": "The competition for talent is as fierce as ever, as the global population ages, the nature of work changes and companies look for skills they need to grow—now and in the future. 77% of CEOs we surveyed voiced concern that the skills shortages could hinder their organization's growth. . . . To find these employees, CEOs are increasingly tapping into a more diverse hiring pool—and looking across borders. They are also focused on the structure and future of work, including the gig economy with 28% of CEOs [already] relying more heavily on temporary workers."*

F3 FOCUS

F3 Companies know that to succeed in today's complex business environment, they must rethink the definition of their teams. They manage a workforce of employees and freelancers, creating extended teams and greater business potential. Success amid the Talent Mobility Revolution requires agility—allocating dynamic work to workers and enabling them to complete projects.

---

* Bob Moritz, "4 Concerns that Keep CEOs Awake at Night," World Economic Forum, January 16, 2017, https://www.weforum.org/agenda/2017/01/4-concerns-that-keep-ceos-awake-at-night/.

Worker and Machine Collaboration

Extended teams today are not only about including all types of workers. Agile companies also think about their teams as extending to the machines who contribute to them, increasingly robots and other forms of artificial intelligence. These machines augment the workers on the team, automating repetitive work tasks and providing real-time access to data that workers can use to make decisions. Today's leaders think about human-machine interaction as a core part of their companies, training workers to be comfortable interacting with technology and staffing chunks of work across employees, freelancers, and machines. Leaders today must segment and understand work that requires uniquely human skills and work that machines excel at to create the most efficient teams to complete their projects. They do not think of work as a trade-off between workers and machines. Rather, like we saw in the early days of Topia, they know that growing artificial intelligence technologies can augment worker capabilities and be a powerful contributor to the modern team.

Today's leaders also know that as technology advances certain workers' jobs will be impacted by machines. But unlike technology advancements of yesteryear, in the Talent Mobility Revolution, these disruptions can be met with new opportunities for affected workers to use their skills in new jobs. Companies that rethink team composition and make investments in talent mobility and learning will succeed in the dynamic twenty-first-century business environment and support their workers through a changing economy.

Countless businesses are adopting human-machine collaboration as a part of their companies. Japanese holding company Fast Retailing, which owns popular clothing store Uniqlo, pairs workers with artificial intelligence on their teams, implementing an AI-enabled device for its shop assistants. The technology provides real-time data on inventory, orders, and returns, freeing assistants to have more informed conversations with clients. The company, which reported record sales and a profit increase of nearly 39 percent in its most recent financial year, plans to use AI to improve speed to market as part of its strategy to increase revenue by nearly 70 percent by 2021.*

Like Fast Retailing, Morgan Stanley is also augmenting the work of its 16,000 financial advisors through the introduction of AI agents. These intelligent advisors continually learn about their clients and interact with their human coworkers to proactively recommend a range of options that take into account their clients' changing financial situations. Financial advisors then recommend these options to their clients and are better placed to contact clients at the right time with more relevant advice. With human-machine collaboration, these financial advisors can spend their time focusing on their clients' needs and interacting with them directly, relying on machines to do time-consuming pattern and trend analysis.[†]

Accenture Research has shown the rapid growth of AI in business and the importance of worker and machine collaboration to modern teams in its surveys. In a 2018 survey of 1,200 CEOs and 14,000 workers about the future of human and machine collaboration, 74 percent of executives said that they planned to use artificial intelligence to automate some work tasks in the next three years, but 97 percent of them said that they planned to use these machines to enhance worker capabilities. Workers for their part were similarly optimistic—62 percent said that they believed intelligent technologies will create opportunities for their work. Most tellingly for teams of the future, however, 61 percent of senior executives said that the proportion of roles requiring people to collaborate with AI will rise in the next three years.[‡]

---

* Ellyn Shook and Mark Knickrehm, "Reworking the Revolution," Accenture Strategy, 2018, https://www.accenture.com/t20180613T062119Z__w__/us-en/_acnmedia/PDF-69/Accenture-Reworking-the-Revolution-Jan-2018-POV.pdf#zoom=50.
† Shook and Knickrehm, "Reworking the Revolution."
‡ Shook and Knickrehm, "Reworking the Revolution."

"The opportunity for newly skilled individuals to collaborate with increasingly intelligent machines and software will accelerate the shift from an assembly line approach to a more fluid "assemblage' of teams and technology, capable of higher levels of creativity and innovation," write Accenture's Paul Daugherty and Jim Wilson in *Human + Machine: Reimagining Work in the Age of AI*. Companies must ensure that, in this new era of worker and machine collaboration, all of their workers are trained in technology use and digitally fluent.

F3 FOCUS

F3 Companies not only rethink their teams to include a broader set of workers, but increasingly pair human workers with artificial intelligence to augment their capabilities. With this expanded team composition, they harness the Talent Mobility Revolution to drive employee engagement, accelerate innovation, and unleash growth, responding rapidly and gracefully to opportunities and disruptions as they occur.

From Fixed Teams to Dynamic, Agile Teams

In the world of dynamic projects and extended teams of workers and machines, the concept of a fixed team goes away. Rather teams are now dynamic—forming with the people, machines, and skills needed to complete a project, and then "unforming" once the project is completed. To enable this, companies deconstruct their work into smaller chunks each with defined objectives and milestones to complete projects. Each project lasts for a particular amount of time—some happen over months, and some happen over years. When the project is done, the team is no longer needed. Both the workers and machine intelligence are free go and look for the next project where their skills are needed, leveraging the intelligent talent marketplace, as discussed in Chapter 4.

Companies must transform their company culture and operations to support this agile work. Like consulting firms who have long had a similar model, they hire employees with the explicit expectation that work will be dynamic and that they will be working across diverse teams, leaders, and projects with measurable objectives tied to them. They also set expectations that employees will work fluently with local and remote freelancers and artificial intelligence technologies as a part of their teams. They build staffing models around these dynamic projects and their talent marketplace, continuously allocating work on demand and creating teams to complete it. And they reinvent the concept of a manager to orchestrate this fluid movement of people and teams while balancing career and development conversations with employees.

Spotify is one of the most well-known agile companies, and one that we looked to at Topia in designing our product development teams. Spotify runs its product teams in "squads," small, cross-functional, self-organized, and self-managing teams usually consisting of 6 to 12 people who own product objectives and work as an independent unit to complete them. The company organizes these squads into tribes—a group of squads—for work on a given product area. The leaders of these squads and tribes set overall objectives and ensure the best possible work environment, but unlike at traditional companies, they do not dictate and assign work. They let the autonomous teams figure out the best way to complete the objectives. When objectives are completed, squads will disband and move on to a new cross-functional squad with a new objective.

We looked to Spotify when we designed our product development model at Topia. Chief Product Officer and Teleport Founder Sten Tamkivi created small, nimble, and aligned teams comprised of different skills (e.g., engineering, product management, quality, subject expertise) with objectives and deliverables. We tried to keep these teams aligned in the same region to maximize time zone efficiency and collaboration.

We are in the early stages of traditional companies transitioning to this agile team model used by technology companies like Spotify. But as companies deconstruct their work, shift to dynamic project teams, and redefine their workforce, those that increasingly follow this model will be positioned for success.

F3 FOCUS

F3 Companies know that to harness the Talent Mobility Revolution for success, they must reinvent the way they think about teams. They create teams continuously to complete dynamic jobs and include all types of workers and machines, seamlessly integrating human intelligence and artificial intelligence to accelerate innovation and growth. To make this work, they set clear objectives for teams and unleash them through autonomy and purpose.

Rethinking Management Amid Dynamic, Extended Teams

In traditional companies, managers have long run teams, due to their experience and expertise. Like my manager at Lehman Brothers, they have developed their careers in a particular function taking on greater numbers of direct reports and submanagers. They have planned and assigned work, often in a top-down structure, and at the end of year, assessed work performance in the annual performance review. However, companies today are rethinking the role of the manager amid dynamic jobs and teams.

From Traditional Manager to Manager Coach

The traditional manager is today splitting into two separate functions: a manager coach and a project leader. In traditional companies, managers both assigned work and held development conversations with employees. In today's most innovative companies, we are seeing a decoupling of these functions—it's often not the same person who is an employee's assigned manager who actually leads the work that employee is doing.

One of the most important things to employees is their own development and progression. Even as we shift from fixed roles to dynamic jobs, employees still want conversations on their career and skills growth. They also seek coaching on professional development and navigating company dynamics, and they benefit from leaders who can advocate for them within the company. The best practice at today's companies is to assign a manager to an employee, often the hiring manager, who is accountable for providing that employee feedback and supporting his development in regular conversations. This manager, however, is generally not the person who is working with the employee day to day as the leader of the employee's project teams. In fact, in a world of dynamic projects, employees work across a diverse array of project leaders who plan, assign, and assess work for each project and team. Each employee's manager receives performance feedback from these project leaders to create composite feedback to share with the employee in these development conversations.

In this model, management (the ability to share feedback and hold effective career and development conversations) becomes a skill. Like other skills, the skill of management can be applied across the organization and its employees.

Through nine years leading Topia, I consistently saw that, regardless of the nature of work and skills being developed, our employees always craved a manager to align with and support their career trajectory. The relationship between manager and employee is an important part of a fulfilling work environment. As we matured, we rolled out a model called Continuous Conversations where we encouraged managers to have monthly development conversations with employees, even if they might be working on a project led by a different person.

"Although work is moving to a more project-based model, as we see at Topia, managers still play a critical role for companies and employees," says Jacky Cohen, Topia's leader of People and Culture. "With more dynamic development conversations, however, companies must nurture manager skills so that managers can have these development conversations effectively. This is an emerging area, and one I'm looking at closely now."

F3 FOCUS

F3 *Companies* rethink the role of a manager to be about coaching and development conversations, built on a composite from the multiple project sponsors that employees work for on their project teams. In the Talent Mobility Revolution, employees are continuously mobile across teams and management evolves to support this agile model.

The Role of the Project Leader

While today's managers lead employee development and feedback, project leaders lead project teams that complete the company's work. Project leaders move away from a patriarchal view of leadership, where authority is derived by position and knowledge, to a meritocratic view of leadership, where communication, clarity, and transparency are king. They succeed by staffing the right skills on their teams, setting clear milestones and objectives, and managing their teams to successful completion of project deliverables. They create good working conditions (like at Spotify), share ongoing feedback, and motivate by giving team members autonomy, both in where they physically work and how they work. Confident that workers have the skills to complete their jobs, project leaders move from telling team members *how* to do something to telling them *what* they need to do. Then they give workers the autonomy to figure out how to complete the job, verifying progress.

Project leaders regularly share feedback on employee performance and work. This feedback goes into a composite view of each employee's skills and contribution that is used to assess employee levels, compensation, and development paths, something we discuss in the next chapter. This forms the basis of the conversations that managers have with employees.

Some project leaders lead, while others work across multiple projects, often with overlapping dependencies and deliverables. Successful project leaders have great team-building skills and are able to pull together diverse workers from inside and outside the company and align them around a common project goal. They are high empathy multitaskers, able to orchestrate work across many parties, inspire collaboration, and share dynamic feedback on progress and performance to ensure projects are on track. When conflict arises between different team members, they defuse tension easily with their skills of compromise and communication.

Like Topia's Co-Founder Steve Black in our early days, project leaders are more conductor than commander. They select workers to be a part of their dynamic project teams, intelligently pair them with technology, and then coordinate their diverse team members to ensure expectations are clear, collaboration is high, and deliverables are on time. Consulting firms have long had this model, where an "Engagement Manager" leads multiple different projects—often in different industries—with different people on each team. So, perhaps it's no coincidence that Black came from a management consulting background!

F3 FOCUS

F3 Companies appoint project leaders to lead one or multiple dynamic projects. Project leaders are responsible for staffing teams, setting objectives, and making them happen. They share feedback on employees with managers to create a composite picture of employee performance. Project leaders are the conductors that make the *F3 Company* run seamlessly.

This Talent Mobility Revolution is what I saw starting more than a decade ago at Lehman Brothers, a company built with traditional teams and managers. When I founded Topia, I knew that this model was outdated and wanted to do something different. To accelerate employee engagement, company efficiency, and innovation, I had to rethink the concept of a team and manager. Our teams would have employees, freelancers, and technology working seamlessly together. Our managers would be expected to lead career conversations. And our work would sometimes be led by project leaders. As our own company grew, I saw companies we worked with starting to shift to expanded definitions of teams and new expectations for managers. The companies that made this shift successfully would be best placed to harness the Talent Mobility Revolution to drive employee engagement, accelerate innovation, and unleash growth.

Rethinking teams and management for dynamic jobs is the fifth step for success in the Talent Mobility Revolution. But today, we are just at the cusp of this shift—and many companies remain tied to traditional notions about their workforce, team, and managers. To succeed in the twenty-first century, it's time to rethink this.

CHAPTER SUMMARY

- Traditional companies were designed with functional teams based on hierarchy and led by a manager. Managers' authority was derived from expertise, tenure, and seniority.
- Companies today must move away from a traditional, hierarchical org design to a flat, agile model where dynamic, cross-functional teams form to complete projects with clear milestones and objectives.
- Traditional teams were composed of employees who built a career in that functional area. In the Talent Mobility Revolution, teams should include all four classifications of workers: employees, contractors, freelancers, and gig workers.
- Companies today must increasingly think about creating teams with both human and artificial intelligence. Rapidly advancing technology can augment human skills and unleash greater efficiency and innovation in companies. Companies must invest in building digital literacy across all staff.
- With work based on dynamic teams, companies must rethink the role of a manager. Today's managers are coaches who provide employees feedback and career consultation, while employees work across multiple project leaders in dynamic jobs.

Redefining Career Paths for the Talent Mobility Era

6

My friend Tana has a modern career. She graduated from college with an interior architecture degree and then started working at a well-known New York architecture firm. She then worked for a makeup company in New York doing visual merchandising, before moving to design retail stores for another beauty brand in Los Angeles. During these tours of duty, Tana "loaned" her design skills to large, multinational firms for given periods of time. Each of her stops was different—sometimes designing traditional office buildings, sometimes cosmetic packaging and counters, and sometimes sleek retail stores. With each job, Tana furthered her set of experiences, building out a résumé filled with projects and skills.

While working at these companies, Tana also built her own residential interior design business—as a member of the freelance economy. She designed high-end homes for clients she sourced at dinners, parties, and weddings she attended. She advertised through a website she created that showcased her work, through prior clients, and through interior design networks. She worked on her residential interior design projects "on demand"—as and when she sourced them and had time to balance them with her daily work at her companies. To complete these projects and augment her own skills, Tana built collaborations with other members of

the freelance economy—independent contractors who are paint-
ers, plumbers, project managers, and builders—who collaborated
with her on her residential projects. She worked on these projects
at night or on weekends, alongside her jobs in architecture, visual
merchandising, and retail design at companies.

With all of her work, Tana grew her skills, project portfolio,
and network, creating a modern résumé that she could leverage into
subsequent jobs. As her skills grew, she positioned herself for a multitude of subsequent "tours of duty"—whether at companies, in the
freelance economy, or both—where she could continue to grow.
Tana thought most about the skills she was developing, not about
a title she might acquire or the promotions she might get in a traditional career ladder.

Careers today are increasingly nonlinear. Instead of a career
ladder, today we increasingly see a career zigzag. People like Tana
develop skills over a multitude of experiences across companies,
departments, and the freelance economy. These skills are transferrable across many different jobs. As they grow in volume, these
skills open doors to new opportunities across geographies, industries, companies, and clients. For many companies, it's common to
hire workers who have had numerous different careers, assessing
relevant skills versus traditional titles, roles, and promotions.

This was the case for many of the people we hired at Topia. We
had an engineer who had been a surgeon. We had a quality assur-
ance (QA) leader who had been a pharmacist and taught himself
QA at night. We had a customer support manager who had been a
real estate investor. We had a sales leader who had owned a restaurant. And we had two Co-Founders of a technology company who
had been a management consultant and an investment banker who
taught yoga classes to fund the early company costs. Through the
years, we learned that recruiting for skills almost always trumped
hiring for titles on a traditional résumé.

Many workers today watched their parents lose "lifelong jobs"
during the 2008 recession. Many lost faith in the promise—and

value—of a traditional career at a traditional company, instead trading it for opportunities to develop their portfolio of experiences and skills. Today's workers increasingly see their careers as fluid and nonlinear. They have periods where they work full-time as an employee at a company. They have periods where they freelance in the gig economy. They have periods where they go to a course to develop new skills. And they have periods where they do a combination of all of these. In each career segment, they match their skills with job opportunities, and often become a part of a dynamic team, like Tana's architecture and interior design teams.

F3 Companies know that, in the talent mobility era, people work differently: They trade career ladders and regular promotions for experiences, skills development, and flexibility. They loan their skills to different projects across different companies, teams, and industries. At the same time, *F3 Companies* know that agility is key to succeeding amid the frequent disruptions and opportunities today. They rethink their roles, teams, management, and career paths to be dynamic, seamlessly and continuously matching workers with the skills they need to projects and teams.

Companies and business leaders who cling to a traditional view of careers will miss out on opportunities to attract and engage today's top talent. Those that succeed will rethink how career paths, résumés and rewards evolve for agile work, getting the skills they need to respond to disruptions and opportunities as they strike. In this chapter, we look at the changing nature of careers amid the Talent Mobility Revolution.

Traditional Career Paths

In Chapter 4, we discussed my grandfather's experience working at Mead Paper Company, a traditional manufacturing company founded in the late 1800s. Companies like Mead were designed with fixed roles, fixed teams, and hierarchical management structures.

Employees like my grandfather joined to perform a specific job with a specific title, with an implicit promise of stable employment, salary, and benefits. Each year during the annual review cycle, his performance was evaluated by his manager, and if he did well, he might be eligible for a promotion or a salary increase. If he got a promotion, it was celebrated at home with the family—my grandmother loved to host family dinners, almost never following a recipe as she cooked—and recognized by a more senior title within the company.

Titles, Hierarchy, and Career Ladders

For many years, employees thought about career paths as a linear ladder to climb, where each rung was the next level or title to achieve. (This literally became known as the career ladder!) Companies were designed in a hierarchical way, supporting long-term, top-down planning and traditional, patriarchal management models. Countless children were told by parents to "go to school, study hard, get a good job, work hard, and then retire." Workers put in a couple of decades at a company with the promise of progression in titles and salary during their tenure, and by their sixties, expected to enjoy retirement supported by a company pension. London Business School professors Lynda Gratton and Andrew Scott call this the "three stage approach to working lives: education, followed by work, then retirement" in their 2016 book, *The 100 Year Life.**
Through much of the twentieth century, this was the mindset of the workforce.

The traditional career path looked like this:

---

* Lynda Gratton and Andrew Scott, *The 100 Year Life: Living and Working in the Age of Longevity* (Bloomsbury, 2016).

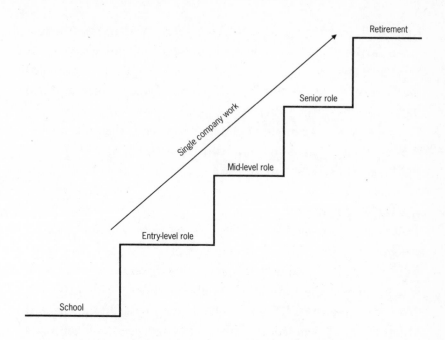

In many ways, my father's career was like this as a community college teacher. He progressed through the ladder of academia over many years to eventually lead a department and be responsible for the management of staff and the achievement of its goals. When my father reached retirement age, he left his teaching position and received a pension and benefits in exchange for his years of service. (Unlike many traditional workers, however, my father was already embracing some of the parts of modern career paths. Alongside teaching, he wrote and produced plays, loaning his skills to community theaters as a freelance worker, a prelude to the career paths and gig workers of today.)

Academia, like traditional companies, operates on tenure, titles, and promotions, supporting hierarchy and linear career paths for employees—who often have to wait to get to a particular level to voice opinions or contribute to decision making. Wharton professor Peter Cappelli and NYU professor Anna Tavis discuss this evolution in their 2018 *Harvard Business Review* article "The New

Rules of Talent Management": "After World War II, when manu-facturing dominated the industrial landscape, planning was at the heart of human resources: Companies recruited lifers . . . groomed them years in advance to take on bigger and bigger roles, and tied their raises directly to each incremental move up the ladder. The bureaucracy was the point: Organizations wanted their talent prac-tices to be rules-based and internally consistent so that they could reliably meet five-year (and sometimes 15-year) plans."*

The Traditional Résumé

Traditional career paths were detailed on the traditional résumé, a document that evolved over more than 500 years to be the de facto standard for conveying career progression and success. It is believed that the traditional résumé originated with Leonardo da Vinci in the late 1400s, when he wrote a letter to the Duke of Milan where he detailed his skills and experience. Over the years however, the traditional résumé moved away from listing skills to a more standard log of the traditional career path and its promo-tions: Where did you attend school? Where did you start work? What levels have you progressed through? Future employers looked at the résumé to judge how "senior" someone was, measured by the titles he had achieved, and how quickly progression had been, measured by the promotions. For the most part, traditional résumés did not showcase skills or potential—rather, they were backward-looking documents detailing experience across business areas and titles. After all, in a world where careers were linear and workers largely stayed in a single business, diverse, transferrable skills were not important.

Banks, like Lehman Brothers, have long trafficked on the tradi-tional résumé and linear career path. Each entry-level analyst, like myself, wanted to progress from first-year analyst to second-year analyst to third-year analyst to associate, vice president, and so on.

---

* Peter Cappelli and Anna Tavis, "The New Rules of Talent Management: HR Goes Agile," *Harvard Business Review*, March–April 2018.

Each year, we updated our résumé to show that we had made it through another year and gotten a small adjustment to our title. When people switched banks, they often did it to leapfrog a year of progression. Typically, the only way to accelerate a linear career path was to convince another bank to hire you at a more senior level, something I successfully did when I moved from Lehman Brothers to Standard Chartered Bank. Looking back, it seems so futile, but at the time, I thought it was very important to progress my title as quickly as possible!

When I founded Topia, I wanted us to recruit for skills and values, not what it said on a résumé, something I discussed a lot with both Rachael King, Topia's first VP people, and Jacky Cohen, who today leads the function. In some cases, we did this well. In other cases, particularly when we needed to quickly fill headcount, we did not. But we all knew this was the future of recruiting and résumés.

"We need to turn the traditional résumé on its head," says Rachael King. "It should not be about 'I've done these jobs at this time.' But it needs to be based on skills—to promote what you've done and your achievements instead of jobs. With this, however, we need a wholesale redesign of recruiting across companies, both when recruiting from internal and external talent pools. We need companies and recruiters to source skills not titles and for technologies to become much better at classifying and matching people to jobs based on the skills they have. This also really helps in building diverse teams. It's not about where you've been in the past or the opportunities you've been given, it's about the skills you've developed and how they apply to new opportunities. This skills and project based world really democratizes opportunities for workers."

The Annual Performance Review

Traditional companies have long used an annual performance review to assess employees' performance and evaluate opportunities for salary increases and promotion along the career ladder. The annual performance review emerged from the long-term, top-down planning approach of traditional companies. The idea was that each year, a manager knew what employees would do, and at the end of that year, he could assess whether his employees were successful or not in achieving the goals: whether financial targets, production output, or new sales. The unit of measurement was the year—and all feedback, reviews, and promotions operated alongside it.

During the year, employees often didn't know how they were performing: they didn't get regular, dynamic feedback. If they acquired new skills late in the year, they could get missed in the annual review. Conversely, if they performed well in the first part of the year and not as well in the final part, they could be penalized in the annual review due to recency biases. If the business environment changed, with new disruptions or opportunities emerging, the company often had to wait for the annual cycle to finish before updating plans. In this structure, it's not hard to see how employees could become disengaged ("punching the clock" as it was colloquially known), and businesses could miss significant opportunities without agile operations.

The output of annual reviews was a grade that dictated performance during the year. Former GE CEO Jack Welch is well known for evolving this into a forced ranking performance structure—segmenting employees as "A," "B," or "C" players. By the early 2000s, as many as 60 percent of Fortune 500 companies had adopted forced ranking systems in their annual performance reviews.*

Each year at Lehman Brothers, we went through the annual performance review and ranking ritual. Managers would enter performance reviews into a central system that would then crunch these reviews into a performance grade that dictated our bonus. On a set day each year, you would walk into a conference room and sit with an HR manager who would deliver your performance grade, bonus, and continued progression. I remember being shocked both that I had to wait a year to get feedback on my performance and

---

* Peter Cappelli and Anna Tavis, "The Performance Management Revolution," *Harvard Business Review*, October 2016.

that someone was delivering this information without any context on my performance; I had mistakenly expected that this conversation would happen with my manager, who planned my work, not with an HR manager that I had never met before. I remembered this experience acutely as we designed Topia's talent management processes to be agile and manager-led (see Chapter 5 for details on the evolving role of a manager at an *F3 Company*).

Cappelli and Tavis discuss the history and future of the annual performance review in their 2016 *Harvard Business Review* article "The Performance Management Revolution": "Appraisals can be traced back to the U.S. military's 'merit rating' system, created during World War I to identify poor performers for discharge or transfer. After World War II, about 60% of U.S. companies were using them (by the 1960s, it was closer to 90%). Though seniority rules determined pay increases and promotions for unionized workers, strong merit scores meant good advancement prospects for managers. At least initially, *improving* performance was an afterthought."

However, innovative companies now recognize that with dynamic project work and teams, nonlinear career paths and agile performance management will increasingly be the norm. Cappelli and Tavis note that "regular conversations about performance and development change the focus to building your workforce needs to be competitive both for today and years from now."

"There must be a different focus on employee development than there has been. Development has historically all been around promotion and level, and how that corresponds to a career ladder," says Rachael King, who brought this lens to designing Topia's talent management processes. "People are still entering the workforce expecting quick recognition, promotion, and salary increases. But we need to look at experience exposure in breadth and depth, and the skills being developed versus traditional experience. We need to recognize and reward that in the right way for agile companies and modern employees."

How Career Paths Are Changing

In Chapter 3, we met my friend Daniel, a consultant who works from many different locations—cafés, coworking spaces, and client offices—as he completed his work. Like many workers today he values flexibility and *location movement* as a part of his work (see Chapter 3 for more details on location movement). But before Daniel became a roaming consultant, he got a Harvard law degree and practiced at a prestigious law firm, worked as an investment banker, and wrote movie scripts. Today, he is starting a digital health technology company, writing a TV series, and continuing his work as a consultant. Like Tana, Daniel is a quintessential modern worker. Careers today look more like theirs than my grandfather's at Mead Paper Company.

Nonlinear, Dynamic Careers

Today's workers increasingly work across companies, sectors, and jobs during their careers. Gone are the days where an employee joined a specific company and department with a "job for life" and clear career ladder to climb. Driven both by the changing preferences of today's workers and company transformations to agile work amid the Talent Mobility Revolution, careers are now nonlinear and dynamic. Business is changing faster than ever, and businesses must be agile to capitalize on opportunities and respond to disruptions as they happen. At the same time, shifting employee demographics mean that workers today increasingly value autonomy and flexibility above career ladders and paychecks. They work for *both* companies and themselves as a part of their careers—spending time as employees and freelancers and working across a series of tours of duty like Tana and Daniel do.

A 2018 article in *Forbes* cited research from edX that 29 percent of Americans ages 25 to 44 have completely changed fields since starting their first job post college, while research from Deloitte shows that 43 percent of millennial workers plan to quit their current job in the next two years.* But nonlinear careers are not limited to millennials. According to JP Morgan, "The Federal Bureau of Labor Statistics (BLS) recently reported that nonlinear job-hopping was no longer something reserved for entry-level working teenagers. Rather, across various fields and various shades of color, career flux has become an acceptable norm."[†]

In this world, there is no linear career path. Career ladders look more like career pretzels, moving in a circular continuum rather than to an end goal of retirement:

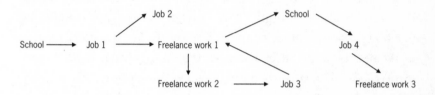

All of this means that traditional companies must expand their thinking about the right employee profile for a given job. They must look to skills and how they translate across jobs, rather than looking to experience within a given business area. All of this requires a fundamental redesign of recruiting processes to be based on skills, and assessing their transferability, rather than being based on experience, a transformation we lay out in the next section.

In Chapter 1, we met Peggy Smith, CEO of Worldwide ERC, an HR industry group that educates and connects more than 250,000 corporations, thought leaders, learners, stakeholders, and mobile people. In her role, she has watched the shift from traditional linear careers to dynamic nonlinear careers driven by shifting employee demographics and business needs.

---

* Anant Agarwal, "Why Today's Professionals Are Taking the Career Road Less Traveled," *Forbes*, October 31, 2018, https://www.forbes.com/sites/anantagarwal /2018/10/31/why-todays-professionals-are-taking-the-career-road-less-traveled/ #7ab590e8466b.
† JPMorgan Chase & Co., "The Next Episode," *The Atlantic*, https://www.theatlantic .com/sponsored/jpmc-2017/the-next-episode/1742/.

"People coming into the workforce 10 years ago watched their parents work for traditional employment and career models, and they saw them lose a lot during the recession," says Smith. "At the same time, the ACA came into law, and all of a sudden people could get health insurance independent of their employer. This gave them a sense of empowerment and leverage; 'I am now going to drive my career and skills, and not let one company do it for me.' It provided a newfound freedom to workers.

"The other thing is that, in this generation, no one is disillusioned that a company can be bought, disrupted, or go out of business," continues Smith. "So instead workers are demanding flexibility in job content, remuneration, skills development, employment models, and the experiences they are getting. Workers are increasingly dictating their employment model—full-time work in one project, then volunteer time, or time in the gig economy or experiences abroad. Throughout all of this, what you're seeing is people placing greater value on time due to the recognition that time and employment are not finite."

F3 FOCUS

F3 Companies recognize that careers are nonlinear. They know that workers will work inside companies and as members of the freelance economy, often with breaks in between to learn and develop skills. They look to the breadth and depth of the skills and experiences of workers, rather than their titles and expertise in a given business function, to assess fit with projects and teams. Then, they celebrate the nonlinear career paths of their workers.

From Recruiting for Titles to Recruiting for Skills

Titles and experience were the foundation of traditional careers. The currency of nonlinear careers is skills and outcomes—goals achieved and impact made as a part of the dynamic jobs that a worker does inside and outside of the company. In the talent mobility era, these skills—and project experiences—become the blueprint of the worker, dictating what she can offer her next project team.

Innovative companies categorize each worker's skills in their talent marketplace. When they look to fill the next project team, they query their system for workers with the skills they need for the project team. Companies look at the breadth and depth of skills and the historical achievement of project objectives to set employee level, pay, and staffing paths. They move away from a hierarchical model of management and ladders to a standardized leveling system that ties pay to competencies and contribution.

After categorizing workers based on skills, companies should assign competency benchmarks to the skills developed and the projects completed, forming the basis for assessing seniority. This should all be logged in the talent marketplace system and aligned to job descriptions when recruiting for project teams—for example, what skills and competencies are needed for a team? Companies then need to transform their recruiting model to source candidates based on skill and competency keywords instead of title keywords. Traditional recruiting practices search for and filter candidates who have had particular job titles at particular companies to create candidate short lists. In a skills-based world, titles are irrelevant. Recruiting today should reflect that and, once skills and competencies are logged, search for these.

"Job benchmarking and recruiting needs to shift from levels to skills," says Rachael King. "There will always still be some hierarchy in companies, but we are moving to a much flatter structure. As employees complete projects, I think about these projects like building blocks that get attached to their profile. Each of these building blocks has an impact from a development, level, and compensation perspective. The future of benchmarking employees and their compensation will be based on skills and competencies—in fact, quite a few of the salary reports, like PayScale, are already moving this way—and this translates to recruiting that needs to be much more based on this. In reality, we are just at the beginning of this transformation, however, because it requires a comprehensive redesign of systems and the way we classify workers, their skills and the competencies they've developed."

F3 FOCUS

F3 Companies reclassify their workers based on skills and the competencies they've developed across dynamic projects. They redesign their systems to categorize this and adapt their recruiting processes to source project teams based on skills and competencies, and their compensation models to benchmark in the same way.

Innovating on the Traditional Résumé

In 2018 *Fast Company* published an article entitled "Four Reasons Resumes No Longer Work." The article posits that the traditional résumé's focus on experience over skills, organization by job titles, disregard for gig work, and static format make the traditional résumé—the document used for more than 500 years—irrelevant for today.

As companies shift away from traditional career paths and titles to fostering careers based on skills and dynamic jobs, the structure of the traditional résumé no longer makes sense. Rather, many companies are pivoting to more skills, certification, or rating-driven models to measure workers' fit for a job. LinkedIn's skills endorsements are an example of this, as are the skills and reviews commonplace in freelancer systems like Upwork and TaskRabbit. Many companies also increasingly give tests as a part of their hiring process to assess candidates' skills—valuing performance on these tests over any number of titles on a traditional résumé. At Topia, we followed this model, and had candidates not only tell us about what they had accomplished in prior roles, but also do mock presentations and complete engineering tests—which is why we often ended up with engineers with nontraditional backgrounds as some of our top performers.

"Many of the best people don't even have a résumé today," says Joanna Riley, Founder and CEO of Censia. "Companies know this, and need a solution to find and engage the right talent. Companies work with Censia because we have mapped a global workforce of hundreds of millions of professionals based on skills by aggregating publicly available data and applying algorithms to create a skills profile. They are saying to us, 'help me find a worker with these particular hard and soft skills and competencies from the work they have done, and their career trajectory. We will teach them the rest.' The traditional résumé can't do this, and I 100 percent think the traditional résumé is dying."

F3 FOCUS

F3 Companies know that traditional résumés are not an appropriate way to assess workers' skills and competencies. They, instead look to innovative systems that categorize workers' skills and make competency tests a part of their interview process to assess workers' skills. F3 Companies know that with the right skills and competencies on their project teams, they will be ready to capture opportunities and respond to disruptions in the Talent Mobility Revolution.

Agile Talent Management and Nonlinear Careers

When Rachael King and I sat down to design our agile management processes at Topia, we were emphatic: no annual performance reviews. I had vowed after experiencing these at Lehman Brothers that no company I ran would ever have this structure. Rachael, for her part, had developed a strong belief in dynamic projects, clear milestones, and regular feedback on performance. Instead, we decided, we would champion "continuous feedback" (I often called this "being human": tell people how they were doing as and when they did something. But Rachael, very rightly, vetoed this nomenclature!).

We started by simply telling our small team that we wanted people to give regular, honest feedback to team members as work was completed. Over time, we implemented a formal objectives and key results (OKR) process that set annual, quarterly, and monthly objectives for project teams with a framework for regular performance feedback. We then set up an annual cross-calibration process where project leaders contributed feedback that formed a composite assessment of employee skills, competencies, and performance that managers shared with them.

Innovative companies know that static annual reviews done by static managers don't work in a world of dynamic talent mobility, where employees move regularly between jobs and geographies. Rather, they rethink performance management structures to align to dynamic on-demand work across many jobs, teams, and leaders. The best practice is the OKR framework used by many companies, including Topia.

Setting Project Objectives and Measuring Success

As companies shift to be agile, they deconstruct the company's work into projects with clear milestones and objectives that the team completes. These objectives form the basis of measuring the success and performance of teams. As we discussed in prior chapters, many technology companies have been operating like this for years, the result of their agile software development processes. As a part of the Talent Mobility Revolution and increasing movement between jobs, traditional companies are now restructuring their work into discrete projects and goals.

Project goals should be put into a comprehensive objectives and key results (OKR) framework across the company that becomes a core part of the company's operating model. Popularized by Google, OKRs are measurable and regular goals set by leaders that are tracked as projects progress. The best practice is to set OKRs quarterly, with monthly OKRs aligned to each quarterly goal and regularly adjusted as needed as work progresses. (In fact, according to talent management company Reflektive, companies who manage goals quarterly see 30 percent higher returns than companies who manage goals annually.)* Generally, project teams have project OKRs and clarity on how these align to company OKRs. Each worker—whether an employee or freelancer—has his or her own OKRs aligned to the project OKRs that can be easily measured. This framework should be adopted as employees move to new jobs or new geographies (whether through frequent travel, relocation, or assignments)—both types of movement should come with clear and measurable expectations on what success looks like.

Employees should update the status of OKRs as work happens, providing transparency and real-time status on project milestones. The best practice is for all OKRs to be logged in a talent management system (at Topia, we use BetterWorks, a competitor of Reflektive) for easy review and look back. At the end of each project, leaders review how successfully the project team was in completing the project OKRs—and how each individual contributed to the team's outcome. With OKRs set and tracked, managers can then easily pay

---

* Reflektive, "Understanding the Difference: Traditional vs. Agile Performance Management," March 6, 2018, https://www.reflektive.com/blog/agile-performance -management/.

freelance workers based on performance and review employees for ongoing contribution and skills development. Overall, this iterative planning and assessment process helps companies respond quickly as business conditions or project statuses change.

With OKRs the currency of contribution, the traditional notion of tenure and career ladders goes away. Rather, companies recognize now that workers come from different backgrounds with nonlinear careers. It's the skills they contribute, the competencies they develop, and their success completing OKRs that drives career progression.

Since leaving Topia, Rachael King has been implementing OKRs across traditional companies, helping them start the transformation to working with agility. She advocates that "this transition should first start with companies mapping their company goals and the work that goes into completing them. From there, work should be broken down into discrete projects with measurable OKRs."

However, King cautions that companies "must be careful about the connection between OKRs and reward. If employees only include OKRs that they can easily achieve to maximize their compensation, then you miss the concept of work planning and setting ambitious goals for project teams to figure out through their ingenuity and initiative. OKRs must become a standard part of the company's operating model, not only a talent tool."

F3 FOCUS

F3 Companies know that amid globalization, demographic change, and automation—the forces of the Talent Mobility Revolution—agility is king. To make agile performance management work, they adopt the OKR framework, setting and tracking dynamic goals and outcomes. With this in place, they set up a cross-calibration process that supports employee progression amid nonlinear career paths.

From Annual Reviews to Agile Feedback

With dynamic projects, teams, and careers, companies swap the annual performance review for regular, dynamic feedback. They train project leaders to provide continuous feedback during the course of projects and as OKRs progress. And they train managers to deliver composite reviews of project performance and provide career coaching. They log all of this feedback in their talent management system, where they can easily refer back to it when needed. For freelance workers, this structure drives payment for contribution to projects. Simply, if the worker did his job as expected, he will be paid for it. For employees, this contributes to an overall picture of skills development and contribution to the company, which is discussed annually in a cross-calibration process, which I detail in the next section.

In the *Harvard Business Review* article "HR Goes Agile," Cappelli and Tavis discuss the evolution of the annual review, noting: "As individuals worked on shorter-term projects of various lengths, often run by different leaders and organized around teams, the notion that performance feedback would come once a year, from one boss, made little sense. They needed more of it, more often, from more people. Overall, the focus is on delivering more-immediate feedback throughout the year so that teams can become nimbler, 'course-correct' mistakes, improve performance, and learn through iteration—all key agile principles."[*]

Reflektive is one of the systems that enables agile performance management, and therefore an expert on helping companies shift to this model. "A coach coaches in real-time during a game, reacting to their team's performance and providing in-the-moment guidance to help the players improve and the team win," the company writes. "The coach doesn't wait until the end of the season to start coaching. The same principle applies to performance reviews. The

---

[*] Peter Cappelli and Anna Tavis, "The New Rules of Talent Management: HR Goes Agile," *Harvard Business Review*, March–April 2018.

traditional method of performance management—waiting until the end of the year, or doing biannual reviews, simply doesn't work.

"Agile performance management utilizes regular check-ins and 360-degree communication—managers provide constructive feedback to employees and vice versa, which strengthens the team as a whole," they conclude.*

F3 FOCUS

For *F3 Companies* agile performance management doesn't just improve the feedback loop, it underpins the entire talent mobility model—supporting dynamic jobs and teams, and skills matching versus linear career paths. To make this work, *F3 Companies* adopt the objectives and key results (OKR) framework to set project milestones and goals. They then review workers' OKRs to assess contribution and development.

Talent Reviews, Indicators, and Career Progression

As we discussed in Chapters 4 and 5, companies today have an expanded view of their workforce and create project teams with employees and freelancers. For freelancers, career progression doesn't matter; they complete their project work, build their skills, and collect their payment. For employees, however, there is still a desire for career *progression*. Even in a world of nonlinear career paths and more frequent and fulfilling tours of duty across jobs and geographies, employees still want to grow their status and salaries. The question is how to provide and communicate progression in a

---

* Reflektive, "Understanding the Difference: Traditional vs. Agile Performance Management," March 6, 2018, https://www.reflektive.com/blog/agile-performance -management/.

work environment that is increasingly flat and defined by dynamic jobs and teams.

With dynamic projects, employees may work with a variety of project leaders over the course of a year. These leaders need to provide feedback on employee contribution to create the composite view of skills and competencies that a manager will communicate. In this complex mosaic, OKRs are the GPS. The OKRs completed across the different projects denote what an employee contributed and what competencies were developed or acquired. These are the basis of a talent review process that replaces the traditional annual review.

In the talent review, company leaders and sponsors come together for a series of meetings to review the contribution of each employee at the company. Using the OKRs from each project as the blueprint, they review each employee's performance, impact, and competencies developed across their projects. Project leaders who have worked with the employee provide anecdotal evidence to support the conversations. For each employee, company leaders should look at the OKRs as well as *how* they were done, assessing whether the employee continues to work in line with the company's values and culture.

The best practice is for talent reviews to happen quarterly as a part of management meetings. At the end of each year, the leaders should look at the prior three quarters of data and agree on a talent indicator for each employee, taking into consideration both project performance and potential for subsequent contribution. This rating should drive an upward or downward multiplier on any variable compensation and form the basis of a discussion for any forward progression for the employee. After the indicator is set, employees should be reviewed against a leveling framework that assesses skills, competencies, and development opportunities. Based on these competencies, leaders set each employee's level and learning path, which drives the next dynamic project and the employee's contribution to it. With this process, forward-thinking companies move from a world of vertical career ladders to nonlinear dynamic career paths.

Jacky Cohen, who leads Topia's People and Culture team, thinks about employee levels and career progression as based on "scope and impact." "It's evolving to be similar to the leveling matrices that are found in compensation surveys which span industries. Like these, we need to increasingly look at competencies instead of titles to compare salaries. It's more like: Can the employee tie a knot? Can the employee tie a knot and teach someone else to tie a knot? Can the employee tie a knot, teach someone else to tie a knot, and advocate to senior leadership about why it's important to tie knots?" says Cohen. "Most companies are not near this place yet, though. To do this, you have to fundamentally break down all of the company's work and map it out in a competency-based way with levels assigned. This is a necessary, but major transformation for traditional companies."

F3 FOCUS

F3 Companies use talent reviews, talent indicators, and competencies to assesses employee contribution and potential. This process is collaborative across company leaders, as employees work with multiple project leaders across dynamic teams. Using a dynamic talent management structure, companies support employee career progression in a nonlinear and innovative way.

When I founded Topia, I wanted to rethink our teams, project goals, and feedback structures to embrace nonlinear careers and dynamic feedback. And through my nine years leading the company, I saw our customers starting the same journey as they transformed for the talent mobility era. *F3 Companies* rethink career paths, résumés, and performance management to unlock seamless talent mobility across jobs, teams, and geographies. With dynamic goal setting and measurement, they can quickly spin up project teams. They dispense with the structures of a traditional company, instead thinking about career paths as a nonlinear mosaic where an employee will work across many projects, teams, and business areas.

Redefining career paths is the sixth step for success in the Talent Mobility Revolution. Leaders who do not start to adopt these practices and shift their mindset about career paths will struggle in the future of jobs. Today's Talent Mobility Revolution brings growing disruptions and opportunities—only companies and teams built on agility and diverse skills will succeed.

In this section, we looked at how to redesign work at an *F3 Company* and covered the next three steps to talent mobility transformation: (1) rearchitecting roles to be dynamic jobs, (2) evolving teams and managers for dynamic jobs, and (3) redefining career paths. With an *F3 Company* set up and work redesigned to be agile, we now turn to look at how to make your *F3 Company* run smoothly. In Section 3, we look at the nuts and bolts of an *F3 Company*, covering policies, compensation and benefits, and operations and systems.

CHAPTER SUMMARY

- Traditional career paths were built on hierarchy and ladders. Today's career paths are increasingly nonlinear, which means companies must rethink their approach to recruiting and managing talent.

- Companies traditionally relied on a résumé detailing experience and titles to showcase an employee profile. Today's companies recruit for skills, not titles, increasingly sourcing and staffing project teams for skills that are needed.

- The annual performance review has long been a part of employee management. Companies today adopt agile talent management practices, breaking work into dynamic projects, assigning clear objectives to projects, and regularly assessing progress.

- Project goals should be based on the OKR framework. OKRs should be set quarterly and reviewed with the same frequency. At the end of the year, company leaders should come together to create composite views of each employee's skills and competencies.

- In the talent mobility era, employee skills and competencies form the basis of career progression. These skills are the basis of matching workers to dynamic jobs. This creates fluid rather than linear career paths.

OPERATING A FLAT, FLUID, AND FAST COMPANY

7

Creating Policies to Manage Talent Mobility

In 2013, I was sitting at a client meeting discussing how to transform the business's policies for increasing talent mobility. The company has a large amount of employee mobility, driven by a headquarters in a second-tier city, and a corporate culture that values diversity, customer experience, and employee career empowerment. Additionally, the company was growing quickly. Employees moved to start new jobs at the HQ, open offices in new locations, and provide maternity cover, among other reasons. We were looking at how to govern all of this employee movement—that is, how to create a framework that simultaneously enabled it and managed the company's costs and compliance, while supporting families with a great relocation experience.

Our client was steps ahead of many other companies at the time. It's leaders had already centralized their budget for geographic movement (global mobility) and started to think about an expanded talent mobility definition and alignment with the broader talent and business strategy. But they were struggling to make it all happen, and that's what we were discussing—specifically how to innovate in policies and frameworks.

I have had the "policy redesign conversation" with countless companies around the world since then. It generally starts with looking at how to transform traditional corporate relocation from a back-office, reactive part of HR to a core part of talent development strategy. It almost always touches on selection (how to select the right employees for the right opportunities), tracking success (how to ensure goals are clearly met before an employee moves on to another opportunity), compliance (how to support increasingly frequent mobility in line with current tax, immigration, and geopolitical frameworks), and cost (how to manage budgets and approvals). In more recent years as the Talent Mobility Revolution has taken off, the conversations have almost always moved on to then discuss the policies for job, location, and employment movement, and how to bring this all together under one talent mobility definition and leader (see Chapters 1 and 2 for further discussion).

Companies today know that their talent mobility is rapidly expanding—both in volume and breadth—and that their policies must evolve to enable and manage it. The Chief Talent Mobility Officer should own and design these policies as a part of the transformation, but they must be adopted as a core part of overall business operations and strategy. As we discussed in Chapter 1 in our expanded definition of talent mobility, enabling employee movement—across geographies, jobs, locations, and employment—is the foundation of an *F3 Company*. But supporting continuous movement of workers inside and outside of a company can be easier said than done. Your policies are the framework to make this happen. Any company or business leader that wants to make talent mobility work must reinvent its policies for the talent mobility era. Those that do will reap the rewards in employee engagement, innovation, and growth. Those that do not will lose out to their more forward-thinking competitors.

In the last two sections, we looked how to set up your *F3 Company* and redesign work to be dynamic. We now turn to look at the nuts and bolts of operating an *F3 Company*. We start by looking at policies—the governing framework for employee movement. We will then look at how to innovate in benefits, systems, and operations to enable your *F3 Company* to drive employee engagement, accelerate innovation, and unleash growth.

Designing Policies for Geographic Movement

Traditional Corporate Relocation Policies

In Chapter 1, we looked at how today's geographic movement originated from the traditional corporate relocation of past years. In past years, corporate relocation was, for the most part, business-directed—that is offered (sometimes strongly suggested) to an employee by the company and manager. It was governed by a set of robust policies that helped to convince the employee and his (almost always, his!) family to accept a relocation or expatriate assignment in a different location. Over time, employees grew to expect that if they took opportunities abroad, they would have the opportunity to enjoy more compensation and benefits.

Corporate relocation had two types (which still exist today):

- *Relocations.* A permanent move to a new location where the employee becomes employed by the new ("host") location
- *Expatriate assignment.* A fixed-term move to a new location (often abroad) where the employee remains employed by the original ("home") location and is expected to return at the end of the assignment

Typically, the policies for these included a set of relocation benefits (shipping, temporary stay at arrival, support in finding housing and schools, language and cultural training, local destination support like a car and driver or a housecleaning service), tax advice, and ongoing salary and employment adjustments, such as a housing, hardship, or cost of living adjustments. For expatriates, taxes, social security, and other pensions were almost always "equalized," that is adjusted to ensure employees could be in no way worse off than they may have been in their home market. In fact, in most instances they were better off.

Because almost all geographic movement was at the request of the company, there was no need to think about how people were selected for moves or whether there should be a shared responsibility between the experiences and skills the employee developed and the contribution the company got from the employee's work. Rather, the corporate relocation function focused on how to get the employees to accept the opportunity and fill the business need.

This was the setup for people who accepted expatriate assignments at Lehman Brothers in 2006, like my colleagues Victoria and Darren. After a few years working in New York, they had both taken the opportunity to spend the third year of their analyst program working in Hong Kong and helping to expand the investment banking team there. They came to Asia as traditional expatriates: employees of the US entity with the explicit expectations that they would return to New York after their year of services in Hong Kong. They had a traditional set of corporate relocation benefits: end-to-end relocation support, corporate housing, tax advice, immigration support, cost-of-living adjustments, and Chinese language and cultural classes.

My experience, however, was different. After many interviews in English and Mandarin during my senior year of college (I don't think Lehman Brothers actually believed a blond American could speak business-level Mandarin!), I had been hired directly to Hong Kong. This was rare; normally employees worked in their home country and office for a number of years before earning a transfer to an office abroad. I would not follow the traditional pattern of working two years in New York and then accepting an expatriate assignment for my third year. Instead, I graduated from college, completed a monthlong training program in New York, and then got on a plane directly to Hong Kong. This without precedent, or policies.

I remember sitting in training in New York when a colleague who had interned in Hong Kong asked me if I'd "sorted my serviced apartment yet." I had no idea what a serviced apartment was or what she meant. I'm not sure what I thought I was going to do, but at that moment, it suddenly dawned on me that I was moving across the world and had no plan for where I was going to live when I arrived. I also remember learning that real estate brokers in Hong Kong were paid by the renter, and that a very large security deposit was expected. Without a paycheck yet, I had no idea how to pay for it. I also remember getting a letter saying that I had a housing allowance—a welcome surprise after having been hired as a Hong Kong local employee. With my mobility experience outside of the company norms, Lehman Brothers apparently hadn't quite figured out what to do.

As with many of my experiences at Lehman Brothers, I was seeing the future Talent Mobility Revolution emerge—a world where employees would move continuously with shared responsibility between company and employee. As we discussed in prior chapters, many employees today move for tours of duty across offices and jobs at all stages of their career. But in 2006, very few did. Corporate relocation worked within a transactional framework and clear set of policies. I challenged this when I moved outside of the bounds of the traditional corporate relocation policies. Today, this is increasingly the norm—and companies are transforming their frameworks and policies to enable it.

"I see a big shift in employee expectations and mobility demands," says Susanna Warner, VP International Mobility at Schneider Electric, a Fortune 500 global power company that is 182 years old and generates revenue of $25 billion annually. "Employees are much more mobile today in many more ways; in particular, we see much more voluntary mobility than we ever have in the past. Right now, I am in the midst of transforming our processes, policies, systems, and employee experiences to ensure we are set up to achieve our talent and business goals for tomorrow."*

New Policies for Geographic Movement

As talent mobility has ballooned, so too have the frequency and configurations of geographic movement. As we discussed in Chapter 1, *F3 Companies* expand their definition of geographic movement to include relocations, expatriate assignments, frequent travel, long-distance commuting, project-based moves, and rotational or training programs. Within each of these, there are a near infinite number of permutations for employee and business needs. And in addition to this, companies often have to consider job, location, and employment movement as a part of these—an employee may relocate for a new job in a new project team in a new business area in a new geography, or a freelance worker may take new a tour of duty across the country with a need to both long-distance commute and work-from-home some days, to name just a few setups.

At the same time, geographic mobility has shifted from almost exclusively company-driven to being in much more demand from employees who value the experience, learning, and lifestyle balance (one spouse may ask for a relocation to align with another spouse's move) that comes with these tours of duty. This means that, in certain instances, employees are willing to fund part or all of their mobility—in the way I funded part of mine at Lehman Brothers, valuing the opportunity to work in Asia and learn about the economies of other countries. Increasingly policies for geographic mobility are shifting from a patriarchal model of companies funding everything to a model of "shared responsibility" between company and worker (again, like my experience at Lehman Brothers).

Managing this near continuous movement across locations and configurations can be a nightmare for a traditional company, but using an evolved policy framework, *F3 Companies* make it happen

---

* Interview with Susanna Warner, VP International Mobility, Schneider Electric, December 19, 2018.

seamlessly and unlock benefits in employee attraction, retention, and engagement and rapid innovation and business growth.

Susanna Warner joined Schneider Electric in January of 2017 to transform the traditional corporate relocation program (today called "International Mobility"). She had previously worked in global mobility at LafargeHolcim, a Fortune 500 cement and construction company, and AXA, a Fortune 500 insurance company, but also had tours of duty in talent acquisition and employee development. This gave her a unique perspective on the emerging Talent Mobility Revolution that she brought to her new role at Schneider Electric.*

Schneider Electric itself had already started transforming for the talent mobility era and the preferences of today's employees. The first time I visited its offices in suburban Paris, I expected the venerable global power company to have a traditional office design with cubicles and offices. As soon as I entered, I was struck by the bright colors, open plan designs, and modern imagery on the walls. It was clear that Schneider Electric already had a forward-looking view of work.

"Because I've been in various walks of life, my third taste of global mobility was very different than the others," says Warner. "I could make the connection between mobility and sourcing talent, developing leaders, retaining employees, staffing client projects to drive revenue, and building local and regional hubs."

Schneider Electric's HR leadership team had already initiated an ambitious HR transformation program focusing on building a globally inclusive but locally empowered company, gravitating and attracting talent around three main geographic hubs. Instead of operating under the leadership of an HQ-centric organization, this approach enabled people to have equal opportunities for growth, build locally empowered teams for customers, and drive a more diverse environment to foster innovation and creativity. Over a

---

* Interview with Susanna Warner, VP International Mobility, Schneider Electric, December 19, 2018.

three-year period, Warner and her team focused on policies, digitization, and experience to support this HR transformation. Their goal was to "really position employee mobility as a key enabler of talent strategy and the HR transformation," enabling opportunities for mobile employees but also ensuring that mobility was purposeful and aligned with the overall talent and diversity strategy. The project started by tackling the policies and frameworks for geographic movement.

"It was initially a traditional relocation and expatriate program," says Warner. "The mobilities tracked and facilitated by the global mobility team were focused on traditional expatriate assignments, mainly of senior leaders or experts, driven by the business.

"We started by rolling out new policies for employee mobility aligned to our business and talent needs," continues Warner. "Policies framed each purpose of global mobility—from expatriate assignments to one-way relocations to short-term projects—and structured them within a framework of three mobility drivers: development, leadership and transformation, and knowledge transfers. We also included a specific category for self-driven mobility—designed for those who put their hand up for a tour of duty in another location or team. Self-driven mobility is today our biggest segment and the fastest growing.

"We ensured that selection for global mobility was closely linked to our talent management approach. For example, when selecting a candidate, we needed to ask ourselves: is this someone who we have identified as a high potential and needs to have a development opportunity? Or, is this someone with specific skills that are required for a particular project team?" says Warner. "This gives us a rigorous framework across selecting and managing our growing geographic mobility."

Nick Pond, Mobility Leader EY People Advisory Services, has seen Fortune 500 companies undertaking similar approaches. "Companies are increasingly linking talent strategy and tours of duty across geographies and designing strategic workforce planning around how to build [locally], buy [gig economy], or move [geographic movement] talent to match business needs they have. On the demand side, you have employees increasingly asking for these opportunities," says Pond. "To do this, companies are increasingly redesigning their roles to be dynamic, project-based jobs, rewriting their mobility policies to encompass more scenarios, and aligning global mobility opportunities to a nine-box model. All of this creates a clear link between talent and business strategy."*

F3 FOCUS

F3 Companies transform and broaden their policies for geographic mobility to address the continuous and diverse movement of the Talent Mobility Revolution. They then tie this to their talent and business strategy, dynamically matching employees to new opportunities across geographies and jobs. With this updated framework, F3 Companies harness the Talent Mobility Revolution to drive employee engagement, accelerate innovation, and unleash growth.

Four Steps for Success with Geographic Movement

In the prior section, we looked at how *F3 Companies*, like Schneider Electric, are transforming their frameworks for the Talent Mobility Revolution. I've summarized the four steps for geographic mobility success below:

Set an overarching policy framework. Your talent mobility policy framework should first recognize that today, there is an expanded set of geographic movement. It should include a clear definition for each of our six core configurations: relocations, expatriate

---

* Interview with Nick Pond, Partner, EY People Advisory, December 17, 2018.

assignments, short-term project moves, extended travel, commuting, and rotational or training programs. For each of these, you should design a core set of benefits, including the employment model, and relocation, tax, immigration, cost of living, and ongoing destination benefits (such as language training and on-the-ground support). Typically, this framework will include a set of benefits demarcated by location (usually three bands based on distance), family size (single, married, or married with children) and driver (self vs. business directed). Your final policy framework will look something like this:

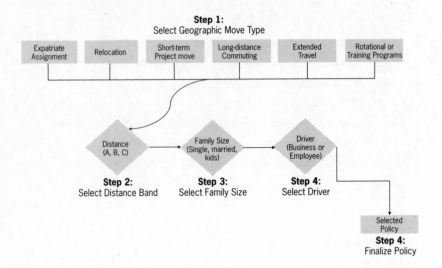

This framework, including the definition of each move type, decision tree for drivers, and core benefits, is your blueprint for geographic movement. Designing it is the first step in transforming your policies.

Build flexibility by shifting from a fixed benefit to a points model.
Traditional policies typically structured their benefits in a "use-it-or-lose it" model—that is, each employee received a set of benefits that must be used on a specific thing (e.g., shipping, serviced apartment,

or destination support). With growing amounts of geographic movement and diverse configurations to address company and individual needs, your new global mobility policy model should swap fixed benefits for points that can be applied to any benefits in a pool. After designing the core benefits for each of your geographic mobility policies in step 1 above, you should translate these benefits into a number of points tied to each benefit. Then calculate a number of points for each geographic mobility policy. Then leave it up to the employees to decide how they want to use them across the pool of benefit options (for example, an employee may want to swap shipping benefits for a longer stay in a serviced apartment). Today's employees traffic in autonomy and flexibility—and they likely know better than any manager does what they need!

Align tours of duty to a nine-box talent grid. Like Schneider Electric did, tie employee tours of duty to a "nine-box model" in your talent review discussion (see below for further details on this). Ensure that employees are being offered the correct geographic movement opportunities (tours of duty) for where they fall in the nine-box. Tie a learning agenda required in their tour of duty to the nine-box (for example, if an employee is moving to a Honolulu for a three-month project in a new business area, give him or her a learning agenda both about that new business area and the local culture). Use your talent management system to keep clear track of the nine-box and tours of duty the employee has had and how that contributes to the employee's skills development and career growth. Here's what your nine-box should look like aligned to mobility opportunities:

	Improvement	Good	Great
Potential — Upward multiple levels	Identify root case and additional tour of duty	Stretch opportunities/ tours of duty	Stretch opportunities/ Significant investment in tours of duty
Upward movement	Performance management	Recognition/ Tour of duty development plan	Stretch opportunities/ Tours of duty
Right current level	Performance management	Engagement Tour of duty leveraging skills	Recognition/ Tour of duty leveraging skills

Performance →

Adopt a set of mobility drivers. Like Schneider Electric did, overlay a set of "mobility drivers" to your policy framework and nine-box model to ensure each geographic mobility tour of duty can be classified against business and talent goals. We suggest using four classifications, each defined below: Project, Corporate, Development, and Retention.

- *Project.* Geographic movement as a part of a project team where skills are matched, often with job movement included
- *Corporate.* Geographic movement as part of a broader corporate goal such as opening an office or supporting training or expansion
- *Development.* Geographic movement to support employee development, generally leveraging the output from the nine-box during the talent review discussions
- *Retention.* Geographic movement to support employee retention, generally as part of an employee-requested move to fulfill her own flexibility, growth, or experience goals

F3 FOCUS

F3 Companies know that amid the Talent Mobility Revolution, they'll have near constant geographic mobility. They bring structure and success to this by transforming their staid corporate relocation policies with a four-step model that includes setting an overarching policy framework, building flexibility by shifting from a fixed benefit to a points model, aligning tours of duty to a nine-box talent grid, and adopting a set of mobility drivers.

Creating Policies for Job Movement

Traditional Policies for Job Movement

Job movement is a relatively new concept amid the Talent Mobility Revolution. As we've discussed in prior chapters, traditional companies like Lehman Brothers and Mead Paper Company hired full-time employees into fixed roles in a given organizational department and team led by a traditional manager. The expectation was that—with time and contribution—employees would progress through positions of increasing seniority (the career ladder) toward an end goal of retirement. In this setup, movement laterally between departments and teams was rare. In fact, as I built Topia, I heard countless stories at HR conferences about business units blocking lateral moves and internal hiring as they sought to "hold on to" existing talent in their teams.

If an employee wanted to learn new skills or try a different career area, she was often on her own going against organizational bureaucracy and expectations to advocate for an internal transfer. Sometimes this worked; sometimes it didn't. If it didn't, an employee might resign from the company and try to execute this switch by going to another company. Most often the way to navigate to a new job in a new business area was by going back to school to learn new skills, and then going through a formal recruiting program in another business area. There really were no policies or precedents for enabling job movement at traditional companies.

When I did my MBA at London Business School, there were countless people from around the world using business school to make this switch. My class included hospitality professionals who switched to marketing, accountants who switched to investment banking, procurement specialists who switched to management consulting, and public relations managers who transitioned to technology firms, among many other scenarios. Like many employees at traditional companies, the only way to switch between industry segments and jobs was to take a break and reset at business school. Developing skills and transferring them to another team or department was almost unheard of.

My friend Anna encountered these organizational roadblocks when she advocated for a change of job and geography at one of the world's largest PR and marketing firms. Anna was a top performer in New York, recognized across the firm for her high leadership potential and contributions. However, after a number of years in healthcare public relations in New York, she was ready for a change—like many millennials, she wanted the opportunity to learn new skills in a new business area and do a tour of duty in a different office. Put into the language of the Talent Mobility Revolution, she wanted job and geographic movement. Her company, however, struggled to make this happen. Anna was bounced around the firm to speak to many different people in different departments and human resources. She visited offices around the world, met with people, and pleaded her case. She loved the firm and wanted to stay—but she wanted to do something new. Ultimately—due to organizational bureaucracy and friction—the company couldn't make any job or geographic movement happen for Anna. Instead, they asked her to sit tight, keep doing her regular job, and wait and see if anything came about in the future. Anna, like many ambitious millennial workers, did not wait. Instead she resigned and joined a nonprofit that gave her the opportunity to work across diverse areas and countries, accelerating her skills development. The company lost both significant institutional knowledge and a rising star because they couldn't make job and geographic mobility happen. They were seeing firsthand how strong the forces of the Talent Mobility Revolution are.

"Historically, things like headcount, visas, compensation, and compliance were challenges to mobility," says Rachael King, Topia's first VP People. "In addition to this, there was often a lack of visibility and talent planning across managers and teams, especially outside of the leadership levels. With traditional siloed organizational designs, rather than taking a global approach to talent and business goals, opportunities for talent mobility were often not identified, or when they were, there was often not the talent planning to successfully repatriate someone back to their next opportunity. The irony is that companies would often lose people overall amid this siloed approach."

New Policies for Job Movement

Schneider Electric is going beyond its global mobility transformation to further facilitate job movement. "The ultimate goal is to create an internal jobs market and application process. We want to make this reactive (where employees apply) and proactive where we can map employee skills against open jobs and algorithmically recommend them for them. This additional step will help provide more agile and global talent solutions (part-time projects as well as full time roles, cross-functional as well as cross-border opportunities); it is currently in pilot phase," says Susanna Warner.

As we've discussed in the prior section, Susanna's vision is the goal for *F3 Companies*. Implementing it allows them to harness the Talent Mobility Revolution to drive employee engagement, accelerate innovation, and drive growth. According to Deloitte, 76 percent of "high-performing companies" regularly tap into internal talent pools.* This starts with setting the right policies for job movement.

After deconstructing work into projects and segmenting project jobs into core jobs (performed by employees), context jobs (performed by freelancers) and repetitive jobs (automated), companies design policies to govern how workers apply to jobs, how workers are selected for jobs, and how company leaders support job movement.

- *How workers apply for jobs.* Workers (both employees and freelancers) should be encouraged to look for new jobs (or projects) regularly via the talent marketplaces. For employees, this requires a cultural shift to thinking about work as project tours of duty—and must become a part of your standard employee onboarding program and ongoing cultural norms. The jobs graph in the talent marketplace should clearly indicate which jobs are core jobs and therefore best for employees, and which jobs are context jobs and therefore best for freelancers. Additionally, the algorithms in the jobs marketplace should continuously recommend employees— based on the skills they have—to project leaders as they kick off new projects. Employees should only be allowed to apply for or be recommended to new jobs when they are coming to the end of a given project.
- *How workers are selected for jobs.* The project leader for each team should be responsible for reviewing the skills and competencies of each worker who has applied or been matched to a given job. Policies should ensure that employees can only be considered for new project teams as they complete a prior project—to ensure structure and reliability

* Deloitte, Denise Moulton, "Talent on the Move! Inspiring Better Employee Experience Through Internal Mobility," July 17, 2018, https://capitalhblog.deloitte.com/2018/07/17/talent-on-the-move-inspiring-a-better-employee-experience-through-internal-mobility/.

for project teams. When employees are not staffed on a project (traditionally called "on the bench" at management consulting firms), they should have preference in staffing considerations, provided their skills and competencies are a match. For freelancers, selection should be based on skills, availability, and cost, which is generally listed in the freelance marketplace.

- *How leaders support job movement.* You should set expectations and policies to ensure company leaders support and enable job movement. Company leaders should have training to think about their contribution to the overall company objectives as their first priority and to embrace the project-driven work structure, shifting away from the traditional org design and department-first mentality of the past. Leaders should get confidence in completing their projects well, with clear policies in place that job movement cannot be done midproject, but when employees have completed a project.

"Improving internal mobility in an organization starts with a change in mindset and culture," says Deloitte in the 2018 article "Talent on the Move! Inspiring a Better Employee Experience through Internal Mobility." "Today's talent no longer views mobility as a privilege, but as an *expectation*. To compete for and develop top talent, companies should find a way to integrate employee mobility into the range of the employee experience," Deloitte concludes.*

---

* Deloitte, Denise Moulton, "Talent on the Move! Inspiring Better Employee Experience Through Internal Mobility," July 17, 2018, https://capitalhblog.deloitte.com/2018/07/17/talent-on-the-move-inspiring-a-better-employee-experience-through-internal-mobility/.

F3 FOCUS

F3 Companies know that amid the Talent Mobility Revolution, job movement is critical. They unlock job movement with policies for how workers apply to jobs, how workers are selected for jobs, and how leaders support job movement. These policies ensure that job movement only happens when projects are completed giving structure and stability to teams. They support these policies with a shift in operational and cultural norms around job movement, starting with updated onboarding programs for employees and leaders.

Structuring Policies for Location Movement

Traditional Policies for Location Movement

As we discussed in Chapter 3, traditional companies operated with the expectations that employees came to the office each day to work for a set number of hours. If they had personal or family needs to balance, they had to happen outside of working hours. There were no policies for location movement (work-from-home or work-from-anywhere); rather the policy was that if you needed to take time off to be home or to pursue a personal travel experience, you took defined PTO (personal time off) and logged it in the internal HR system. If you wanted to live in a rural location and work for a company in a city, you had to commute there; there was no concept of extending work opportunities to skilled professionals outside of local urban markets. Companies even made it difficult to work during business travel. In many cases, access to company networks and systems was limited to when you were physically in the office, and USB ports (for easily transporting files to access) were blocked—like at Lehman Brothers and Standard Chartered Bank.

In 2009, while I was working at Standard Chartered Bank in Singapore, my father was nearing the end of his life. After a 10-year battle with stage 4 colon cancer, the doctors had called to say that he didn't have much longer to live and I should return to the United States to see him. I quickly called my boss, Rai, told him what was happening, and asked to work remotely for a few weeks. Without flinching, he looked me in the eye and said one word: "Go." While I was in Boston with my father, I worked remotely—joining conference calls, completing financial models, and more. For my boss and me, it worked fine (and Standard Chartered made it easier than Lehman Brothers to access files and connect). I was deeply grateful for this flexibility and for Rai's support.

When I got back to Singapore, however, I got a call from the COO of our fund. I had gone over my holiday allotment and she was requesting that they deduct it from my pay. Incensed by both the fixed, traditional policy and the fact that I had been penalized for working remotely while my father died, Rai worked on my behalf to get a policy exemption granted. Standard Chartered did ultimately grant the exemption, but it took months, hours of Rai's time, and countless amounts of emotion and anger from me. Standard Chartered, like Lehman Brothers, was a traditional company with traditional location expectations: you were in the office or you were taking structured vacation days. Nothing in between. After this experience, I became completely disengaged with Standard Chartered—and its archaic view of work—and vowed to go to business school and design a different future in what would become Topia.

"Offices used to be necessary because of the way companies thought about work, but also because of the cost of equipment in the industrial age," says Sten Tamkivi, Chief Product Officer at Topia and Founder of Teleport, which developed with a remote working culture. "Imagine a world when desktop computers cost a ton of money and were in one stationary location. People needed to come to the office to use hardware like this and access binders and papers where things might be written down. But in the information technology era, equipment has become much cheaper—people have laptops, mobile phones, and iPads. Now we are even living in a world where I don't even have to take a computer out of my bag at home to access files, check e-mail, or communicate with colleagues, I can do it all from my phone. In this world, work 'place' disappears. Knowledge processing or creative economy jobs can be done from anywhere."

New Policies for Location Movement

With growing talent mobility and reduced office space footprints, videoconferencing has grown rapidly to a $16 billion market today. The market is predicted to grow 20 percent each year through 2022 as location movement expands, making it a $41 billion market by 2022. With the growth in location movement, Krish Ramakrishnan designed videoconferencing platform BlueJeans specifically for remote work—with noise canceling technology ("so you don't hear the dog barking or lattes being made"), easy troubleshooting ("so you don't need corporate IT support in the office") and a format for large meetings ("not a bunch of tiny screens only"). As talent mobility and remote working grows, Ramakrishnan has set a new mission for the company—"better than being there."

"We don't look at ourselves as a videoconferencing provider anymore," says Ramakrishnan. "We look at ourselves as a platform for modern meetings. We're trying to build a product that improves upon meetings—like watching sports on TV in your living room can be better than from the bleachers."*

Today's *F3 Companies* know that location movement is core to their talent and business strategies. More broadly, enabling greater location movement and distributed jobs is important for spreading job opportunities to skilled professionals living outside of traditional urban hubs. Companies must enable more distributed and remote work with clear policies for the way that teams work and the systems they use. Policies for location movement should have

* Interview with Krish Ramakrishnan, Founder, BlueJeans, December 3, 2018.

four pillars: in-person time, working hours overlap, systems adoption, and meeting etiquette.

- *In-person time.* Companies with significant location movement should set policies for when and how teams get together. The best practices for policies is likely one annual, in-person company meeting, paired with quarterly team meetings.
- *Working hours overlap.* One of the most difficult things about significant location movement is that employees may be working across many time zones without much overlapping worktime. The best practice for policies is to mandate that, regardless of where an employee is working from, he needs to have a minimum number of hours of overlap of working time. If an employee decides to move to Maine when the rest of the team is in Seattle, he should expect to work later in the evening.
- *Systems adoption.* Companies should set clear expectations for the systems they use to enable remote work, typically a videoconferencing system (like BlueJeans), a messaging system (like Slack) and a collaboration system (like Box or Google Docs). (We discuss how to set up systems for talent mobility in Chapter 9.) Policies should set use expectations to adjust traditional employee norms and ensure everyone is included—e.g., videoconferencing before phone calls or watercooler discussions, and messaging before e-mail before sporadic brainstorms. This helps to foster collaboration, communication, and inclusion amid location movement.
- *Meeting etiquette.* With lots of location movement, meetings will generally have some employees in the office, some at home, and some "on the road" (in transit or traveling). To make meetings effective and ensure no one feels like a "second-class citizen," companies should adopt policies that require meetings to be done by videoconference and that

all employees dial in from a location where they are alone and quiet—from a desk, not a conference room, and a home office not a noisy café. It is very challenging when part of the team is in a conference room and others are alone, so you should smooth this with clear policies to ensure that everyone is operating in the same way. Policies should also clarify that meeting notes are documented immediately and circulated via the messaging platform and stored centrally.

Sten Tamkivi articulates his own framework that he used at Teleport: "Write liberally, meet regularly, and congregate occasionally." He champions documentation of meeting notes and a company-wide shift from in-person meetings to messaging software, meeting in offices sometimes for collaboration, and congregating in annual and quarterly meetings.

* * *

In Section 1, we discussed Automattic, which owns content management system WordPress.com and operates a fully distributed team. Automattic has clear policies that touch on the above four pillars: the entire company meets for a week annually, teams meet regularly in person, messaging platforms are used widely, and notes from calls and meetings are immediately documented on its proprietary internal system. All of this makes a significant amount of location movement and flexibility work well.

Stella and Dot, which was founded to create flexible economic opportunity for women, operates a distributed engineering team, where the vast majority of the 100-person strong team work remotely. CEO Jessica Herrin says that distributed work is "a muscle that needs to be developed."

"People need to learn the skill of being at home and working remotely," says Herrin. "You must be very clear from the top about expectations and norms. We insist on people using a video camera for meetings and sending out pre-reads because we found that this radically enhances presence and preparation. We also insist that people join meetings from a quiet location. Working from home does not mean you're working while driving or eating or something else. It means you're present and working from home. As a company, you must develop the right communication tools, culture, and policies around that."

F3 FOCUS

F3 Companies know that amid the Talent Mobility Revolution, location movement is an important and growing part of their business and talent strategy. They support this with clear policies to make it work, including in-person time, working hours overlap, systems adoption, and meeting etiquette. Or, to summarize—"write liberally, meet regularly, and congregate frequently."

Policies for Employment Movement

The rise of the freelance economy is an important—and new—part of the Talent Mobility Revolution. *F3 Companies* design frameworks to leverage skills from both their employees and freelancer workers as a part of their dynamic project teams (see Section 2 for further discussion on dynamic projects). They do this by first deconstructing work into projects that fall in three tiers: core, context, and automate. Core is work that is critical and differentiated to the business success, and therefore should remain done by employees. Context is work that is noncore but specialized and can be completed with skills from the freelance economy (and done from anywhere, including parts of the country that might not normally access jobs at companies in urban locations). Automate is work that is repetitive and gets done by artificial intelligence over time. This is the framework that companies should apply to their expanded definition of the workforce and adopt to govern employment movement.

Companies should centralize management of all of these workers under their total talent management umbrella. When hiring freelancers, companies should agree on a base compensation for their work up front and have a variable compensation component for completing project objectives successfully within a given time frame and quality.

Stephane Kasriel, CEO of Upwork, works with many companies to help them adopt freelancers as a part of their teams. He says that the hardest part of companies in setting up the framework of "core, context, and automate work" is taking the time to deconstruct existing work into small enough chunks that they become projects with clear jobs that fall in that framework. Upwork itself has done this work and successfully staffs its work along this framework.

F3 FOCUS

F3 *Companies* champion employment movement as a part of their talent mobility strategies. They deconstruct work into a three-tiered framework of core, context, and automate work, which they staff across employees, freelancers, and artificial intelligence. With this framework, they access a broad range of skills and extend job opportunities beyond their local markets.

This is the Talent Mobility Revolution that I have seen sweep across many companies and parts of our economy over more than a decade. To harness it, companies must comprehensively transform their policies for geographic, job, location, and employment movement. These frameworks provide structure for this changing world and help companies drive employee engagement, drive innovation, and unleash growth. Increasing movement—and the policies that enable it—also extends jobs beyond the local markets where companies operate, creating economic opportunities in new areas of our country.

Creating policies to manage talent mobility is the seventh step to success in the future of jobs. Companies that succeed in the Talent Mobility Revolution create clear policies to support increasing employee movement. Those that do not risk losing out to more agile and more rigorously managed competitors.

CHAPTER SUMMARY

- Traditional corporate relocation policies are not fit for purpose for the diverse geographic movement of today. Companies must transform to consider the many permutations of relocations and travel.
- Companies should transform policies for geographic movement with a four-step model that includes setting an overarching policy framework, building flexibility by shifting from a fixed benefit to a points model, aligning tours of duty to a nine-box talent grid, and adopting a set of mobility drivers.
- Job movement is an important part of how companies and workers work today. To enable this, companies should design policies for how workers apply to jobs, how workers are selected for jobs and how leaders support job movement. Then they should change cultural norms starting with their onboarding processes.
- Workers no longer work from a set office location. Instead companies must enable location movement with policies to make it work, including: in-person time, working hours overlap, systems adoption and meeting etiquette.
- Employment movement is a growing part of the Talent Mobility Revolution. Companies must think of their workforce as including employees, freelancers, and artificial intelligence. Then they should deconstruct work into core, context and automate work and staff across their worker types.

Transforming Compensation and Benefits for Talent Mobility

"I'd like to update our holiday benefits to be in line with our global culture," Jacky Cohen, Topia VP of People, told me in 2018. We had just finished launching equal parental leave for men and woman—something both Jacky and I felt was deeply important to continuing to build a company rooted in diversity and fairness. Now Jacky had her eye on a similarly innovative approach for our holiday benefits, or paid time off (PTO).

Spotify, she explained, was well known for offering floating holidays, a set number of annual holiday days for all global employees that could be used anytime, replacing the divergent public holidays in each country and state. Employees could use them as they wished—if they wanted to take them on public holidays, they could; if they didn't, they could; if their religion dictated time off that was not a recognized local public holiday, they could take time off and celebrate. This approach smoothed public and company holiday variances across global locations and supported a global culture of working everywhere. I immediately loved it.

At Topia, we had already taken our holiday benefits a step further than most companies. I had founded the company in London in 2010, where the European Union mandates a minimum of 20 holiday days per year, but the local market often dictates 25 days per year, which we adopted at Topia. As we expanded to the United States (and other countries), I felt strongly that we should embrace our founding identity and keep this entitlement for all global employees. After all, why should an employee in the United States work more than an employee in the United Kingdom, and perhaps be perceived as more committed when the annual talent review comes along? Similarly, why should an employee in the United Kingdom have the opportunity for more health and wellness time, and perhaps be able to be more present while at work? None of it seemed fair. Everyone at Topia got 25 holiday days per year as part of being a Topia employee, regardless of where they lived.

But due to great variances in public holidays across states and countries, our employee time off still varied greatly, causing regular discussions internally. Jacky's floating holiday proposal would fix all of this—and also recognize that individuals may want to celebrate holidays at different times. So, we started looking into it.

Like many forward-thinking companies, however, we encountered administrative and compliance bottlenecks to rolling out what we wanted to do. We didn't have the resources to manage the intricacies of managing this in the many countries where we operated and ensure we maintained compliance with local laws. So, we made a compromise. We gave everyone the same number of days off—PTO and local public holidays—but we did it with a set calendar, selecting which days would be the public holidays. Like many companies, we phased our transformation, ensuring we could balance an innovative approach for the talent mobility era with the reality of operating a growing business.

One of the most difficult things about managing a company with significant movement between geographies, locations, and jobs is the different local expectations for compensation, benefits, and employment protections, balanced with the local laws and norms, which can vary widely across states and countries. As employees increasingly work across different cities, states, countries, and their own homes—working everywhere—traditional compensation, benefits, and employment protection models may no longer be fit for purpose.

F3 Companies rethink their compensation and benefit structures to enable talent mobility. This includes salary and bonuses, holiday and leave entitlements, and healthcare and retirement, all of which we'll cover in this chapter.

As the talent mobility era takes hold and people increasingly work across companies, geographies, and employment types (as employees and freelancers), America's long-held social contract between employer and employee must also evolve. For decades, companies provided benefits like healthcare, retirement plans, and leave to employees. However, with the growth of talent mobility and the freelance economy, we must fundamentally rethink the structure of work—including social support, benefits, and protections—for our new era. We must ensure all workers, regardless of employment type, have a living wage, antidiscrimination protections, health and safety standards, the right to collectively represent themselves, and support to balance families and careers. While there are many benefits of employment mobility, its growth brings challenges in ensuring that all workers enjoy both new work opportunities and a healthy, safe, and fair environment for work.

Companies and business leaders that want to succeed in the talent mobility era must rethink their compensation and benefits models, creating a new worker value proposition. Those that do this will attract and retain top talent and skills; those that don't will lose out to their more forward-thinking competitors. This chapter looks at how to transform the structure of work, including compensation, benefits, and worker protections, for the talent mobility era.

Rethinking Compensation Models

How Employees Were Traditionally Paid

As we've discussed in prior chapters, traditional companies hired employees to fixed roles in fixed teams with defined compensation for that role and seniority. Compensation increases were tied to two things: tenure and promotions within the team (see Chapter 6 for more information on linear career paths). Traditional compensation was generally a base salary and a small annual bonus. In most cases, the annual bonus was expected, the result of working for the year. Compensation levels were either based on a minimum wage with some additional amounts dictated by seniority and tenure, or set in line with the role and local market norms, generally dictated by a cost of living index in a particular market.

When employees moved—generally a relocation or traditional expatriate assignment (see Chapters 1 and 7 for further details on how these worked), compensation was adjusted to ensure that employees were not "worse off." In nearly all instances, they were much better off—companies enticed them to accept expatriate assignments by increasing their salaries through a series of cost of living, relocation, hardship, housing, car, school, and foreign service allowances (also called premiums) and tax equalizations, which almost always meant higher compensation. Base compensation was converted to the local currency and then adjusted by a cost of living multiplier (rarely did these go down) with the allowances added on top. If an employee went on to another expatriate assignment (as was common in certain industries like oil and gas), the same process happened. Colloquially, this is known as "the expat package." The process was both cumbersome and expensive for companies. But since it happened rarely (and even more rarely repeatedly for the same employee), it worked.

In the traditional model of employee movement, it was rare for employees to move between departments or functions when mobile. Rather, these expatriate assignments were used to fill specific *geographic* needs. Company org designs and departments still remained vertical and siloed—different from the complex matrix of movement across geographies and jobs we see today.

At Topia, we always have naturally attracted employees who had experiences living around the world as children—often with parents working as expatriates or in the army. Our first sales hire had this profile. His father worked for Schlumberger, one of the world's largest oil services companies, and was a "serial expat." He is Dutch, but he and his parents had spent time in Holland, Qatar, Azerbaijan, and France. While he worked for us, his parents went off on another assignment to Angola. His family moved on a traditional expatriate package, supported with corporate housing and other living benefits. In each community, they socialized with other expatriates who followed a similar path, creating a type of global community.

"The traditional expatriate assignment was long the compensation model adopted for any type of geographic movement," says Peggy Smith, CEO of Worldwide ERC, whom we met in Chapter 1. "Expatriates were maybe, max, 5 percent of a company's workforce, so it was fine for companies to invest a lot of money for them and take significant time managing them. Traditionally, they were also almost always experienced, senior-level employees. Let's say with a back of the envelope calculation, we generally knew that it cost three times an employee's base salary when considering all of the benefits and equalization."

"However, over the last 10 years or so, we've seen a significant shift in this approach," continues Smith. "Traditional expatriate assignments still exist, but companies are shifting to a much more fluid concept of global mobility, where many more employees move . . . but in many more structures. You see one-way moves, hiring moves, rotations, commuting structures, frequent travel, and short-term assignments for projects. Underlying this is a shift to much more dynamic project-based work across all parts of companies and much more remote and distributed work. With all of this, there's a very different cost, compensation, and management model for companies. I haven't seen many of them—at least the larger companies—fully make the transformation to this yet."

How to Set Compensation Amid Talent Mobility

With increasing geographic, job, location, and employment movement, setting compensation can be challenging. Should you adjust an employee's salary with a cost of living adjustment if she works in another location for three months? What should you do when an employee elects to move to lower-cost geography? Or, does projects in multiple places? Or, works remotely while traveling the world? Or, works four days per week balancing childcare needs alongside work, but contributes significant hours over the weekend? And how do you compensate a remote freelancer doing the same work on the same project team as a full-time employee in the office? These are just some of the scenarios amid the Talent Mobility Revolution. And all of them introduce compensation complexity.

Continuous movement is a growing part of today's workforce. For geographic movement, companies should consider two compensation structures: local benchmark or global benchmark.

- *Local benchmark.* This compensation model is based on the traditional model. In a local benchmark model, compensation is set based on a local market norm based on a cost of living index. The goal is to be competitive in the local market with local employees. If an employee moves from a lower to higher cost of living market, compensation is adjusted upward; similarly, if an employee moves the other way, compensation is adjusted downward. (Note that this can be a challenging conversation, and expectations should be set early for this operating norm with all employees). For traditional business-driven expatriate policies, it remains common to offer tax equalization benefits, but the numerous allowances of prior years are less common, except in hardship locations, like moves to certain African countries. For permanent one-way relocations or hiring relocations, tax equalization is generally not used. Companies should adopt policies that dictate that compensation is only adjusted to the local market when an employee is there for more than six months consecutively, such as for a long-term assignment or relocation. Otherwise, living adjustments should be covered in the benefits for the given policy, with things like corporate housing or per diem allowances (see Chapter 7 for further details on policies).

- *Global benchmark.* This compensation model is increasingly looked to as a way to support the continuous movement of employees in the talent mobility era. In a global benchmark model, compensation is tied to a fixed global norm, and all employees have their pay set to this global norm (which replaces the local cost of living indices). Effectively, this decouples compensation from local markets and means that all global employees with similar competencies and skills are paid consistently, making it easy to work from everywhere. The HR team gets new efficiencies by not going through complex salary adjustments with each move—an unrealistic expectation when there are so many of them! Adjustments needed for cost of living considerations for moves to certain places or with certain personal circumstances are still considered, but they are dealt with on a case-by-case basis. To get started, companies may first apply this model to a specific subset of employees who they expect to be regularly mobile across geographies, locations, and jobs (for example, high potential employees). This mobile talent pool may also be employed by a global employment company (GEC; see Chapter 9) that administers a global benefits model and eases legal friction (see the rest of this section and Chapter 9 for more details on GECs).

The Talent Mobility Revolution not only brings compensation challenges with geographic and location mobility, but also questions on how to compensate external freelance workers, who are increasingly part of project teams. The standard compensation methodology for freelance workers is to agree to project compensation up front as an hourly, daily, or monthly fee. In certain instances, companies may also agree on a project fee up front, but it can often be difficult in this dynamic world of work to know how long projects will take.

Catherine Stewart is Chief Business Officer at Automattic, which as we discussed in prior chapters owns content management site WordPress.com and operates a fully distributed global team of more than 800 people. Despite Automattic's successful model, Stewart acknowledges that setting fair and equitable compensation amid talent mobility is still one of the most difficult things to do. Automattic uses a combination of the local and global benchmark strategies today.

Schneider Electric has tried to solve this for certain employees with what Susanna Warner calls an "international compensation package." She describes this as a compensation structure that is disassociated from a particular country with an expectation that employees will be regularly working across different countries as a part of their career, a type of global benchmark model. The company hasn't yet widely rolled it out but sees it more as applicable for a certain population of high potential employees who would move regularly as a part of their leadership development.

F3 FOCUS

F3 Companies know that with growing talent mobility, traditional compensation models are not fit for purpose. They look to the global and local benchmark models to innovate in their compensation approach and enable continuous movement across geographies and locations. As they evolve, they often select a specific subset of high potential, mobile employees to first adopt a global benchmark model. *F3 Companies* also frequently hire freelancers for their teams and agree hourly, daily, or monthly rates up front.

Bonus Methodologies for Talent Mobility

As we discussed in Chapter 6, *F3 Companies* redesign their annual reviews and bonus processes to be agile, championing an objectives and key results (OKR) framework to set project goals and sharing continuous feedback with workers during projects. At the end of the year, they have a talent review, where project leaders and managers come together to review employee contributions (based on the OKR framework) and competencies. They then apply a talent indicator that corresponds to employee bonuses, compensation increases, and leveling. Levels are based on breadth and depth of competencies and skills and are consistent across the company, regardless of the functions or teams the employee has worked on.

F3 Companies structure their compensation to include a material portion of employee compensation as variable bonuses, rewarding achievement of both the company goals and individual goals (as dictated by the OKRs). The bonus amount (typically a percentage of base compensation) is dictated by employee level. A key tenet is that bonus payouts are dictated by output in dynamic projects (detailed in OKRs), not, as at traditional companies, an expected portion of compensation for time put in. The talent indicator drives the amount of bonus paid to an employee. Like all parts of the Talent Mobility Revolution, bonuses are agile and tied to performance.

Like many companies, we followed this model when we designed our talent management processes. We made variable compensation and an agile bonus process part of our talent strategy. Based on our employee levels, we set bonus percentages that were consistent across teams and offices. We used an OKR framework to set dynamic goals tied to projects (as discussed in Chapter 6) and held talent reviews to discuss employee contributions.

Rachael King, Topia's first VP People, believes that over time, this model may shift to be even more agile. "In a similar way to how the annual review is disappearing, there is an argument to say that compensation and bonuses shouldn't be structured that way either when work is contributed more in projects or 'chunks,'" says King. "I think there will always be a core salary for an employee because that's the nature of employing someone rather than hiring a freelancer, but the bonus part could become much more agile over time and tied to what is being delivered across dynamic projects. I think this will change in coming years as the Talent Mobility Revolution accelerates to reflect how we are actually managing and retaining people."

F3 FOCUS

For *F3 Companies* performance is king. They move away from set annual bonuses to variable compensation models with payment tied to contribution across dynamic project teams, measured by OKRs. They set variable compensation as a percentage of base compensation and ensure it is consistent across the company. With an innovative and agile compensation approach, *F3 Companies* harness the Talent Mobility Revolution to drive employee engagement, accelerate innovation, and unleash growth.

Reinventing Employee Benefits

Innovating in Vacation and Time-Off Benefits

F3 Companies dispense with the idea that vacation days are fixed and tied to norms in each location. Instead, they know that when employees are constantly mobile, they will be working across many different geographies and locations. Therefore, they move from a fixed vacation model to either a floating or unlimited vacation model. I explain each of these below.

- *Fixed vacation model.* This is the historical standard and remains in place at many companies today. In this model, employee vacation days are provided based on country and market norms. Employees of each country get the national public holidays in that country off, plus a set number of PTO days that is in line with the market norms. Like Topia, some companies adopt a "fixed plus" vacation model, enhancing the traditional model by equalizing the number of public holidays and PTO days globally.

- *Floating vacation model.* This is an innovative approach that companies like Spotify take. In this model, all employees get a set number of public holidays (e.g., 25 days) that they can use whenever they want to during the year, in addition to their normal PTO entitlement. Employees can elect to use these days to cover some public holidays that they would normally take, or they can use them when they wish. This approach brings consistency and recognizes that employees have different religious and personal needs, allowing them to celebrate and worship as they wish.

- *Unlimited vacation model.* In this model, employees are able to take unlimited amounts of vacation throughout the year. There is no tracking of days off or maximum amount allowed. Instead, employees are expected to handle their time off responsibly. In reality, many also work remotely during portions of their vacations and stay connected to their projects and teams. This approach eliminates any inconsistencies globally and gives employees full autonomy to manage their work and life needs. This approach is popular with technology companies like Automattic and Netflix, and has also been adopted by Virgin, among others.

"Time away works differently at Netflix," writes the company on its jobs website. "We don't have a prescribed 9-to-5 workday, so we don't have prescribed time off policies for salaried employees, either. We don't set a holiday and vacation schedule, so you can observe what's important to you—including when your mind and body need a break. We believe in working smarter, not harder."

F3 FOCUS

F3 Companies like Spotify, Automattic, and Netflix enable greater talent mobility by removing barriers in employee benefits, starting with their employee vacation policies. They recognize that with greater movement, disparities between locations can bring friction, and they smooth this with fixed plus, floating, or unlimited holiday models.

Managing Retirement Benefits

In the talent mobility era, managing retirement benefits can be another area of friction. Geographies across the world have different approaches to statutory retirement support (e.g., Social Security in the United States), as well as local norms for companies in given markets (e.g., 401(k) in the United States). When employees are geographically mobile, they may forgo some of these retirement benefits.

When employees are moving between geographies, it can be difficult to smooth gaps associated with country-led retirement schemes. In most instances, there is no way to transfer a government-provided retirement account between locations, and it would be impractical in a world of constant movement. Certain companies include retirement or social security equalization in their policies for geographic mobility (see Chapter 7) to ameliorate some of this. Many however, look to smooth this exposure through company-provided plans or other benefits that employees get through talent mobility.

Companies can pursue two models for retirement benefits that they provide: a local retirement model or a global retirement model. As the Talent Mobility Revolution continues to grow, companies will increasingly look to innovative retirement savings approaches to ease friction from talent mobility. We outline both the local and global retirement model below.

- *Local retirement model.* This is the traditional retirement savings structure that companies have followed, and most still do today. In this model, employees receive a company-sponsored retirement plan that is in line with the norms in the local market where the company operates and the employee is employed. For example, in the United States this is generally a 401(k) plan; in the United Kingdom, it is typically a private pension. Employees are typically able to contribute to these plans tax-free to save for their future retirement. Depending on the company, there may also be a company contribution component, such as company matching in 401(k) plans. This varies by company—and is generally a benefit provided by larger companies. At the same time, employees working in a given market generally have a portion of their salary deducted to pay into a national retirement plan, like Social Security in the United States. In the talent mobility era, this local retirement model can create friction as retirement accounts (public or company-provided) remain in different locations while an employee works around the world. In this model, when employees move to a new location, the company ties the employees' retirement schemes to a home market and equalizes them for contributions, similar to how other tax equalization is handled (certain countries also have social security treaties for long term assignments, but this can be increasingly complex with shorter durations).

- *Global retirement model.* Companies may increasingly look to a global retirement model in the talent mobility era. Similar to a global compensation benchmark, employees become a part of a single global retirement scheme that is often headquartered and administered offshore in a place like Jersey, United Kingdom. Employees and companies can pay retirement contributions into a global plan regardless of where they are physically working. Typically, these plans are denominated in US dollars or British pounds (GBP), and as

contributions are made, they are converted from the local contribution currency to US dollars. When they retire—regardless
of where they live—employees can withdraw these savings for
their retirement. Nationally run retirement savings plans operate in the same way as above through equalization or treaties.

When I worked abroad, I had a local retirement model. In Hong
Kong and Singapore, I was able to withdraw the funds I had contributed to the public schemes when I left the country. In the United
Kingdom, the money I contributed to the national plan stays in the
plan even though I now live back in the United States.

Public and private retirement plans are complex to administer
and manage amid continuous talent mobility. Like compensation
and holidays, today's companies increasingly look to a private
global retirement model to smooth differences across markets and
make up for challenges with national plans amid talent mobility.
Companies may adopt this for all employees or for a segment that
they expect to be mobile. To make this—along with the global
compensation and holiday models—work, companies may set up a
global employment company (GEC) to employ a subset of employees that are expected to move frequently (see Chapter 9 for further
detail on managing entities and GECs).

F3 FOCUS

F3 Companies know that growing talent mobility makes managing
retirement savings difficult across both public and private plans.
They manage differences in public retirement savings plans through
equalizations and treaties, or they compensate employees for
losses with other benefits and opportunities. They increasingly look
to smooth differences in private plans by adopting a global retirement model for all or part of their employees.

Enhancing Family Leave

Like the challenges in normalizing compensation and retirement, talent mobility brings with it similar challenges for family leave. Family leave is critical to supporting diversity in the workforce and giving employees both vibrant work and personal lives. Yet family leave policies vary greatly by geography, even by state in the United States. And the United States sadly does not yet offer any paid parental leave—one of the only advanced countries that does not.

In 1993, the US Congress passed the Family and Medical Leave Act (FMLA), which mandates a minimum of 12 weeks of job-protected, unpaid leave for mothers. Certain states support adjusted maternity leave, including four states that fund a portion of a mother's salary for a part of it, or include leave for fathers in it. However, in most cases, fathers must use vacation days for the birth of a child. Other countries, such as the United Kingdom, provide up to a year of maternity leave, with employers required to pay a statutory amount for up to 39 weeks and 2 weeks of paternity leave. There are also great variances in expectations for other types of parental leave, for example to care for an aging or sick parent, or to mourn the loss of a loved one, as I did with my father while working at Lehman Brothers. More often than not, caring for a parent also requires traveling to a different place and working remotely from there.

These great variances, across countries and states, make it difficult to normalize employee benefits in the talent mobility era and to appropriately support working families in an era where both men and women regularly work. But companies now recognize that work-life integration is in high demand from today's employees. With increasing talent mobility and the absence of sufficient and consistent statutory parental leave policies, companies should adopt consistent family leave policies to support families. They should also champion location movement, one of the building blocks of talent mobility, to allow for flexible work while away from the office or to care for families.

The best practice for family leave is to offer a minimum amount of paid parental leave for mothers and fathers, taking into consideration all configurations of a modern family. Companies should also include a minimum amount of paid family leave to care for a sick parent or mourn a death in the family. This, coupled with work-from-home models and flexible work arrangements, balances variances across locations and helps employees balance work and family. Although this can be expensive for small and growing companies, the benefits in attracting, retaining, and engaging today's top talent far outweigh the costs. Small companies should start their transformation with what they can support, and evolve from there, just as Topia did in evolving our vacation days. The principle—and starting the journey to greater support and consistency—is the most important first step.

In 2018, Topia rolled out equal paid parental leave for men and woman. We followed a similar staged model as we did with holiday days. We introduced paid parental leave for both men and women who welcomed new children. Although we wanted to offer more paid leave than we did, we started this journey with what we could realistically support for all men and women at our company. Just as we'd done with our holiday policies, we were balancing the benefits we wanted to offer with business realities. When we announced our new policy in a company all-hands meeting, people were very grateful—and we even received hugs from some of the male employees!

F3 FOCUS

F3 Companies know that balancing work and life is a key demand from today's employees—and a critical part of attracting, retaining, and engaging top talent. Companies should adopt minimum paid parental and family leave policies for mothers and fathers. These should be consistent across locations, ensuring support for employees regardless of the variances in statutory policies across countries.

Delivering Employee Healthcare

One of the core tenants of the structure of American work has been that companies provided healthcare to their employees. Unlike Canada and most European and Asian countries, healthcare in America has historically been provided by employers. In the talent mobility era, with increasing job movement, freelance work, and entrepreneurs, this structure must change so that the government provides a minimum level of healthcare to all workers regardless of where and when they are working.

Amid the Talent Mobility Revolution, employees increasingly work from everywhere all the time—at home, at the office, on the road, and many other places all around the world. This continuous movement brings with it challenges in delivering employee healthcare. If an employee is working between 10 different countries over a couple of months period, how does his or her healthcare coverage work? How do you ensure employees are covered for a one- or two-month assignment in another location? What should you do for freelancers who work similar hours to employees on the same project team but don't get healthcare provided by the company or country?

Similar to the global compensation and retirement models we've discussed, companies increasingly look to global healthcare plans to support employees who continuously move between geographies. Similar to retirement models, often companies offer a local healthcare plan tied to an employee's home location (e.g., the United States), plus a global healthcare plan administered offshore, often through a global employment company (GEC) (see Chapter 9 for further details). Like compensation and retirement, the global healthcare model often starts with a particular segment of employees who are presumed to be continuously mobile, while others remain on traditional local plans in given countries. Certain companies also provide emergency healthcare plans (often delivered through companies like International SOS) to cover employees who travel regularly.

As freelancers become a larger part of their workforces, certain companies are innovating in their traditional benefits model to provide freelancers healthcare options. Certain companies offer a healthcare plan that freelancers can buy into. As freelancers become a larger part of our workforce, we should update the US federal employment law to account for the changing the structure of work. This should classify freelancers and gig economy workers as a new type of worker and provide a mechanism for collective bargaining, benefits, and protections within the flexible on-demand structures of the freelance model, something we discuss further in the subsequent section and in Chapter 10. Until we get to national healthcare and an update to federal labor laws, however, companies should provide their freelancers with healthcare plans that they can buy into and benefit from the bargaining power of the company.

F3 FOCUS

F3 Companies know that delivering employee healthcare can be challenging when employees are continuously mobile. They look to global healthcare models to enable talent mobility and consider providing emergency healthcare plans for those traveling regularly. They should also increasingly provide healthcare options to freelancers, stepping in where the traditional structure of employment fails workers.

Supporting Employee Wellness

With work from everywhere comes constant connectivity to e-mail, videoconferencing, and messaging systems (see Chapter 9). In this virtual work world, the concept of location and time zone goes away; gone are the days where you worked 9-to-5 and then relaxed in the evening with family without any thoughts of work. This brings with it challenges in employee wellness.

Companies today must develop employee health and wellness programs to ensure employees have strong mental and physical health amid the Talent Mobility Revolution. Often these programs include mindfulness initiatives, such as meditation offerings in person or via applications, coaching programs, and employee wellness platforms where employees can allocate a set of points to classes, like yoga or Pilates, that they may want to take outside of work. Employee health and wellness is a growing part of the Talent Mobility Revolution, so that companies can ensure the benefits of continuous connectivity and talent mobility without negative effects.

F3 FOCUS

F3 Companies know that the Talent Mobility Revolution brings great benefits to employees in autonomy and flexibility, but also means potentially working outside the traditional 9-to-5. They implement health and wellness programs to ensure mindfulness for employees amid the constant connectivity and movement of the talent mobility era.

Evolving Employee Protections Amid Talent Mobility

Traditional Employee Protections

As we've discussed in prior chapters, one of the key elements of the Talent Mobility Revolution is the growth of on-demand freelancers as a part of project teams, a trend that is set to accelerate in coming years. In a 2018 survey by Upwork, 57 percent of HR managers said they plan to increase their utilization of freelancers in the next 10 years,*which is driven by demand from both companies and workers.

The growth of the freelance economy has positives for companies and workers. Many companies—often located in urban coastal cities in America—report challenges finding skilled workers for open jobs. These urban employment markets often have very low micro-unemployment rates and high costs of living that can make it prohibitive for people to move for work opportunities. Moreover, many people in America—across all demographics—value living in their local community near family and friends; however, often they can't find good paying jobs there. There is an ongoing discussion about incentivizing companies to move to or set up in new locations—often outside of popular urban coastal cities. However, another way to look at this is to incentivize companies to hire a greater number of remote freelance knowledge workers spread throughout the country, whether in rural areas like Truckee, California, or midwestern cities like Indianapolis. Freelancers can work from anywhere, loaning their skills out to companies based in urban coastal cities, and remain living in their communities.

The structure of employment in America, however, must shift to support freelance workers with some of the traditional employment protections and benefits. Until this happens at the government level, companies that leverage freelance workers as a part of their teams should extend their traditional employment protections to all workers.

Throughout the twentieth century the US government, in partnership with our unions, passed legislation mandating protection for employees working at companies. Some key legislation included setting a minimum wage for work, ensuring antidiscrimination in the workplace, and setting health and safety standards for work environments. Freelancers do not enjoy any of these employment

---

* Upwork, "Future Workforce HR Report," 2018.

protections under the law or any collective bargaining rights. While many workers today value the flexibility, diversity, and work-life integration of working in the freelance economy, significant questions abound about how to ensure these workers are protected.

The best practice is for companies to extend basic employment protections to all workers and make this a part of their culture and operating norms. These should include protections for antidiscrimination, sexual harassment, and health and safety at a minimum. Upwork sets a strong example for its customers and follows this policy to protect all of its workers under similar company policies.

F3 FOCUS

F3 Companies have an expanded view of their workforce that includes employees, contractors, and freelancers. They extend a minimum level of employment protections to all workers, including freelancers. This should include protections for anti-discrimination, sexual harassment, and health and safety.

Innovating in Benefits for Freelance Workers

In the absence of nationally led healthcare and other benefits, companies that use freelancers should think about how to extend their benefit models and employment protections to their whole workforce. Companies should include healthcare and retirement buy-in options to freelancers. These can be structured as plans where the freelancer can elect to participate, continuing to provide flexibility and ensuring freelancers are not classified as employees. With the company's buying power, these plans could provide lower cost healthcare options to freelancers than if they purchased healthcare on their own. The best practice is to set this up via a portal for freelancers and make it entirely optional—healthcare for those who want it; retirement savings for those who want it. To further support workers, companies should include web-based trainings on health and financial literacy (including savings for retirement). In the shift to the freelance economy with more variable pay and less company-led savings, there is increasing responsibility on workers to understand how to plan and save. Companies have an obligation to support their workers with this knowledge in an easy and accessible way.

Given that the nature of freelance work is "on demand"—that is, work happens when a worker wants to take a job (and often in addition to other work)—holiday and family leave policies are not relevant. In fact, one of the things that workers value in the freelance economy is the opportunity to balance work and life obligations through flexibility—working when and where it's convenient for them.

F3 FOCUS

F3 Companies extend healthcare and retirement benefits to freelancer workers with options to buy into plans. They pair this with education for freelance workers on financial and health literacy to support them in planning and saving for their personal needs amid the talent mobility era.

As I built Topia, I worked with many companies as they worked through their compensation and benefits models amid growing amounts of talent mobility. As the freelance economy grew and companies started to increasingly leverage nonemployee workers for project teams, I participated in discussions with companies and government leaders about how to evolve traditional worker protections and benefits for the growing freelance economy. The structure of employment needs to be updated in America, as the Talent

Mobility Revolution and freelance economy increasingly take hold. For the near term, however, companies that want to harness talent mobility for success should evolve their benefits to both enable more frictionless employee movement and ensure all classifications of workers are supported and protected.

Transforming compensation and benefits is the eighth step of talent mobility transformation. Companies and business leaders that innovate in their compensation and benefits models will win the war on talent, continually attracting the people they need to fuel their business. Those that don't will lose out in the Talent Mobility Revolution.

CHAPTER SUMMARY

- In the talent mobility era, companies must evolve traditional compensation models. Companies should consider global and local benchmark models and adopt variable compensation tied to performance of project OKRs.
- Vacation and time-off entitlements can vary significantly across geographies, creating friction amid talent mobility. Forward-thinking companies look to fixed plus, floating, and unlimited holiday models to remove friction and treat employees equally.
- Public and private retirement models differ across geographies. With geographic movement, companies should consider equalization approaches for public retirement savings. They should look to global private retirement models for employees who are continuously mobile.
- Employees today value family leave. Companies should offer a minimum amount of paid family leave for new children, family illness, or death, ensuring entitlements have consistency across geographies.
- Healthcare structures vary wildly across geographies, and companies with frequent geographic movement should look to global and emergency healthcare benefits to support employees. With constant connectivity, companies should also adopt wellness programs as a standard.
- With an expanded definition of the workforce, companies should ensure minimum benefits and employment protections for freelancers. This includes optional healthcare and retirement programs, as well as protections for antidiscrimination, sexual harassment, and health and safety.

Transforming Systems and Operations for Talent Mobility

9

When Susanna Warner went to Schneider Electric to lead its global mobility department, she knew that the HR transformation already underway posed one of the most complex global mobility challenges that she had faced in her career. Warner, however, brought a unique background to the leading energy management company. She had worked in talent management, international mobility, and compliance, so she brought both a strategic and operational lens to the job. Her mandate was to set up talent mobility for the future—and in doing so support the global power company's international business footprint and recruiting of top talent.

In order to support the HR transformation, Warner included with the policy review already underway (as discussed in Chapter 7) a three-year transformation plan with one major theme each year. Her next two years focused on digitizing systems and enhancing the employee experience amid a talent mobility world. In parallel, Schneider Electric initiated transformation to link geographic mobility with job mobility, launching a talent marketplace, as we also discussed in prior chapters. As she drove the changes in policies, systems, and operations, Schneider Electric itself was moving to an increasingly distributed work model, introducing further need to unify all of the parts of talent mobility in the digitization roadmap.

The goal of Warner's digitization phase was to unify talent mobility systems and operations in modern digital systems, first looking at geographic movement to ensure she knew where all her mobile employees were at a given point in time so that she could manage tax and immigration compliance and geopolitical risk. After this, the mobility team started to focus on the "consumer facing" experience for geographically mobile employees—the systems, vendors, and partners that employees engaged with to manage their relocations, travel, and virtual work experiences.

Warner's team started with more than 50 Microsoft Access databases that the HR team used to manage employees who were geographically mobile. This meant that Schneider Electric, a company of 144,000 employees, was largely managing its mobile talent from spreadsheets, and entirely separately from the other company systems, such as core HR, payroll, and finance, and external vendors, such as compensation providers, real estate firms, and immigration providers. The team started thinking about how to unite the more innovative systems like relocation experience applications, a talent marketplace for job matching, and employee collaboration software. The team had to first digitize the nuts and bolts of geographic movement to ensure that all the basics could actually be managed within the frameworks of the company's operations and global legislation. This required implementing a global mobility management (GMM) system to replace the databases.

We worked with Schneider Electric's global mobility team as they implemented Topia's global mobility management (GMM) system to digitize these nuts and bolts of geographic mobility. Their journey is not unique. Over my nine years leading Topia, I saw countless companies like Schneider Electric start the journey to transform their systems and operations for the Talent Mobility Revolution, often starting with implementing a GMM system. Like Schneider Electric, many of them were large, venerable, international, publicly listed brands that had been operating as traditional companies for decades. They started these transformations because they knew that, in order to succeed in the twenty-first century, they needed to make talent mobility the basis of their business and talent strategies. To do this, they had to transform their operations to make it happen. They realized that companies that could execute this transformation successfully would succeed in the twenty-first century and continue to win the global war on talent; those that didn't recognize the need, or succeed in execution, would lose out to their more agile, innovative competitors.

While many business leaders recognize the forces of the Talent Mobility Revolution—globalization and automation—few know how to practically implement the operations and systems to make the talent mobility transformation we've discussed in this book happen. This is particularly acute because much of the world's legislation—across employment, tax, and immigration law—was set up for the traditional way of working. At the same time, increasing geopolitical uncertainty and security threats make the reality of managing talent mobility more complex than ever.

With these forces all converging, companies need a clear operational and systems roadmap to harness the talent mobility revolution for success. This chapter shares how to set up systems and operations to harness the Talent Mobility Revolution to drive employee engagement, accelerate innovation, and unleash growth. It is the final puzzle piece to transforming into an *F3 Company*.

How to Employ People and Get Them Paid

The Traditional Employment and Pay Model

Traditionally, employees were employed by one entity with their payroll running from that entity. As we've discussed in prior chapters, talent mobility across locations, jobs, and employment was rare; however, a small portion of employees did move geographically for expatriate assignments or relocations. One of the main differences between these two policies was the entity that the employee was employed by: expatriates stayed employed by the entity in their home country; relocations moved to be employed by the entity in the host country. The entity that the employee was employed by then dictated where the employee's payroll was run and in what currency. So, if relocating employees moved to a new entity in the host country, they were set up on the new local payroll and received their paychecks from there in the new local currency. If an employee instead moved as an expatriate, she would remain an employee of the home entity and have a payroll processed from there in that currency. Certain expatriates also received a split payroll, a portion paid by their home country payroll and a portion by their host country so they could cover local living expenses.

Lehman Brothers, as we've discussed in prior chapters, was a traditional company with traditional geographic mobility operations. When I relocated to Hong Kong for a permanent relocation, I became an employee of the Hong Kong entity and received my paychecks in local Hong Kong dollars. When I spent multiple months working on a project in India, but not relocating there, I continued to be paid by the Hong Kong entity in Hong Kong dollars. When colleagues moved from New York to Hong Kong for one-year expatriate assignments, they continued to be paid in US dollars from the US entity.

Entity and Employment Strategy for Talent Mobility

The overarching assumption in the traditional employment and pay model was that employees worked in geographies where the company had an entity and operating presence, whether as local employees or expatriates, and they were employed and paid from one of these entities. In the talent mobility era, however, this is changing. The continuous movement of the talent mobility era challenges the assumption that every worker will be working from a location where the company has a local entity and payroll operation. With frequent geographic and job mobility, and work-from-everywhere and work-from-home models, employees increasingly demand the flexibility to work where they want to even if a company doesn't have an entity there. At the same time, freelancers with nontraditional payroll structures are becoming a greater portion of the workforce.

All of this introduces operational complexity for companies today. Current US employment law classifies workers as employees (W2 workers) or contractors (1099 workers). Employees must be hired by an entity, set up on the company's payroll, and receive the corresponding employee benefits and protections, as we discussed in Chapter 8. Contractors must fall under certain requirements for hours worked for a single company so as not to be classified as employees. When contractors work for a sustained period of time from a location where a company does not have an entity, there can be a risk that they are deemed to be employees and create a "permanent establishment" in that market. Then the company is required to pay local taxes and classify workers as employees.

As discussed in Chapter 1, conversations on entity and employment strategies for talent mobility and the growing work-from-everywhere structure was a constant point of discussion over the years at our Customer Advisory Board meetings at Topia. Talent mobility leaders are accountable for managing the risk and operations of employee movement. Business leaders often say yes to work-from-everywhere models—in a drive to attract, retain, or engage key employees—without understanding the operational complexity it introduces. I have heard stories of talent mobility leaders reviewing company messaging channels to identify anyone who may be working somewhere that introduces company risks, fighting with business leaders about their decisions, and scrambling to set up entities to avoid tax exposure.

Forward-thinking companies know that employees will be continuously mobile, and they intentionally design a multitiered entity and employment model to support this. It should look like this:

- *Contractor/freelancer employment.* In this model, workers are hired as contractors, not full-time employees, and companies do not bear responsibility for benefits or taxes.

The worker bears all risk for local tax payments and generally signs a contract detailing that he is not an employee and bears any and all employment liability. This model should be used when hiring workers as freelancers on project teams, for contracted part or fixed-term work on project teams, or when a company does not have an entity or permanent establishment (PE) in a given market. (Although beyond the scope of this book, it's important to note that contractor status can be abused to take advantage of workers, leaving them with unpredictable hours, low wages and no benefits, and the company with higher profits. This is a big issue for the working and middle class in America today, and must be rectified.)

- *Professional employer organizations (PEOs).* A PEO is a local organization that employs and pays local workers on a company's behalf. Workers are not formally employed by the company but are able to get the local benefits as employees of the PEO. Often companies treat their PEO workers as if they were full-time employees and also expand the benefits provided to be in line with their traditional employment benefits. It's common for companies to transition contractors to a PEO model if they work with the company for an extended duration or in a largely full-time capacity creating employment risk. The PEO employment model mitigates employment and tax risk for companies and outsources operations and administrations to local experts.

- *Employment by entity.* When a company has a critical mass of workers in a given market and/or workers it wants to hire as full-time employees, it generally sets up a local entity that employees can be hired from. In this traditional model, employees are classified as full-time local employees. The best practice is for companies to tie their entity expansion to hiring a critical mass of workers in a given market.

- *Employment by global employment company (GEC).* Certain companies use global employment companies to employ employees who are continuously geographically mobile and reduce the associated operational friction. This model has been historically used by energy companies for their "career expats" and may grow common again in the talent mobility era as we discussed in Chapter 8.

Automattic employees can elect to work from wherever they want—from a rural hometown to a bustling urban metropolis to a remote emerging market. As you would expect, Automattic has a number of entities around the world through which employees are hired and paid. However, it also frequently has workers who want to work in markets where Automattic doesn't yet have entities, so it hires these workers as contractors, but culturally engages them as if they were employees. Managers include them in project teams and don't discuss or differentiate internally between their full-time employees and contractors—very much embodying the tenants of an *F3 Company*. When Automattic reaches a critical mass of freelancers in a given location—for example if numerous workers decide they want to live and work from Mexico—it considers establishing an entity and hiring them as full-time employees of the Mexican entity.

"Distributed teams expose you to different regulatory risk," says Chief Business Officer Catherine Stewart. "It's important to keep in mind local employment and tax policies."

We found a similar challenge at Topia. When we acquired Teleport in 2017, its distributed team structure meant that there were a number of employees working as freelancers from locations around the world. Similarly, as we expanded our sales footprint into new markets, such as Germany and Australia, we found that the overhead of setting up an entity often did not make sense. Like Automattic, we pursued a multitiered employment strategy hiring freelancers to contribute to teams part-time, using PEOs to hire team members in markets where we did not have an entity but needed to hire staff and setting up entities once markets justified a permanent presence.

"The employment model that we follow at Topia with contractors, PEOs, and employees is the best practice for employment in the talent mobility era," says Jacky Cohen, who leads Topia's People and Culture team. "Outside of a PEO, today there is really no other way of hiring people in markets where you don't have an entity, while having the confidence of being compliant and giving the best employee experience."

F3 FOCUS

F3 Companies know that in the talent mobility era, workers will work from all over the world. They enable talent mobility with a clear strategy for their entity and employment models, considering: contractors, employees, PEOs, and global employment companies. This framework gives structure and risk management.

Payroll Setup for Talent Mobility

Traditionally, payroll systems were set up in each market where a company operated and used to pay salaries and withhold local taxes. Amid the Talent Mobility Revolution, companies will have a diverse set of entities and workers that includes employees, contractors, and PEO-employed staff. In addition to this, employees will move frequently between entities and payroll systems as they work across geographies, jobs, and locations. Companies should follow the guidelines below for paying their different classifications of workers:

- *Paying contractors and freelancers.* Freelancers may be hired directly or through traditional staffing agencies. When hired directly, companies pay their project fees in an agreed-upon gross amount. The worker then bears responsibility for paying taxes. Therefore, the company does not need a local payroll system to administer these payments. Freelancers hired through staffing agencies may be paid by the agency, which then bills the company. Similar to this model, modern freelancer marketplaces like Upwork also now offer payroll management services, where they essentially act as a PEO for freelancers and pay salaries, and bill the company.

- *Paying via PEO.* When workers are employed by a PEO, the PEO is responsible for processing the local payroll, handling withholding taxes, and administering statutory local benefits. The PEO then bills the company regularly for these costs and the PEO's services fees.
- *Paying employees.* Employees are paid through local payroll systems, which also process the local taxes. When employees move geographically, they may be transferred to a new local payroll, continue to be paid from the home country payroll, or have a hybrid setup where part of their paycheck is paid to them in the currency of their home office and part is paid in the currency of their new location. Because payroll systems are generally locally run, it's important for all local payroll systems to be linked to the central global mobility system to ensure equalization and other benefits are calculated and withheld correctly. (See the following sections for an overview of the systems roadmap to enable talent mobility.)
- *Global employment company (GEC) payroll.* In prior sections, we discussed the setup and potential for using a global employment company to employ, pay, and administer benefits to employees who are continuously mobile. Companies who employ this model can pay employees offshore in a standard currency like US dollars. This model has been used in the past to pay those who frequently go on expatriate assignments, but we may see it come back as talent mobility grows.

How to Manage Compliance and Risk

Location Tracking and Compliance

When we founded Topia in 2010 and started speaking to HR leaders about their challenges from growing geographic movement, almost all of them told me that their biggest issue was tracking their employees—that is, knowing where their employees are and what they are doing at any given point in time. This is the "first order problem" of talent mobility—if companies can't track employee locations and projects, all of the more complex strategic and operational tasks are irrelevant. Additionally, it's impossible for companies to carry out their duty of care for their employees without clarity on where they are!

You might think this sounds crazy. I certainly did. But when you think about it further, it's not. With growing talent mobility, employees are constantly on the move—across geographies, coffee shops, hotels, and homes—as well as working dynamically across project teams. And many of the workers at a company are not even full-time employees. Traditional HR systems were designed as a system of record with basic information for each employee: name, address, age, compensation, office, manager, department, entity, team, and so on. Since employees were in the office each day and had fixed roles, companies could easily look at their HR system and see where an employee was working. When expatriate assignments or relocations happened, the HR team updated the information in the HR system. But since these happened infrequently and generally lasted for a decent amount of time, this process didn't cause too much friction. Travel systems were used to plan trips and process expenses but didn't provide dynamic movement information, let alone link to the HR system to provide a single view of employee location.

In the talent mobility era, however, companies must track a complex employee footprint across geographies, locations, and teams. Without a global mobility management (GMM) technology system in place, tracking employee location is virtually impossible.

When we founded Topia, we made this one of the first focuses of our global mobility management system. We helped companies centralize their employee movement data in our system to provide a single place where HR teams could access all this data. This started with initiating each geographic mobility experience in the system, and then updating it as an employee footprint evolved. Through the years, we saw companies get many benefits from this centralization—from rapid responses to locating employees who may be at risk, to reviewing nationalities amid immigration law changes, to ensuring employees did not overstay their tax and immigration authorization (one of the biggest fears for companies in the talent mobility era).

"At the same time that working everywhere is getting more common, governments are getting tougher in protecting their borders," says Nick Pond, Mobility Leader, EY People Advisory Services. "Company and employee demands don't always marry up easily with the realities of government. People can't just pick up and work where they want. Companies need to invest in the frameworks to make it happen within the constraints of today's rules and regulations."*

---

* Interview with Nick Pond, Partner, EY People Advisory, December 17, 2018.

F3 FOCUS

F3 Companies implement a global mobility management (GMM) system, setting up the infrastructure to track employee geographic locations and movement. With this, they ensure that they can operate talent mobility seamlessly without safety or compliance concerns.

Tracking Tax and Immigration Compliance

When I was researching Topia, I heard many stories about employees who had violated tax and immigration authorization. Often this was from traveling across borders to work regularly without the right visa—like an employee who commuted between the United States and Canada without a work visa. Sometimes it was employees who overstayed a visa in a particular country, not realizing that it had expired—like an employee we heard of who was deported when a work visa expired. Other times, it was employees whose taxes were not calculated correctly by local payroll systems and then found themselves with big tax liabilities after returning home from an assignment. All of this stemmed from companies not being able to easily track where their employees were and how long they were in given states and countries and to ensure necessary tax and immigration compliance. Many companies hadn't even implemented the basics of a global mobility management system, let alone the complex calculations and alerts for tax and immigration compliance.

Once companies implement a GMM system to track their employee footprints, they should ensure global tax and immigration logic is set up to flag risks as they arise—for example when immigration thresholds are hit (whether through travel, days in country, or renewal dates); when permanent establishment becomes an issue from working time in a given location where the company doesn't have an entity; or what tax calculations need to be done based on the time working in a given state or country. GMM systems should come with this tax and immigration logic included and able to automatically prompt talent mobility teams, employees, and external service partners to take action when needed. Automating this in the GMM system streamlines the management of mobile talent and ensures employees can work everywhere while still meeting the compliance constraints of existing tax and immigration frameworks.

F3 FOCUS

F3 Companies enable talent mobility by adopting systems and automation to power it. They implement GMM systems to track employee footprints and then apply tax and immigration logic that flags risks and recommends actions based on each employee's time traveling to and working in a given country or state.

Responding to Geopolitical and Security Risks

With systems in place to track employee locations and ensure tax and immigration compliance, companies can then rapidly respond to geopolitical and security risks, an increasingly frequent consideration amid today's uncertain world. If an event happens in a particular location, the company can quickly pull a real-time log of the employees in that location and use it to check their safety. If a law changes in a given country, companies can quickly categorize who may be affected and respond to it promptly.

In November 2015, a series of coordinated terrorist attacks took place in Paris, France. With a GMM system in place to track employee location, companies were able to quickly identify which employees were in Paris and start to contact them. Similarly, in January 2017, President Donald Trump issued an executive order restricting entry into the United States for citizens of certain predominantly Muslim countries. At the time of the executive order, many companies had employees of these nationalities either already in the United States, on their way to the United States, or with upcoming plans to come to the United States. Using the GMM system, companies were able to quickly identify who might be affected by this change of legislation and make alternative plans for them. We saw companies change the locations where they were hosting meetings, divert project teams to be based in other locations, and have certain team members long-distance commute to the United States rather than moving.

Eric Halverson, Head of Global Mobility at eBay, spoke about this experience at an industry conference in San Francisco shortly thereafter. "When the executive order happened, all of a sudden, we had to categorize our entire global workforce to know where people were, what nationality they held, and their visa status," said Eric. "We had to leverage our systems and do it quickly. As the world becomes more globalized with geopolitical disruptions continuing to occur, I expect this rapid categorization and response will become an increasing need, and systems to power it will be critical."

F3 FOCUS

F3 Companies use their GMM systems to categorize their employees and respond promptly to geopolitical incidents, risks, and legislative changes. With data on employee movement centralized, companies can protect and support their workers well amid growing talent mobility.

Managing Costs and Budgets

Scenario Planning to Fill Open Jobs

With constant talent mobility, companies also must manage dynamic scenario planning about how to move employees, budgeting for the cost of moves and managing the approval processes with business and finance owners. Traditionally—with infrequent movement—this process was handled as a one-off by global mobility (a part of HR), finance, and the managers involved. With near continuous movement, however, this manual process is inefficient and cumbersome. Therefore, companies automate talent mobility workforce planning, budgeting, and approvals in their global mobility management (GMM) systems, allowing for complex considerations of different scenarios for filling open jobs and real-time approvals for managing workers.

As we've discussed in prior chapters, the best practice is for companies to set up a talent marketplace listing open jobs and categorizing workers' skills. When a job needs to be filled—remember, this happens continuously tied to dynamic projects—companies source potential candidates from inside the company (for development, skills match, or movement tied to disruption of a traditional job) and outside the company (full-time candidates and freelancers). As discussed in Chapter 5, the first screening of a candidate is for whether the worker has the skills needed for the job. Once a potential worker (or set of workers) has been identified with the skills required for the job, the company runs dynamic scenarios on how to staff them on the project team. For example, a company may compare hiring a new employee locally for the job, relocating an existing employee whose job has been disrupted by automation and investing in a learning program for the new job, expatriating a more senior employee who doesn't require an investment in a learning pathway but is more expensive to relocate, hiring an employee in another location and supporting frequent travel or a long-distance commute to the new job, or hiring a freelancer who is completely remote. In summary, these scenarios should consider the worker type, location type, geographic movement, policy, and costs for the workers and job in a mix of configurations:

- **Worker type.** Scenario planning should look at hiring a new employee, existing employee, or freelancer to fill the job.
- **Location type.** Scenario planning should consider whether a worker needs to be physically at a job or whether he can work remotely and be hired from anywhere.
- **Geographic movement.** Scenario planning looks at the location requirements and then considers geographic movement configurations. If a worker needs to move to be physically at a job, scenarios should look at relocations and expatriate assignments. If a there is location flexibility, scenarios should look at short-term assignments, frequent travel, commuting, or fully remote work.
- **Policy.** Scenario planning should look at the policy for the different configurations above, taking into consideration the benefits provided and compensation, tax, cost of living, and retirement adjustments.
- **Cost.** Scenario planning should look at the costs of each of these configurations and compare them versus the contribution that the worker is likely to make to the company.

In the talent mobility era, there is a near infinite set of configurations for how a job can be filled by new employees, existing employees, and freelancers. To enable this, companies adopt a GMM system that can dynamically run a near infinite set of configurations and iterations, so that company leaders can make real-time decisions on how to fill jobs in the right way.

One of the most popular parts of Topia's GMM system is Topia Plan, our cost projection and workforce planning application that allows companies to run parts of these scenarios. Traditionally, these projections were done in spreadsheets by the global mobility team or, in more recent years, outsourced to consultants at a Big Four accounting firm or relocation company, who charged high prices and then sent back a spreadsheet. Over the years, I heard countless stories from customers who were frustrated by this structure—if they needed to run another scenario or make a change, they waited days and paid another price for another spreadsheet. Or, if they needed to talk to a business leader tomorrow, the spreadsheet might not be ready. Companies adopted Topia Plan and saw dramatic improvements in their planning and approval efficiency. Many of them set up Topia Plan with the global mobility team running these scenarios on behalf of hiring managers; some of them took this a step further and trained recruiters, HR business partners, and managers across the business to run these scenarios—empowering them to easily plan how to fill their dynamic jobs internally or for clients (e.g., at consulting and engineering firms). This transformation dramatically increased efficiency across our customers and enabled business leaders to continuously consider how to fill dynamic jobs. In short, they could all embrace agile work.

F3 FOCUS

F3 *Companies* use their GMM systems to do dynamic scenario planning about how to fill project teams. When they have an open job, they run scenarios that consider worker type, location type, geographic movement, policy, and cost to find the most effective staffing solution for the job. They train business and HR leaders across the company to use this system bringing agility to the whole company.

Approving and Initiating Talent Mobility

After running scenarios and selecting a worker for a job, the GMM system supports an approval workflow with the business and finance leaders. Each of the designated approvers can easily review the configuration and cost of the selected worker, submit any questions, and seamlessly click on an approval button, replacing countless conversations and e-mails of the past. The GMM system keeps a log of questions and approvals for future reference, removing previous confusion that may have arisen without central documentation. The GMM system should send the approved cost to the finance system, where it can be accrued for in the appropriate management accounts, with the costs tracked going forward.

Once approved and logged in the finance system, the GMM system should automatically initiate a move, sending a notification to the worker, project owner, and any external service providers that may be required, such as immigration or tax firms. By initiating all geographic, location, and job mobility in the same system, companies create a single database of all mobile employees that they can use to dynamically track employee location, managing geopolitical and compliance risks (as discussed above). If there is a learning program tied to the worker's move, it should be tied to her profile in the GMM system so that the development of competencies for the job can be tracked. We take a closer look in the next section at the full talent mobility systems roadmap.

Topia Plan's approval and initiation workflow was another popular part of our offering. Our customers had been used to sending many e-mails to discuss selected workers and obtain approvals. This process was inefficient and cumbersome for them. With Topia Plan, this moved from days of back-and-forth to minutes of review and approval.

F3 FOCUS

After selecting a worker for a job, *F3 Companies* use their GMM systems to obtain approvals from business and finance leaders and store their history in the GMM system. Once approved, the GMM system initiates a move, creating a central log of all mobile employees that drives tracking, risk, and compliance management. With a GMM system in place, companies automate key operations for talent mobility, unlocking agility.

Systems to Enable Talent Mobility and Engage Workers

Core Talent Mobility Systems Map

The GMM system is a critical part of enabling efficient talent mobility. But it is just one system in an overall talent mobility systems roadmap that makes talent mobility work. Implementing and adopting this systems roadmap is an essential part of transforming to be an *F3 Company.*

The talent mobility systems roadmap should include three core systems bidirectionally linked to one other and to a broader set of company technology platforms. This system structure should also connect to an ecosystem of offline service providers who carry out services like immigration, tax, relocation, and healthcare that support mobile employees. The three critical talent mobility systems are the talent marketplaces, global mobility management system, and learning system. Below we take a look at what they are, how they work with one another, and the other systems and service providers they should connect to:

- *Talent marketplaces.* As discussed in Section 2, companies should shift from fixed roles to dynamic jobs that include employees and freelancers. To enable this, companies should adopt a talent marketplace for employees and freelancers. The jobs graph should list all open jobs and the skills required for them. The skills graph should categorize employees, their skills, and competency levels. These should work seamlessly to recommend workers for jobs.

- *Global mobility management (GMM) system.* As discussed above, the GMM system is the backbone to make geographic, location, and job mobility work. It handles scenario planning to fill jobs, approvals for selected workers, initiations for moves, tracking and compliance for mobile employees, and a broad universe of logistics for geographic mobility, including initiations to external service providers, status updates on external services, and document storage. It should also handle compensation, payroll, and withholding adjustments when workers are working in different geographies.

- *Learning system.* In many cases, a worker is matched to a new job without all of the skills required for it. This may be particularly acute when a prior job is disrupted by artificial intelligence and a worker gets a new job that requires him to develop new skills or competencies. In these scenarios and others, employees may have a learning program associated with their new job and administered by a learning system. Companies should link their learning systems to their GMM system and talent marketplaces.

These three systems—the talent marketplace, global mobility management system, and learning system—are the backbone of supporting efficient talent mobility. You can also think of this as enabling continuous "matching, moving, and learning." These three core systems should then be linked to the other company systems and service providers. Overall, the systems roadmap should look like this:

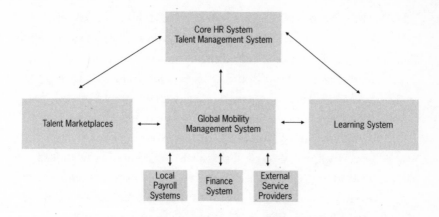

F3 FOCUS

F3 Companies know that, to succeed amid the Talent Mobility Revolution, they must digitize talent mobility and set up the systems to enable it. They set up "matching, moving, and learning" by implementing a talent marketplace, global mobility management (GMM), and learning system as the foundation of their talent mobility transformation. They then integrate these with other core systems and service providers.

Employee Engagement and Collaboration Systems

The final piece to unleashing talent mobility is setting up the infrastructure for virtual work. With increasing geographic, job, and location movement, workers need robust collaboration and engagement systems to work seamlessly while outside the office. The key systems for workers in the talent mobility era are collaboration software, messaging applications, and virtual meeting technology.

- *Collaboration software.* With employees working virtually from places around the world, the need for digital collaboration increases. Gone are the days—like at Lehman Brothers—when files could only be accessed from the office and collaboration required printing documents and discussing them in person. In the talent mobility era, employees access files and collaborate from everywhere. To enable this, companies adopt collaboration software based in the cloud to support virtual work and access. Popular systems are: Box, Dropbox, Google Docs, or SharePoint. These should be adopted by all people in the company. Certain teams may also adopt niche collaboration software for their functions, such as NetSuite for finance or Confluence for product roadmaps.

- *Messaging applications.* With continuous movement and work everywhere, companies adopt messaging applications for worker communication. They shift from in-person conversations and e-mail to dynamic messaging applications, like Slack, that allow people to participate in multiperson conversations digitally and review what's been discussed. This shift must start from the top with the company leaders adopting messaging applications and must become a part of the cultural and operational norms within the company, with expectations set in onboarding programs. Messaging applications should become the central hub where information, such as management reports, is shared and accessed even if it is produced in another system, like a business intelligence platform.

- *Virtual meeting technology.* With distributed teams and continuous movement, companies move from in-person to virtual meetings. Companies should adopt virtual meeting technology, like BlueJeans, and champion video-conferences as the standard for all meetings. Adopting a "videoconference-first" strategy ensures that all workers, regardless of location, feel included and equal. As virtual meeting technology evolves, companies may begin to adopt virtual reality meeting systems where workers don headsets and meet with others as avatars in a virtual setting.

Many technology companies use these systems as a part of their standard operations. Increasingly traditional companies are also making this transformation. When I worked at Lehman Brothers, we accessed files from the office, had meetings in person, and social media messaging was blocked—even LinkedIn. When I founded Topia, we immediately adopted Google Docs and Box for collaboration, Slack for messaging, and WebEx (later BlueJeans) for virtual meetings. When we acquired Teleport, Sten Tamkivi and the founding team had taken this a step further: they used collaboration systems for almost everything they did and set clear guidelines for using them.

"At Teleport, virtual and remote working was a core part of our founding principles," says Tamkivi. "We set rules for which system to use when and for what. This is important so that everyone knows how to work, where to find things, and no one misses anything. This might sound mundane, but it actually makes people's lives simpler. It doesn't take away employee freedom per se, but rather starts to align them around default behaviors for using these systems that make it easier for everyone to work from everywhere."

F3 FOCUS

F3 Companies adopt a core set of systems to enable work everywhere. This includes collaboration software, messaging applications, and virtual meeting technology. They then champion clear expectations for workers using these systems, aligning behavioral and cultural norms. With this, they truly unlock the Talent Mobility Revolution.

The Talent Mobility Revolution is the result of the seismic forces of globalization, automation, and demographic change. It has almost entirely changed the nature of work and the way that companies need to operate to be successful in the future. Much of what we have discussed in these three sections may seem difficult to enable and manage. But by implementing a core set of systems and championing adoption of them across the business, companies seamlessly harness the benefits of talent mobility—increased employee engagement, innovation, and growth. Peggy Smith, CEO of global trade body Worldwide ERC, puts it succinctly:

"In the next five years, companies are going to be very chaotic on the surface. For someone used to pretty org charts and fixed roles, the new project-based way of working will seem very complex," says Smith. "But under the hood, companies will be incredibly efficient. They'll be agile to respond to disruptions and opportunities. They'll apply the concept of mobile talent to see results for business and customers' wants much more quickly. They'll tap into vast networks of workers to mobilize and bring people together to complete projects. And these workers will develop their own vast networks because they will work with many different people for short bursts of time."

Transforming systems and operations is the ninth and final step to success amid the Talent Mobility Revolution. To succeed, companies must restructure their business and talent operations across employment strategy, workforce planning, and payroll. They must implement a new set of systems to power their *F3 Company*, following the talent mobility systems roadmap. Companies that effectively make this operational change will be set up to harness the benefits of talent mobility for their businesses and workers.

In these three sections, we looked at the nine steps of talent mobility transformation. Any company that follows this playbook will be ready for success in the Talent Mobility Revolution. We conclude the book with a final chapter on how to unleash the *Flat, Fluid, and Fast* economy everywhere, looking at how to transform traditional companies, start new companies, and reinvent government policies.

CHAPTER SUMMARY

- Companies used to employ and pay workers through an entity. With an expanded talent pool, companies now must pursue an employment and payroll model with freelancers, employees, professional employer organizations (PEOs), and global employment companies (GECs).
- With increasing geographic movement, the burden of care for workers increases. Companies adopt global mobility management (GMM) systems to track where employees are and manage geopolitical, security, and compliance risks.
- With dynamic jobs, there are many ways to fill them. Companies use the GMM system to dynamically plan work across new hires, employees, and freelancers, considering location, policies, and costs.
- Talent mobility can appear freewheeling and complex, but with a clear systems infrastructure, companies can seamlessly enable continuous "matching, moving, and learning."
- The talent mobility systems infrastructure should include a talent marketplace, global mobility management (GMM) system, and a learning system, all linked to one another, and to other core software systems and external providers.
- With growing virtual work, companies must transform their systems and operational norms to adopt critical systems for collaboration, communication, and virtual meetings. They must make new norms for virtual work a core part of their operations.

UNLEASHING THE FLAT, FLUID, AND FAST ECONOMY

10

Transforming, Launching, and Incentivizing Flat, Fluid, and Fast Work

In 2013, I was sitting in Luxembourg, as part of a multicity talent mobility roadshow with a client. We had recently launched Topia's first relocation product and were piloting it with a few companies that were transforming parts of their talent mobility program to meet the demands of their growing millennial workforce, international operations, and recruiting needs. At this client, we had started to implement changes first in certain European locations as part of a pilot population before considering a global rollout. Together with their other partners, I was now meeting with an array of company talent and business leaders across their European offices—London, Dublin, Luxembourg, Frankfurt, Munich—to introduce the proposed changes, educate them on the context for the changes, and build local change champions.

Many of America's most innovative technology companies were both *F3 Companies* and traditional companies when it came to talent mobility. From disruptive business models to dynamic project teams, many of these companies were designed to be agile amid the talent mobility era. However, like many fast-growing technology companies I've worked with over the years, talent mobility processes often lagged business strategy. Instead of making talent mobility a key part of operations and business strategy, this client, like so many others, had set up it up to mirror the corporate relocation designs of traditional companies. With rapid growth and strong demand to fill open jobs, some visionary talent leaders now recognized that it was time to innovate. I had met one of the talent mobility leaders at just the right time in 2013. And now we were—together with their other partners—looking at how to help the company harness the talent mobility revolution as it rapidly scaled.

After working together to redesign things for the future, we had kicked off a change management roadshow to make this transformation a reality. And that is how I found myself sitting in Luxembourg in the dead of winter—cold, exhausted, and excited—doing a presentation on transforming talent mobility for millennial workers.

Over the years running Topia, I have worked with countless traditional companies as they transformed for talent mobility. For some, this meant a wholescale redesign of talent mobility across the areas we've discussed in this book—from strategy to org design to policy changes to operational transformation. For others, it was implementing and connecting a new set of talent mobility systems, often starting with Topia's GMM system, to support a new talent mobility strategy that had been adopted. For each of these, effective change management and company alignment were a critical part of a successful transformation.

At the same time, I watched many companies (like Automattic, Upwork, Netflix, and many others) start and grow with talent mobility at their core. These companies have agility in their DNA and are able to respond as disruptions and opportunities hit. They are increasingly the employers of choice for today's talent. And this talent increasingly can work from anywhere—giving employees greater flexibility, companies larger talent pools, and workers around the nation the opportunity to connect to jobs outside of their local area.

With this model, companies can also increasingly be started from anywhere, like Teleport and Skype, which were founded in

Estonia. Gone are the days where companies had to be based in a few urban hubs to attract the talent they needed. Today's companies can be based in cities and towns throughout the world, accessing skills from a global talent market and allowing founders to live in their communities and create local jobs. With the principles of talent mobility in place, these companies make frequent travel a part of their operations, with people working from dispersed locations and traveling to urban hubs for meetings as needed. With 62 percent of new jobs in America since the 2008 recession created by small businesses and increasing numbers of traditional jobs at risk from automation, it is crucial to our economy and workers that we rethink the structure of work. This should include incentives for companies hiring remote workers from outside of urban hubs, and updated benefits, protections, and labor classifications so that workers may comfortably work in the freelance economy. To underpin this, we must update our education curricula to help students understand different job opportunities and career paths in this new economy.

This book has provided a lens into the Talent Mobility Revolution and a playbook on the steps to transform for success amid its forces. But once companies and business leaders know what to transform, they must make it happen across complex, global companies. At the same time, the Talent Mobility Revolution brings with it the possibility to start and grow new companies throughout the country in different ways, bringing opportunities to many. Once company leaders and entrepreneurs understand this, they must make it happen with new designs and norms at their companies. To make all of this happen in a way that is fair and inclusive for workers, government leaders and unions must rethink the structure of work as we have known it for decades.

We conclude the book with this final chapter that looks at how to unleash an *F3 Economy* across America by implementing the changes we've discussed at traditional companies, starting new companies with these principles at their core, and evolving government policies to ensure all workers can benefit.

Transforming Traditional Companies to Be *Flat, Fluid, and Fast*

In the first nine chapters of this book, we covered the nine steps to becoming an *F3 Company* and looked at how traditional companies should adopt them. Bringing all of these together into a comprehensive change management and rollout plan is the final and, arguably, most complicated part of this transformation.

Implementing a transformation successfully requires a comprehensive change management program. There has been lots written about change management across business literature, but in my experience, there are certain key elements to successful large-scale talent mobility change management. These elements include a transformation team, change management roadmap, critical context, global kickoff, pilot population, key stakeholders, support classification, change management roadshow, and information hub. Whether you're making changes for talent mobility at a small company, large company, or within a team, you can apply these principles.

Principles for Successful Change Management

Companies have been designed a particular way for many decades, and changing their norms, operations, and behaviors can be incredibly difficult. A comprehensive change management program and team can make this happen.

Successful change management first requires setting up a dedicated *transformation team* led by your new Chief Talent Mobility Officer. As you start your journey, your first hire should be your Chief Talent Mobility Officer (CTMO). As discussed in Chapter 2, the CTMO often does not come from a traditional HR background—rather, she often comes from another part of the business. Regardless, she should bring exceptional leadership, communication, and transformation management skills. Once hired, she should immediately assemble a cross-functional transformation team.

This team should have representation from across the company, with particular expertise in project management, communication, and internal selling. This is the team that will design your new *F3 Company* using this book as their guide and align your company behind it.

Once the transformation team is assembled and has established the design and goals for your new *F3 Company*, they should create a comprehensive *change management roadmap*. The roadmap should be a large, master project plan with work streams for key activities, milestones, and dependencies. This is the plan that guides your transformation and its progress should be tracked in regular team and management calls, as well as reported in summary across the company.

Large-scale change management is difficult to implement because changing established human behaviors is hard. But, it's easier when people understand why change is being asked of them. Successful change management starts by setting *critical context* about *why* you are undertaking this transformation journey. Successful execution and adoption of your talent mobility transformation requires that everyone in the company understand the reasons, goals, and benefits of the transformation. You should design and lead a comprehensive program to educate the company about this context. This should start from the first day of your change management program and continue throughout it.

Once you've built your transformation team, designed your change management roadmap, and started your education program on your critical context, it's time to hold a *global kickoff* for your talent mobility transformation. The global kickoff is a meeting, usually virtual, with everyone in the company to introduce the transformation initiative and team. If your CTMO has not yet been introduced to the company, you can introduce her here. Otherwise, she should lead this kickoff. Before this meeting, you should ensure that key company leaders understand the critical context so that they can support employee questions after the meeting.

The global kickoff should present an overview of the transformation initiative and set expectations for the major milestones in the roadmap. It should also clearly tell employees where they can find more information and how to ask questions about what's happening. Establishing clear communication and expectations starts to establish alignment across the company, which will be important going forward.

F3 FOCUS

F3 Companies implement talent mobility transformation with a comprehensive change management program led by the Chief Talent Mobility Officer. They create a transformation team, set critical context for employees, and host a global kickoff to provide an overview of the initiative and set expectations for what's ahead.

Pilot Populations and Segmenting Your Organization for Transformation

When launching a talent mobility transformation across a company, it's helpful to start with a pilot population where you can roll out change first. With this population, you can launch new initiatives, gather feedback, iterate on that feedback, and then be well prepared for the broader rollout. Across Topia's customers—from large global investment banks to consulting firms, consumer goods companies, and many more—I have seen the best practice be to first adopt changes in a pilot population, iterating on feedback from that population before rolling out across the company.

One of the key parts of becoming an *F3 Company* is the shift to being an agile organization with movement across geographies, jobs, locations, and employment. Inherent in this is deconstructing work into dynamic projects that can be done by employees, freelancers, or artificial intelligence. But not every part of your company can be agile immediately. For example, accounts payable analysts may continue with business as usual until automation becomes a priority, while data scientists may have skills that immediately get loaned across projects.

To identify an appropriate *pilot population*, you should first segment your workforce into those who would naturally become agile, project-based workers and those who are likely to remain in fixed roles for the near term, and then select your pilot population from your agile workforce. Because the nature of talent mobility is movement, it is best if this pilot population is "horizontal"—that is selected from across the company and not demarcated by geography or department. With a pilot population identified, your transformation team can execute the various parts of their transformation plan and easily gather feedback from them.

F3 FOCUS

F3 Companies select a pilot population where they first roll out the parts of their talent mobility transformation and gather feedback. The pilot population should come from the identified agile workforce and be from multiple geographies and business areas.

Building Support and Launching Change

As you start to implement your transformation, it's important to identify the *key stakeholders* for change. While you will communicate your critical context to all of your employees in the global kickoff, all of your employees will not be key stakeholders. Once you've identified your key stakeholders, you should identify who supports your change and who does not, assigning a *support classification* to each stakeholder. These support classifications are:

- *Champion.* A champion fully supports the change. She is willing to put her own time and reputation on the line to advocate for the change. She can eloquently articulate the critical context, explain the milestones of the change management roadmap, and rally people in support of the change. Champions should be included as close partners to the transformation team. They are your allies and incredibly important.
- *Coach.* A coach supports the change and shares important feedback from the company that is useful in how you position and share things to the broader company. Unlike a champion, however, a coach does not put much of his own time or reputation behind the change.
- *Supporter.* A supporter is generally positive about the change. A supporter agrees with the change but tends to be passive. She does not actively advocate for the change (as a champion does) or share regular feedback and advice (as a coach does).
- *Neutral.* A neutral is not positive or negative about the change. He politely listens and generally does not engage in any way, positively or negatively.
- *Detractor.* A detractor does not support the change. She is actively negative and advocates against it, regularly sharing concerns and criticism. If pushed, a detractor may block parts of your change and work to rally support against it.

It is important to classify each key stakeholder so that you can take actions to amplify the support for your change and to neutralize your detractors, who can create difficult roadblocks for talent mobility transformation. It is unlikely that your detractors will become supporters of your change, so your goal should be to neutralize them. Generally, this is best done in one-on-one conversations helping them understand the critical context more deeply. You should assign a champion to work with each detractor with a clear objective to neutralize them. You should also leverage your champions to convert coaches and supporters to new champions, and neutrals to new supporters. For these one-one-one conversations, champions should be trained deeply on the critical context and change management roadmap, and able to answer skeptical questions from stakeholders. Often detractors and neutrals just need more time to understand the critical context and roadmap to get comfortable with it.

The support classifications of your key stakeholders are important as you kick off your *change management roadshow*, the final component of a successful rollout. The transformation team should visit offices around the world to introduce the transformation and what's ahead. It's important that this is done in person and in fairly intimate settings, so that the team can establish relationships with key stakeholders in local offices and build local champions to continue to carry the flame of the transformation once the team departs. These sessions should be run as a presentation covering the critical context, change management roadmap, and immediate next steps, but also have a significant portion of time allocated for questions so that everyone is heard.

During these sessions, you should direct the key stakeholders to the *information hub*. The information hub should be a website (or location on an intranet) that the transformation team creates and updates to provide details on the transformation, including presentations, frequently asked questions (FAQs), key milestones, and status updates. The information hub should be updated regularly as new information and FAQs emerge. It is essential that progress toward the important milestones is up to date so that everyone can track progress of the talent mobility transformation and see the progress toward becoming an *F3 Company.*

With these change management principles, any company can follow the nine-step transformation outlined in this book to become an *F3 Company* and then successfully embed this change across the company.

F3 FOCUS

F3 Companies implement successful change by identifying key stakeholders and aligning their support for the talent mobility transformation. They then invest in a change management road-show to introduce the transformation across the business and host discussions and questions with employees. Finally, they create a comprehensive information hub that gives everyone in the company details and status updates about the transformation.

Building New Companies That Are Flat, Fluid, and Fast

We've now looked at the nine steps to becoming an *F3 Company* and how traditional companies can implement them for agility and success amid the Talent Mobility Revolution. But the *F3* principels are not just for large or traditional companies. They are for all companies in all parts of the world that want to succeed amid the forces of globalization, automation, and demographic change.

Small businesses are the economic engine of America. Since the 2008 recession, small businesses generated more than 62 percent of all net new private sector jobs created, and 42 percent of the American workforce is employed by small businesses. Small businesses face many of the same challenges and potential disruptions as large, traditional companies, and, like larger companies, they must be able to adapt as disruptions hit. While not all of these transformation activities may apply to small businesses, the principles do.

The *F3* principles also have significant potential for new companies. Greater talent mobility means more movement across geographies, jobs, locations, and employment. It also means that companies can hire remote knowledge workers outside of where they are headquartered. Companies in urban locations can hire workers from around the country, enabling virtual work and travel to offices and cities when needed. Companies in rural or suburban locations can hire workers based locally and around the world and increase efficiencies by pairing lower real estate costs and travel to cities when needed. More than ever today, companies can be started from anywhere.

SeeMe is an art technology company that was set up like this. SeeMe connects emerging artists around the world with buyers. It showcases its artists at a series of major art fairs around the world— selecting those who exhibit through online competitions it runs and covering travel costs for the winners. In essence, these artists are leveraging *F3* principles in their own work—connecting virtually to those who want to purchase their skills and traveling to collaborate when needed!

SeeMe was founded in New York City but operates a distributed team. Certain employees are in New York, but others work remotely from home offices and travel to New York to collaborate. The company also hosts in-person team meetings when team members come together at the art shows where their artists exhibit. SeeMe CEO Brendan Burns lives in rural Richmond, Massachusetts, and commutes to New York to work on SeeMe and to teach at Columbia Graduate School of Business. Otherwise, he works from rural Richmond working virtually with his global company of artists and employees.

Brendan is in the process of setting up offices for SeeMe. But he's not centralizing everything in New York, as you might expect. Rather, he's keeping with the company's talent mobility DNA—he expects to have an office in the rural Berkshires in Western Massachusetts and a small office in New York to use to bring the virtual team together and carry out certain activities that need to be based there. Brendan knows that, amid the Talent Mobility Revolution, he can connect with both a global marketplace and his virtual employees through collaboration, messaging, videoconferencing systems, and frequent travel. SeeMe's employees also work across the company on projects as they come up—and to fill in the gaps, SeeMe employs freelancers to augment project teams.

SeeMe embraces the principles of the Talent Mobility Revolution, and with them is showing that technology start-ups can now be founded and run from everywhere, even rural Western Massachusetts.

Founding Values and Norms

When starting an *F3 Company*, it's important to define your culture and operating norms at the outset. This includes your company values, the systems you will use, and the expectations for workers. Your company values should embrace flexibility, autonomy, and inclusion of all types of workers, whether working from the office or home, and whether employees or freelancers. At Topia, our values included "be global citizens," "learn relentlessly," and "collaborate radically" (among others), embracing our distributed team, agile mindset, and focus on teamwork. A part of your success building an *F3 Company* will be in setting expectations early to the people you hire about what kind of company it is. This starts with the values.

After creating your values, it's critical to establish your operating norms early. You should follow Sten Tamkivi's framework to "write liberally, meet regularly, and congregate occasionally" and ensure that all early employees embrace this as a foundation of the company. We have discussed many of the other structures of *F3 Companies* in prior chapters—any company starting today should adopt these as a part of their standard operations from the very beginning. These include building a culture of worker movement, deconstructing work into dynamic projects with OKRs, including all types of workers in your workforce definition, setting clear communications and systems use expectations, and rethinking the purpose of your offices, among others.

It is critical that all of these norms are immediately embraced from the founding team and early employees, and then translated to every person that you hire going forward. During recruiting and onboarding processes, you must clearly communicate your company values and norms. This includes making sure everyone hired knows that a job at your company does not come with a promise of lifetime employment and a linear career path; rather it will include dynamic projects, flexible work, and exponential learning and skills development opportunities across geographies, jobs, and teams.

Finally, when starting a new *F3 Company*, you must understand the talent mobility systems roadmap, but implement it in line with company growth. You should immediately implement a collaboration system, messaging application, and virtual meeting software to make your company run. You may also want to immediately start to leverage a freelancer marketplace to augment your early employees with skills from freelancers before you are ready to hire more employees. As your company grows and geographic, job, and employment movement increase, you should adopt the other parts of the talent mobility systems roadmap.

"It is so much easier to build a distributed, mobile culture from the ground up," says Sten Tamkivi, an expert on distributed teams from Skype and founding Teleport. "I saw this work at both Skype and Teleport, and then not work as well when Skype was acquired by eBay and people were used to working in another way."

"If 100 people are all working in the traditional way in an office, and you hire one remote person, it's not one person who needs to change, it's 101 people who need to change how they interact with each other and the systems they use. This requires a massive cultural shift from everyone. Instead of shouting from a corner office, now you need to post in a messaging application. Instead of having casual conversations at the watercooler, you need to empathize that someone isn't there and wait for the videoconference. It's a very hard transition to do in later stages," continues Tamkivi. "But it's much easier to do from the start—adopting tools, apps, and behaviors from the beginning and aligning everyone around this. Every company in today's era should be founded like this."

F3 FOCUS

When starting a new company, establish your *F3* values, norms, and operations immediately. Companies that intentionally design these and embed them in their DNA will be built to respond well to future opportunities and disruptions. These *F3* principles make it possible for companies and workers to work everywhere, and to unlock economic potential and jobs across America.

Managing Company Growth and Challenges

Many start-up companies—like SeeMe and Teleport—are founded with *F3* principles at their core. As they grow, they will naturally develop operating rhythms and team dynamics centered around particular locations. Companies should develop an office model of "hubs and spokes" with office hubs in particular locations that offer an easy place for workers to congregate and spokes of distributed workers farther afield. To maximize efficiencies amid growth, companies may start to align distributed workers to one of these office hubs, often in a nearby geographic location and time zone. This starts to build some structure on top of the project teams and provides a natural location if workers want to go into an office or need to dial into a regional conference call.

While talent mobility can attract top talent to new companies and unleash innovation, it can also be challenging to manage amid rapid growth. With change, opportunities, and challenges often comes the need to bring people physically together—whether hunkering down amid headwinds or gearing up amid tailwinds. While your *F3* principles will be in your company DNA, it's important to adapt to the needs of the company and workers at different stages. Yahoo famously banned remote work in 2013 when Marissa Mayer took over as CEO and worked to realign and reignite company growth. IBM brought thousands of remote workers back to offices in 2017.

At Topia, there were numerous periods where we asked people to work from the office. This was often when we rolled out new products, completed acquisitions, or made changes to our business, all of which required more communication and alignment across the company. In this way, companies think about talent mobility like a rubber band—staff stretches across locations at certain points and comes together at other points. You should set this expectation early so that employees are not shocked—as they were at Yahoo—when changes are requested to ways of working and talent mobility is limited.

"Communicating and aligning for change—whether positive or negative—often requires face-to-face working," says Tamkivi. "I always say that you build relationships face-to-face and maintain them through virtual work. Not vice versa. Rapid growth, business challenges, or big company changes often require a deepening of personal relationships and trust that must happen, at least for some time, in person. In these times, working together can also just be more efficient."

F3 FOCUS

As new *F3 Companies* grow, they develop office hubs, where workers can congregate and align. Growing *F3 Companies* know that with rapid growth and business change, there will be times when employees need to spend time working in person. In this way, *F3* leaders think about their growing companies like a rubber band: workers disperse for certain work and come together when needed.

Designing Policies to Unleash a Flat, Fluid, and Fast Economy

F3 Companies drive employee engagement, accelerate innovation, and unleash growth. Any traditional company can transform to be an *F3 Company*. Any new company can start as an *F3 Company*. And any team can adopt *F3 Company* principles. To be successful in the twenty-first century, all businesses must be *F3 Companies*.

The forces of globalization, automation, and demographic change have fundamentally changed the nature of work and brought the Talent Mobility Revolution to our forefront. Workers will increasingly work across companies, jobs, and geographies. They will do this as employees and freelancers, in segments or at the same time. They will work from offices, homes, and coworking spaces in all parts of the country. They will develop skills, loan them across projects, and pursue lifelong learning alongside careers. They will see their work become increasingly project-based, both inside and outside companies, with their skills increasingly decoupled from companies. My generation will work across more careers than our parents had job titles.

With this change in work, we can unlock a new future of work, where companies hire workers from a national talent pool, workers can live anywhere—rural, suburban and urban locations—and access jobs throughout the nation, and diversity becomes commonplace.

While there are many benefits to this future of work, it also brings challenges and uncertainty. For decades, work was based on the concept that traditional companies provided stable work, income, and benefits to employees. Employees worked for years, earned a good wage and benefits, and then enjoyed retirement. In the project-based economy, work can be inconsistent. Skilled workers can earn high wages (the highest paid freelancer on Upwork makes $2.5 million per year) and save for gaps in work, but other workers can be left behind or taken advantage of by unscrupulous employers who push full-time work to cheaper contractors to avoid paying benefits and protecting workers. Without the traditional benefits and protections provided to full-time employees and the collective bargaining of unions, these workers can struggle to earn a fair wage, save for retirement and have healthcare coverage, among other challenges. We must work together across government, businesses and unions to ensure our American workers are supported and protected as our economy undergoes the talent mobility revolution. This is our responsibility and most important job.

We must support this shift by redesigning our contract for work in America. Without this, the gains of talent mobility will fall to only a few and inequality will only accelerate. This starts with rethinking our long-held structure of work, and then creating new programs to support workers in our new economy. Finally, we must create tax incentives for workers to transition to new work, entrepreneurs to pursue ideas and continue to create new jobs, and companies to fill jobs with workers across America. These policies will create a new economy for all and ensure continued American economic competitiveness.

Our new contract for work in America should include:

A new structure of work. We must recognize that work is shifting to include an expanded workforce with more on-demand project and freelance work. At the same time, we must also recognize that certain employers are exploiting these trends to avoid paying workers fair wages, overtime pay and benefits. To address this, we should review labor law and consider a classification for on-demand freelance workers that allows employers to provide and pay for portable benefits, protections and fair pay while recognizing the different structure of work. These flexible project workers are different from traditional employees and contractors because they work when they want to, often with flexible schedules and rates set by supply and demand. In many instances, they work alongside other freelance work or employment to augment their income. (We must separately increase the minimum wage to ensure that workers who choose to work in one job are paid fairly and sufficiently.) We must ensure that these freelanceworkers, who value their different way of working, can maintain their flexibility and autonomy, while being protected from unscrupulous business practices and supported in basic needs. To do this, we should create a new classification of worker that extends many of the traditional employment protections (minimum wage, overtime pay, healthcare and other benefits, antidiscrimination, sexual harassment protections, and health and safety, among others) to freelance workers and allows for collective bargaining and representation. Alongside this, we must accelerate educational resources to help workers adapt, smooth income, and responsibly save.

Portable, protected benefits. For decades, companies provided employees a set of protections and benefits, like a minimum wage, healthcare, and retirement savings. We must ensure that as people work across more job types, all workers have access to affordable high quality and portable healthcare and other basic benefits, regardless of employment classification. We should start with creating a public option, that is exists alongside with private insurance, and can be paid for directly or by stipends from employers. Over time this will help to push down healthcare and prescription drug costs across all insurance types as the effects of a larger competitive market take hold. We must increase our minimum wage, across all types of employment, to ensure our workers earn enough to live comfortably in today's America. We must also create a federally mandated paid parental leave policy for all mothers and fathers to ensure diversity in our workforce and care for our next generation. (The US is one of only a few countries that do not provide paid parental leave. The others include Papua New Guinea, Lesotho, Swaziland and Liberia). Finally, this new structure of work must have an updated retirement savings program that all workers can use, directly and with contributions from employers, regardless of employment status. We should do this because our economy is fundamentally changing and we must support all of our workers in this new paradigm. We should also do this because it makes good economic and business sense. When workers have basic needs for health, family, and retirement met, they are freer to be members of families and local communities, start companies, switch jobs, use their skills in the economy, and learn new skills. This creates a fly-wheel of healthy communities, economic growth and job creation, benefiting everyone.

Expanded community college and apprenticeships. As we've discussed in this book, skills are the currency of today's economy. The talent mobility era will be characterized by lifelong learning, starting after high school, as workers continually develop skills to use across projects. To ensure everyone has the opportunity to develop skills for all parts of our economy, we should both bolster our community college system to ensure that everyone has the right to higher education and the opportunity to pursue lifelong learning throughout a career. We should consider funding structured as a forgivable loan tied to successfully completing a course—if successful, students do not need to pay for the course. As part of this program, we should also incentivize public-private technology partnerships to enhance virtual learning programs, expanding access to courses throughout America, reducing overhead costs for running community colleges, and helping students develop the digital fluency that is a hallmark of the talent mobility era. A part of this should be a program to loan laptops to students who may not be able to afford them. Expanded community college gives everyone the right to an education and helps workers continually develop skills for the new economy. At the same time, we should accelerate vocational programs and apprenticeships in partnerships with our unions, supporting learning and employment opportunities across trades. This is good for workers and good for economic growth.

Expanded early education. As the workforce becomes more diverse, we must invest in education and childcare for our next generation. We should expand our current kindergarten system to include pre-K, helping children develop critical skills early, creating new teaching jobs, and supporting diversity across the workforce.

Over time, we should look to expand this to also include subsidized early childcare and nursery school. (The maternal employment rate is negatively impacted by the lack of affordable daycare. The average cost of full-time daycare for a child age four or younger is approximately $10,000 per year.)* The United States now ranks third to last among OECD countries on public spending on family benefits.† (Note that Congress passed the Comprehensive Child Development Act in 1971, a universal childcare bill with bipartisan support, before President Richard Nixon vetoed it.) Expanded early education gives working families the opportunity for both parents to participate in the new economy. This is sound economic policy that spurs economic output, small business creation, and job growth.

Distributed hiring incentives. If you spend time in any of America's large coastal cities today, you won't go far without hearing business leaders complain that they can't find skilled workers. From San Francisco to Seattle to New York, companies frequently talk about worker shortages. At the same time, many other parts of America—from rural California to the rust belt to Appalachia— are filled with workers with both the skills and work ethic these companies need. There are three ways to solve this problem: move workers to jobs, move jobs to workers, or embrace distributed work supporting remote work from hometowns and travel to company offices when needed. Many people do not want to move away from their local communities, and the high cost of living in urban coastal cities can make moving prohibitive. Similarly, it can be difficult and expensive for communities to attract companies to set up local offices and create local jobs. The solution sits with companies leveraging the distributed work and frequent travel of the

---

* https://www.workingmother.com/this-is-what-day-care-looks-like-around-world#page-3.
† https://newrepublic.com/article/113009/child-care-america-was-very-close-universal-day-care.

talent mobility era to hire workers from all over America and bring them to offices when needed. We should economically incentivize companies, often based in low-unemployment coastal hubs, to hire remote workers from other parts of America where unemployment may be high. This brings jobs to workers and allows people to live in their own communities, where they can continue to contribute to their local economy. Similar to incentivizing companies to hire remote workers from other parts of America, we should incentivize knowledge workers to stay or return to rural parts of America and work remotely from there. (In 2019, Vermont launched a "Remote Worker Grant Program" that pays workers up to $5,000 per year to live in Vermont and work for a company outside the state.)* This is sound economic policy that spreads gains from America's companies to workers and communities throughout the country.

Small business and entrepreneur incentives. As our economy shifts, freelance and remote work will become a larger part of work. At the same time, continued job growth and innovation—including solutions to many of our largest challenges—will continue to come from the ingenuity of America's private sector. We should increase incentives to support and accelerate entrepreneurship and small business creation in America—from the microentrepreneurs of the freelance economy, to those starting local businesses—often the backbone of our local economies, to the technologists solving intractable problems. We should provide tax breaks for freelancers on the first portion of their income, recognizing the risks that these workers take, the value they provide companies, and the fact that many people use freelance work to pay for expenses that they can't afford to cover from regular wages. We should make it easier to start and manage small and growing businesses, from subsidized small business loans to more efficient tax policy. Finally, we should recognize that the solutions to some of the most critical challenges

---

* https://www.thinkvermont.com/remote-worker-grant-program/.

of our time—from clean energy to high-risk home insurance to cybersecurity will come from the ingenuity of our entrepreneurs. We must incentivize and direct our entrepreneurs and investors to tackle these intractable challenges for our society.

The new contract for work will unleash a *Flat, Fluid, and Fast* economy across our nation. This will accelerate economic growth, ensure American competitiveness, and support all workers through the transition to the new world of work. We must make this shift to stimulate our future economy and ensure our companies, workers, and nation are all helped, not hurt, by the forces of globalization, automation, and demographic change. In the early years of globalization, we left many workers behind. Today, we have the opportunity to ensure that everyone benefits from talent mobility.

The Talent Mobility Revolution is upon us. Driven by the seismic and converging forces of globalization, automation, and demographic change, the talent mobility era brings frequent disruptions and opportunities to companies and workers. This book has provided a nine-step playbook for companies and business leaders to transform in the face of the Talent Mobility Revolution—to drive employee engagement, accelerate innovation, and unleash growth. Companies today must transform to be agile—unlocking project-based work and continuous movement across geographies, jobs, locations, and employment. The companies that do this successfully will be the winners of the twenty-first century. Those that do not will be left behind and lose out to their more agile competitors.

But the Talent Mobility Revolution is not only for large companies. It will touch all parts of our economy—from multinational leaders to small businesses to teams to start-ups to individual workers to government policy. By following the principles in this book, we can all benefit from becoming *Flat, Fluid, and Fast*.

Index

Academia, 119
Accenture Research, 101, 105
Adaptability, 73–74
Agile bonuses, 175, 176
Agile feedback, 133–134
Agile performance management,
    133–134
Agile talent management, 130–136
  agile feedback in, 133–134
  for career progression, 134–135
  classification of workers in, 85–86
  project objectives and success
      measurement in, 130–132
  sourcing in, 21
  talent reviews and indicators in,
      135–136
Agile teams, 100, 106–108
Agility, 220
  CTMO's accountability for, 43
  as key to success, 95, 117
  reorganizing for, 41–42
  shift to, 224
  as today's business currency, 73
  transforming culture and operations
      for, 107
  at Upwork, 81
AI (see Artificial intelligence)
The Alliance (Hoffman, Yeh, and
    Casnocha), 13
Almasi, Peter, 93, 94
America, new contract for work in,
    235–240
American Dream, xiv
Annual performance reviews, 108,
    121–123, 133
Antidiscrimination protections, 186,
    187
Artificial intelligence (AI), xi, 80, 95,
    104–106, 163–164
Automated (repetitive) jobs, 163–164
Automation, xi, xii
  disruption from, 14, 73
  as driver of talent mobility, 22, 214

jobs at risk from, 220–221
and jobs graphs creation, 80
in managing costs and budgets, 205
opportunities from, 73
as part of teams, 94–95
and talent mobility transformation,
    193
upcoming risks from, 71–72
work disruption by, 5
workers displaced by, 71
Automattic:
  compensation model of, 174
  employment model of, 197
  location movement policies of, 162
  remote workers at, 17
  unlimited vacation model at, 177
  work-from-everywhere model at,
      64–66
Autonomy, 124, 177
AXA, 147

Babbage, Charles, 5–6
Barton, Dominic, 32
Basic income payments, 236
Benefits, 167–169, 176–185
  and employment movement, 20
  family leave, 181–182
  fixed model for, 150–151
  for freelance workers, 187–188
  in geographic movement policy,
      150–151
  healthcare, 183–184, 236
  holiday, 167–168, 177
  local expectations for, 168
  for PEO workers, 196
  points model for, 151
  relocation, 143
  retirement, 178–180
  with traditional employee
      movement, 8
  vacation and time-off, 176–178
  wellness support, 184–185
Bersin, Josh, 72–73

Betterworks, 131
Black, Steve, 93, 94, 111
BlueJeans, 53, 160, 212
Bonuses, 170, 175–176
Boudreau, John, 46
Box, 212, 213
Brain drain, 57
Budgets:
  for employee movement, 34
  managing (*see* Cost and budget
    management)
Building blocks of talent mobility,
  9–22
  bringing together the, 22–23,
    40–42
  geographic movement, 10–13
  job movement, 13–16
  location movement, 16–19
Building *F3 Companies,* 228–233
Burns, Brendan, 229
Business models, new, 83
Business strategy, 17, 142

Campus recruiting programs, 7–8
Cappelli, Peter, 119–120, 123, 133
Career ladders, 118–120
  career zigzag replacing, 116
  in current environment, 125
  in traditional companies, 30
  and traditional offices, 52
  for traditional teams, 96, 97
Career paths, 115–138
  agile talent management of,
    130–136
  changing nature of, 124–129
  nonlinear and dynamic, 124–126
  recruiting for skills vs. for titles,
    127–128
  résumés in, 120–121, 127–128
  as series of job segments, 13
  traditional, 117–123
Career progression, 134–135
Carey, Dennis, 32
Casnocha, Ben, 13
Catalant Technologies, 44
Censia, 86–87, 129
Champions, 226–227
Change, launching, 227–228
Change management, 222–224
Change management roadmap, 223
Change management roadshow, 227

Charan, Ram, 32
Chief Human Resource Officer
  (CHRO), 31–32
Chief Talent Mobility Officer
  (CTMO), 29, 41, 43–48, 142,
  222
Childcare subsidies, 237, 238
CHRO (Chief Human Resource
  Officer), 31–32, 45
City center office locations, 60–61
Classifying workers, 100
  for dynamic jobs, 82–88
  in employment movement, 19–20
  in new contract for work, 235
  by skills and preferences, 90
  skills graph for, 85–87
  by tax status, 82, 195
Coaches, 133
  manager, 95, 99, 109–110
  and performance reviews, 133–134
  in transformation, 226, 227
Cohen, Jacky, 110, 121, 136, 167,
  198
Collaboration, 17, 54–59, 62,
  104–106
Collaboration software, 211–212
Collaboration systems, 211–213
Collective bargaining rights, 187
Community, 56–59
Community colleges, 237
Company norms, 230–231
Company values, 230
Compensation, 167–176
  amid talent mobility, 171–174
  benchmarking services for, 82
  bonus methodologies, 175–176
  differing local expectations for,
    168
  for freelance workers, 131–132
  traditional models for, 169–171
Competencies, 127–128, 135–136
Competition, xi–xii, 103
Competitive advantage, 9
Compliance management, 17,
  200–203
Confluence, 212
Consulting firms, 87
Context jobs, 156, 163
Continuous feedback, 130
Contract for work in America,
  235–240

Contractors, 19, 20
  on extended teams, 100–101
  in multitiered entity and
    employment model, 195–196
  pay models for, 195
  payroll system for, 198–199
  as 1099 workers, 195
  in traditional companies, 34, 82
  (*See also* Employment movement)
Core jobs, 156, 163
Core talent mobility systems map,
  209–211
Corporate mobility drivers, 152
Corporate relocation, 8–9
  at innovative technology companies,
    220
  talent mobility defined as, 4
  talent mobility vs., 23
  traditional policies for, 143–146
  transforming, 142
  (*See also* Geographic movement)
Cost and budget management, 205–209
Coworking spaces, 49, 65
Creelman, David, 46
Critical context, 223
CTMO (*see* Chief Talent Mobility
  Officer)
Culture:
  defining, 230
  distributed vs. office, 50–51
  need for transformation in, 57
  shift in, 231
  to support agile work, 107
  virtual, 64
  work-from-everywhere, 64
  work-from-home, 62–63

Daugherty, Paul, 106
Deconstructing work, 77–81, 106
DeFelice, Manon, 57
Deloitte, 157
Demographic change, xi, xii
  disruption and opportunities from,
    73
  as driver of talent mobility, 22, 72,
    214
  and office/workplace environments,
    56
  and value of autonomy and
    flexibility, 124
  work disruption by, 5

Design:
  of *F3 Company* offices, 58–60
  of organizations (*see* Organizational
    design)
  of traditional offices, 54–55
  of work around jobs, 89
Detractors, in transformation,
  226–227
Development mobility drivers, 152
Disruption(s), xii, 4
  agility in dealing with, 73
  geopolitical, 204
  of income, 236
  increasing pace of, 72
  in jobs, 13–14
  from technology advances, 104
  in traditional roles, 76
Disruption tours of duty, 14, 33
Distributed hiring, 238
Distributed teams, 197–198, 229
Distributed work, 17, 50, 51, 63–65
  incentives for, 238–239
  policies for, 160–161
  at Schneider Electric, 191
  (*See also* Location movement)
Distributed work culture, 50–51
DLF, 34
Dropbox, 212
Dynamic career paths, 124–126
Dynamic jobs, 77–88
  deconstructing work for creating
    jobs graph, 79–81
  moving from traditional roles to,
    77–79
  reclassifying workers for, 82–88
Dynamic projects, 77, 100, 135
Dynamic teams, 95, 100, 106–108

Early education, 237–238
eBay, 11–12, 231
Education, 237–238
Elance, 81
Emotional quotient (EQ), 45
Employee engagement, 51, 122, 211–
  213, 233
Employee engagement and
    collaboration systems, 211–213
  collaboration software, 211–212
  messaging applications, 212
  virtual meeting technology,
    212–213

Employee movement, 10–22
  employment movement, 19–22
  geographic movement, 10–13
  job movement, 13–16
  location movement, 16–19
  organizing for, 90–91
  policies for, 142
  in traditional companies, 33–34,
    170
  by traditional human resources
    departments, 8–9
  *(See also individual types of
    movement)*
Employee protections, 20, 168,
  185–188
Employee value proposition, 17
Employee wellness support, 184–185
Employees:
  career progression for, 109,
    133–134
  critical skills of, 83
  development of, 109, 123
  on extended teams, 100–101
  full-time, 19–22
  management of, 84
  payroll system for, 199
  talent reviews for, 135–136
  team as sense of identity for, 96, 97
  traditional compensation model for,
    169–171
  traditional job movement policies
    for, 153
  traditional management of, 6–10
  on traditional teams, 96
  use of term, 100
  as W2 workers, 195
Employment by entity model, 196
Employment models, 193–200
  changes in, 73
  for talent mobility, 194–198
  traditional, 193–194
  workers' dictating of, 126
Employment movement:
  challenges with, 169
  in *F3 Companies,* 19–22
  growth of, 83
  as part of geographic movement,
    146
  policies for, 163–164
  talent mobility function for, 37
  types of, 19–20

Engagement Managers, 111
Engagement tours of duty, 14, 33
Entity and employment model,
  194–198
Entrepreneur incentives, 239
EQ (emotional quotient), 45
Expatriate assignments, 10
  compensation adjustment with, 170
  defined, 8
  employing entity in, 193–194
  equalized taxes and benefits for, 143
  at Lehman Brothers, 144–145
  pay model for, 194
  in traditional companies, 33, 170,
    171
  as type of corporate relocation, 143
  as type of geographic movement,
    146
Extended teams/workforce, 100–103
EY People Advisory and Consulting
  service, 12

F3 Companies (see Flat, Fluid, and
  Fast Companies)
F3 Company offices, 56–61
  design of, 58–60
  hubs and spokes model for, 232
  location of, 60–61
  purpose of, 56–58
F3 Economy (see Flat, Fluid, and Fast
  Economy)
F3 principles, 88–91, 228–229, 234
"Face time," 52, 53
Family and Medical Leave Act
  (FMLA), 181
Family leave benefits, 181–182
Fast Retailing, 104–105
Feedback:
  agile, 133–134
  continuous, 130
  for employee development, 109, 111
  OKRs as, 135
  and performance reviews, 122, 133
Fine Foods of Virginia, 74
Fixed teams, 77, 95–98, 106
Fixed vacation model, 176–177
Fixed-role jobs, 74–79
*Flat, Fluid, and Fast Companies (F3
  Companies),* 5, 36–40
  agility as core strategy of, 29
  building, 228–233

career paths in, 117
Chief Talent Mobility Officer in,
    43–48
compensation structure at, 175
employee movement in, 19–22
geographic movement in, 10–13
job movement in, 13–16
jobs in (see Dynamic jobs)
location movement in, 16–19
offices for (see F3 Company offices)
organizational design of, 31–32
remote work in, 62
talent mobility function in, 36–42
talent mobility in, 9–22
technology companies as, 219
Flat, Fluid, and Fast Economy (F3
    Economy), 221–240
    building F3 Companies for,
        228–233
    designing policies for, 233–240
    transforming traditional companies
        for, 222–228
Flexibility:
    of geographic movement policies,
        150–151
    of office spaces, 58–60
    of work arrangements, 16–17, 21,
        124
    for work-life balance, 188
Floating vacation model, 167, 177
FMLA (Family and Medical Leave
    Act), 181
Forced ranking performance systems,
    122
Forum for Expatriate Management,
    3–4
"Four Reasons Resumes No Longer
    Work" (Fast Company), 128
"4 Concerns That Keep CEOs Awake
    at Night" (Moritz), 103
Fragomen, 16, 39–40
Freelance economy, 163, 169, 186,
    188, 221
Freelance workers, 19–21
    benefits for, 187–188
    career progression for, 133
    compensation of, 131–132, 172–174
    employee protections for, 187–188
    on extended teams, 100–101
    extending employee protections to,
        186–187

first platforms for, 81
growth of demand for, 185–186
healthcare for, 183, 184, 187–188
hiring, 164
incentivizing companies to hire, 186
innovating in benefits for, 187–188
in multitiered entity and
    employment model, 195–196
in new workforce, 83
payroll structures for, 195
payroll system for, 198–199
retirement benefits for, 187–188
in traditional companies, 34
Upwork platform for, 18
(See also Employment movement)
Frequent travel, 10, 33, 49, 146, 238
Full-time employees (FTEs), 19–22
    (See also Employees)
Future of work, 35, 44, 234–235
    (See also Contract for work in
    America)

GECs (see Global employment
    companies)
Generation Z, xi, 73
Geographic movement:
    compensation structures for,
        172–173
    configurations of, 10–11
    designing policies for, 143–153
    employee demand for, 146
    in F3 Companies, 10–13
    and healthcare benefits, 183
    new policies for, 146–149
    in scenario planning, 206
    steps for success with, 149–152
    talent mobility function for, 36–37
    in traditional companies, 8–9 (See
        also Corporate relocation)
Geographic tours of duty, 14
Geopolitical risk, 203–204
Gig workers, 19, 20
    benefits and protections for, 184
    on extended teams, 101
    in new workforce, 83
    in traditional companies, 34
Global benchmark compensation
    model, 173, 174
Global employment companies
    (GECs), 180, 183, 196–197, 199
Global healthcare plans, 183

Global kickoff for transformation, 223–224
Global mobility management (GMM) systems, 192
  approving and initiating talent mobility with, 208
  compliance management with, 202–203
  cost and budget management with, 205–207
  risk management with, 203–204
  in talent mobility systems map, 209–211
Global retirement model, 178–180
Global workforce skills graph, 86
Globalization, xi, xii
  disruption and opportunities from, 73
  as driver of talent mobility, 22, 214
  geopolitical disruptions with, 204
  and organizational design, 99
  and talent mobility transformation, 193
  work disruption by, 5
  workers displaced by, 71
Globalization tours of duty, 33
GMM systems (see Global mobility management systems)
Goals, 131
Google, 131
Google Docs, 212, 213
Gratton, Lynda, 118
Growth management, 232–233
Guillermo, Kerwin, 14–15, 17

Halverson, Eric, 11–12, 204
Happiness, 61
Health and safety protections, 186, 187
Healthcare benefits, 183–184, 236
Herrin, Jessica, 102, 162–163
Hierarchy, 96–98, 118–120
Hiring:
  applying for jobs, 156
  distributed, 238
  for fixed-role jobs, 75–76
  of freelancers, 164
  in future of work, 234
  implied stability in, 82
  reactive, 84
  selecting workers, 156–157

skills testing in, 129
for talent mobility leadership, 44
by traditional companies, 7–8, 76
to transform traditional companies, 222
Hoffman, Reid, 13
Holiday benefits, 167–168, 177
Home offices, 62–63
Horsley, Robert, 16, 39–40, 42
Hot desking, 58–59
HP, 14–17, 23
HR (human resources), 5–10, 31–32
"HR Goes Agile" (Cappelli and Tavis), 133
Hubs and spokes office model, 232
Human + Machine (Daugherty and Wilson), 106
Human resources (HR), 5–10, 31–32
Human–machine collaboration, 104–106

IBM, 76, 232
Identity, sense of, 96, 97
Immigration, 34, 202–203
Income disruptions, 236
Industrial Revolution, 98
Information hub, 227
Inkwell, 57
In-person time policies, 161
Internal mobility, 76, 153, 154, 157

Jezard, Adam, 60
Job(s), 71–92
  applying for, 156
  defined, 73
  designing work around, 89
  dynamic (see Dynamic jobs)
  F3 principles for, 88–91
  matching workers to, 83, 86–88, 90
  new, since 2008 recession, 220–221
  rethinking concept of, xiii
  scenario planning to fill, 205–207
  selecting workers for, 156–157
  traditional fixed roles, 74–76
Job matching, 83
Job movement:
  in F3 Companies, 13–16
  new policies for, 155–158
  as part of geographic movement, 146
  talent mobility function for, 37

traditional policies for, 153–155
types of, 14
Jobs graph, 79–81, 156
"Jobs World" principles, 88–91
JP Morgan, 125

Kasriel, Stephane:
  on hiring freelancers, 164
  on remote work, 18
  on rethinking talent models, 21
  on total talent management, 84
  on transformation to dynamic jobs, 80–81
  on work-from-anywhere model, 66
Keskkula, Silver, 50, 64
Key stakeholders, 225, 226
King, Rachael, 6–7
  on challenges to mobility, 155
  on compensation and bonuses, 175–176
  on employee development, 123
  on evolution of organizational design, 99–100
  on evolution of teams, 97–98
  on HR leadership, 32
  on job benchmarking and recruiting, 127–128
  OKRs implemented by, 131–132
  and organizational design, 27–28
  and performance reviews, 130
  on résumés, 121
  on traditional company structures, 31
Knowledge work, 98, 186, 228, 239

LafargeHolcim, 147
Leadership:
  and complexity of work-from-everywhere models, 195
  job movement support from, 157
  meritocratic and patriarchal, 110
  (See also Managers; Project leaders)
Learning initiatives, 76, 237
Learning systems, 210, 211
Lehman Brothers:
  author's career at, 8–9
  collaboration system at, 213
  employee movement management at, 34–35
  expatriate assignments at, 144–145
  managers at, 99

office work culture at, 51
organizational design of, 31
pay model of, 194
performance reviews and ranking at, 122–123
teams at, 96–97
traditional office environment of, 53, 54
Leonardo da Vinci, 120
Liao, Jing, 18
LinkedIn, 61, 82, 128
Local benchmark compensation model, 172–173
Local entities, 196
Local retirement model, 178, 179
Location:
  of F3 Company offices, 60–61
  of traditional offices, 55–56
  type of, in scenario planning, 206
Location movement, 16–19
  in F3 Companies, 16–19
  new policies for, 160–163
  as part of geographic movement, 146
  talent mobility function for, 37
  traditional policies for, 158–160
  transforming policies/spaces for, 51
  types of, 17
Long-distance commutes, 10, 33, 49, 146
Lyft, 61

Management, 93–95
  of dynamic, extended teams, 108–112
  evolution of, 98–99
  and internal mobility, 76
  by project leader, 109–112
  as skill, 109
  by traditional human resources departments, 6–7
  (See also specific types of management)
"Management's Three Eras" (McGrath), 98
Manager coaches, 95, 99, 109–110
Managers:
  for dynamic, agile teams, 107
  purpose of, 95
  traditional, 95–100, 108, 109
Matching workers to jobs, 87–88

Maternity leave, 181
Matrix structures, 99
Mayer, Marissa, 232
McGrath, Rita Gunther, 98
Mead Paper Company, 74, 117–118
Meetings, 161–162, 212–213
Mellon Bank, 55–56
Mercer, 75, 78–79, 84–85
Meritocratic leadership, 110
Messaging applications, 212
Microentrepreneurs, 19, 21, 83, 102
Microsoft, 81
Millennials, xi, 5, 56, 61, 73
Minimum wage, 186, 236
Mobile workforce mindset, 39–40
Mobility:
    as an expectation, 157
    drivers of, 152
    (See also Talent mobility)
Modularization of the workforce, 16
Morgan Stanley, 106
Moritz, Bob, 103
Multitiered entity and employment
    model, 195–198

National Cash Register Company, 6
National Labor Relations Act
    (NLRA), 6
Nature of work, 73, 89, 214
Navin, Peter, 46
Netflix, 177–178
NetSuite, 212
Neutrals, in transformation, 226, 227
"The New Rules of Talent
    Management" (Cappelli and
    Tavis), 119–120
Niagara Maid, 74
Nine-box model, 149, 151
NLRA (National Labor Relations
    Act), 6
Nonlinear career paths, 124–126

Objectives, 107, 130–132
Objectives and key results (OKRs),
    130–132, 135, 175
oDesk, 81
The Office (sitcom), 55
Office parks, 55–56
Office work culture, 50–51
Offices, 49–68
    historical evolution of, 51–52

for new talent mobility, 56–61
for remote work, 62–66
traditional, 51–56
OKRs (see Objectives and key results)
Okulicz-Kozaryn, Adam, 61
Onboarding, 231
The 100 Year Life (Gratton and
    Scott), 118
Operational human resources, 6–7
Operations (see Systems and
    operations)
Organizational design, 27–48
    evolution of, 99–100
    in F3 Companies, 31–32
    project-based, 99–100
    of Topia, 27–28
    of traditional companies, 29–35,
        97–98
Outcomes, 127
Owen, Robert, 5–6

Paid family leave, 182
Paid parental leave, 181, 182, 236
Paid time off (PTO), 167, 168
Paternity leave, 181
Patriarchal leadership, 110
Patriarchal model of funding moves,
    146
Pay models, 193–200
    entity and employment strategies,
        194–198
    setup for talent mobility, 198–200
    traditional, 193–194
PayScale, 128
"People Before Strategy" (Charan,
    Barton, and Carey), 32
PEOs (see Professional employer
    organizations)
"The Performance Management
    Revolution" (Cappelli and Tavis),
    123
Performance reviews, 108, 121–123,
    133
Personal relationships, 56, 58
Personal time-off (PTO), 158
P&G (Procter & Gamble), 81, 102
Pilot populations, 224, 225
Pinterest, 61
Policy(-ies), 141–166
    for employment movement, 20,
        163–164

as framework for talent mobility, 142
for geographic movement, 143–153
for job movement, 153–158
for location movement, 158–163
in scenario planning, 206
to unleash Flat, Fluid, and Fast economy, 233–240
Pond, Nick, 12, 35, 147–148
"Post-title world," 88
Procter & Gamble (P&G), 81, 102
Professional employer organizations (PEOs), 196, 198, 199
Project goals, 131
Project leaders, 79, 99, 109–112, 135
Project mobility drivers, 152
Project objectives, 130–132
Projects:
  deconstructing work into, 84, 106
  dynamic, 77, 100, 135
  in jobs graphs, 79–81
PTO (paid time off), 167, 168
PTO (personal time-off), 158
Public-private technology partnerships, 237
Purpose:
  of F3 Company offices, 56–58
  of managers, 95
  of traditional offices, 52–54

Ramakrishnan, Krish, 53–54, 160
Reclassifying workers, 82–88
Recruiting:
  communicating values and norms in, 231
  long-distance, 11
  for skills vs. for titles, 125, 127–128
  by traditional companies, 7–8, 75–76, 101
Redefining workforce, 82–85
Reflektive, 133–134
"Reimagining Work 2020" (Catalant Technologies), 44
Relocations:
  as building block of talent mobility, 33
  compensation adjustment with, 170
  employing entity in, 193–194
  pay model for, 194
  as type of corporate relocation, 143

as type of geographic movement, 10, 146
Remote work:
  BlueJeans platform for, 160
  embracing, 51
  growing amount of, 16–17
  home offices for, 62–63
  incentivizing, 186, 238–239
  policies for, 160–161
  swapping offices for, 62–66
  work-from-everywhere models for, 63–66
Repetitive (automated) jobs, 156, 163–164
Restructuring (see Organizational design)
Résumés, 120–121, 127–128
Retention mobility drivers, 152
Retirement benefits, 178–180, 187–188
Retirement savings program, 236
Riley, Joanna, 86–88, 129
Risks:
  from automation, 71–72
  geopolitical and security, 203–204
Road warriors, 10
Robots, 72, 95, 104
Role(s), 73
  of Chief Talent Mobility Officers, 43–45
  of CHRO in Talent Mobility Revolution, 32
  disruptions to, 76
  fixed, 74–76
  traditional organization/definition of, 74–75
  on traditional teams, 96
  (See also Fixed-role jobs)
Rotation programs, 11, 33, 146

Salary (see Compensation)
Samsung, 81
Scenario planning, to fill open jobs, 205–207
Schema for talent mobility function, 41–42
Schneider Electric, 147–148, 155, 174, 191–192
Scott, Andrew, 118
Security risks, 203–204
SeeMe, 229–230

Segmenting organizations, 224–225
Sexual harassment protections, 187
"Shaping the Agile Workforce" (Accenture), 101
"Shared responsibility" model of funding moves, 146
SharePoint, 212
Short-term project relocations, 11, 33, 146
Silicon Valley, 61, 102
Silos, 30, 99
Sinek, Simon, 14
Skills:
    categorizing, 85–87, 127
    competency benchmarks for, 127–128
    of CTMO, 45–47
    deconstructing jobs into, 77
    developing, 115–116, 237
    indicator ratings for, 135–136
    in jobs graphs, 79–81
    leveraging, 78
    management as, 109
    matching people with, 15
    as measures of worker fit, 128–129
    in new business models, 83
    of project leaders, 111
    recruiting for, 125, 127–128
    and traditional job movement policies, 154
    and traditional résumés, 120
    transferrable, 76, 116
    "uniquely human," 72, 104
Skills gaps, 72, 101, 103
Skills graph, 85–87
Skype, 59, 220–221, 231
Slack, 61, 64, 212, 213
Small businesses, 228, 239
Smith, Adam, 95, 98
Smith, Peggy:
    on career paths, 125–126
    on changes in nature of work, 214
    on corporate relocation, 9
    on employment models, 21–22
    on expatriate assignments, 171
    on HR function, 7
    on investing in transformation for talent mobility, 47
    on talent mobility transformation, 23
Social contract, 13, 169

SoFi, 18
Solutions Consultants*Reworking the Revolution*, 78
Specialization, 95–97
Spotify, 107, 167, 177
Square, 61
Staffing:
    for dynamic projects, 107
    reactive, 84
    scenario planning to fill open jobs, 205–207
    of teams, 110
Stakeholders, 225–226
Standard Chartered Bank, 158–159
Start with Why (Sinek), 14
Stella and Dot, 20–21, 102–103, 162–163
Stewart, Catherine, 64–66, 174, 197
Stripe, 61
Structure of work, 169, 220–221, 235–236
Success, 5
    agility as key to, 95, 117
    in change management, 222–224
    with geographic movement, 149–152
    in meeting project objectives, 130–132
    and notion of work, 51
    reorganization for, 29
Support for transformation, 225–227
Supporters, in transformation, 226, 227
Systems and operations, 191–215
    employment and pay models, 193–200
    to enable talent mobility and engage workers, 209–213
    location movement policies for, 161–162
    managing compliance and risk, 200–204
    managing costs and budgets, 205–209
    policies as core part of, 142
    to support agile work, 107

Talent gap, 101
Talent indicators, 135–136, 175
Talent management systems, 131, 151

Talent marketplaces:
  building, 87–88
  categorizing of skills in, 127
  investing in, 80
  for managing costs and budgets,
    205–206
  in talent mobility systems map,
    209–211
  at Workday, 77, 84
Talent mobility, 3–26
  approving and initiating, 208–209
  building blocks of (*see* Building
    blocks of talent mobility)
  Chief Talent Mobility Officer,
    43–48
  as competitive advantage, 9
  core talent mobility systems map,
    209–211
  creating single function for, 36–40
  definition of, 10, 22–24
  employment models for, 194–198
  in *F3 Companies*, 9–22
  fragmentation of, 28–29, 33–35
  horizontal activities of, 37–38
  new lexicon of, 22–25
  offices for, 56–61
  pay models for, 198–200
  at technology companies, 219–220
  in traditional companies, 5–9
  varying understandings of, 4
Talent Mobility Revolution, xi–xv,
    25, 240
  acceleration of, 47
  CHRO role in, 32
  forces driving, 22, 214
  tapping into, 9–10
Talent mobility systems, 209–211
  global mobility management
    systems, 209–211
  learning systems, 210, 211
  talent marketplaces, 209–211
Talent mobility systems roadmap,
    209–211, 231
"Talent on the Move!" (Deloitte), 157
Talent reviews, 135–136, 175
Tamkivi, Sten, 50
  on building culture, 231
  on change management, 232
  on collaboration systems, 213
  on location movement, 159, 162
  on offices, 55

operating norms of, 230
  at Skype, 59
  teams created by, 107–108
  on traditional managers, 57
TaskRabbit, 129
Tavis, Anna, 119–120, 123, 133
Tax issues:
  classifying workers by tax status,
    82, 195
  compliance, 202–203
  more efficient tax policy, 239
  with multitiered entity and
    employment model, 196
  requirements for employee
    movement, 34
  tax treatment and employee
    movement, 20
Teams, 93–113
  distributed, 197–198, 229
  dynamic, agile, 100, 106–108
  in dynamic jobs, 77–79
  extended, 100–103
  F3 Company principles for, 234
  fixed, 77, 95–98, 106
  measuring success and performance
    of, 130–132
  OKRs for, 131
  project leaders' role on, 109–112
  redesigning, 100–108
  selecting workers for, 156–157
  traditional, 95–98
  transformation, 222–223, 227
  vertical, 97–98
  virtual, 62–63, 229
  worker and machine collaboration
    on, 95, 104–106
  in work-from-everywhere model,
    64–65
  in work-from-home model, 62
Teleport:
  culture of, 231
  founding of, 220–221
  systems setup for, 213
  work-from-everywhere at, 50, 64,
    197
1099 workers, 20, 195
Termination, 75–76
Time zones, with work-from-
    everywhere model, 65–66
Time-off, 176–178
Titles, 88, 118–120, 127–128

Topia, xii–xiii, 3
  acquisitions of, 50, 54–55, 197
  collaboration systems at, 213
  continuous feedback at, 130
  Customer Advisory Board, 11
  early jobs and resources at, 93–94
  employment model of, 197–198
  expatriate experience of employees
    at, 170–171
  first relocation pilot at, 219
  first VP People at, 6–7
  freelancers at, 101–102
  hiring for skills at, 116
  holiday benefits at, 167–168
  managers at, 109–110
  oDesk used at, 81
  organizational design of, 27–28
  paid parental leave at, 182
  product development teams at,
    107–108
  recruiting for skills and values at,
    121
  scenario planning at, 206–207
  Solutions Consultants role at, 78
  spaghetti challenge at, 63
  values of, 230
  working from office at, 232
Topia Plan, 206–208
Total talent management, 84, 164
Tours of duty, 13–15
  aligned to nine-box talent grid, 151
  benefits of, 146
  positioning for, 116
  in traditional companies, 33
  (See also Job movement)
Traditional career paths, 117–123
Traditional companies:
  Chief Human Resource Officer in,
    31–32
  corporate relocation in, 8–9
  employment and pay models in,
    193–194
  fragmentation of talent mobility in,
    33–35
  hiring in, 7–8
  human resources operations in, 6–9
  jobs in (see Fixed-role jobs)
  offices in (see Traditional offices)
  organizational design of, 29–35
  recruiting by, 7–8, 75–76, 101
  rethinking talent models of, 21

  talent mobility activities in, 40
  talent mobility in, 5–9, 33–35 (See
    also Employee movement)
  teams at, 77, 95–98, 106, 108
  technology companies as, 219
  transforming, 222–228
Traditional compensation models,
    169–171
Traditional employee protections,
    185–187
Traditional managers, 95–100, 108,
    109
"The Traditional Office is Dead.
    Here's Why" (Jezard), 60
Traditional offices, 51–56
  design of, 54–55
  location of, 55–56
  purpose of, 52–54
Traditional policies:
  for geographic movement, 143–146
  for job movement, 153–155
  for location movement, 158–160
Traditional résumés, 120–121, 128
Traditional teams, 95–98
Training programs, 11, 33, 80, 146
Transferrable skills, 76, 116
Transformation team, 222–223, 227
Transforming traditional companies,
    191–193, 222–228
  building support for, 225–227
  launching change in, 227–228
  pilot populations for, 224, 225
  segmenting organization for,
    224–225
  for single talent mobility function,
    40–42
  successful change management in,
    222–224
  talent mobility as key to, 4
  Workday's vision for, 77
Transparency, 131
Trump, Donald, 204

Uber, 61
Uniqlo, 104
Unlimited vacation model, 177
Upwork, 18, 21
  city offices of, 61
  deconstructed work and dynamic
    jobs at, 80–81
  highest paid freelancer at, 234

P&G's leveraging of, 102
skills and reviews on, 129
types of work framework of, 164
uses of, 84
work-from-anywhere model at, 66
Urban employment markets, 186

Vacation time, 176–178
Valente, Rubia, 61
Value proposition, 17, 169
Vermont Remote Worker Grant
    Program, 239
Vertical teams, 97–98
Videoconferencing market, 160
Virgin, 177
Virtual collaboration, 62
Virtual culture, 64
Virtual meeting technology, 212–213
Virtual teams, 62–63, 229
Vocational education, 237
VP HR, 31

Warner, Susanna, 145–148, 155,
    191–192
WebEx, 213
Welch, Jack, 122
Wellness support, 184–185
WeWork, 49, 63
Wharton School, 98
"Why More Business Executives
    Should Consider Becoming a
    CHRO" (Boudreau, Navin, and
    Creelman), 46
Wilson, Jim, 106
WordPress.com, 17
Work:
    across sectors, 124
    agile model of, 95
    expanded view of, 101–103
    future of, 35, 44, 234–235
    human and machine skills for, 104
    new contract for work in America,
        235–240

rethinking structure of, 169, 220–
    221, 235–236
types of, 77
(See also Distributed work)
Workday, 61, 77, 84, 86, 88
Worker value proposition, 169
Worker–machine collaboration,
    104–106
Workers:
    classifications of (see Classifying
        workers)
    on extended teams, 100–101
    perspective on careers among, 117
    in scenario planning, 206
    use of term, 100
    worker–machine collaboration,
        104–106
Workforce, xiv
    erosion of social contract for, 13
    extended view of, 100–103
    freelance/gig, 19
    global, skills graph for, 86
    modularization of, 16
    redefining, 82–85, 89–90
    traditional and new, 20–21,
        100–101
    and traditional offices, 52–53
    traditional setup of, 75
Work-from-anywhere, 17, 33, 63–66
Work-from-everywhere models, 49,
    63–66, 101, 195
Work-from-home, 17, 33, 62–63
Working hours, 52, 53, 158
Working hours overlap policies, 161
Work-life balance, 16–17, 182, 188
Work-life integration, 181, 187
Worldwide ERC, 7, 16, 24
W2 workers, 195

Yahoo, 232
Yeh, Chris, 13

Zoom, 64

About the Author

BRYNNE KENNEDY is the Founder of Topia, a talent mobility company sought after by some of the world's largest companies to move their employees between locations and roles. Brynne led Topia for nine years as CEO, during which she also joined TechNet, a group of business executives who promote the growth of the innovation economy. Brynne is currently a candidate for US Congress.